Princeton Readings in Religion and Violence

Princeton Readings in Religion and Violence

Edited and with introductions by

Mark Juergensmeyer and Margo Kitts

PRINCETON UNIVERSITY PRESS

PRINCETON AND OXFORD

Published by Princeton University Press, 41 William Street, Princeton, New Jersey 08540
In the United Kingdom: Princeton University Press, 6 Oxford Street, Woodstock,
Oxfordshire OX20 1TW

press.princeton.edu

Library of Congress Cataloging-in-Publication Data

Princeton readings in religion and violence / edited and with introductions
by Mark Juergensmeyer and Margo Kitts.
    p. cm.
Includes bibliographical references and index.
ISBN 978-0-691-12913-6 (hardcover : alk. paper) — ISBN 978-0-691-
12914-3 (pbk. : alk. paper)   1. Violence—Religious aspects.   I. Juergensmeyer, Mark.   II. Kitts, Margo, no date.   III. Title.

BL65.V55P75 2011
201'.76332—dc22   2011013613

British Library Cataloging-in-Publication Data is available

This book has been composed in Sabon

Printed on acid-free paper. ∞

Printed in the United States of America

1   3   5   7   9   10   8   6   4   2

Contents

Acknowledgments

A SPECIAL WORD OF APPRECIATION goes to Fred Appel of Princeton University Press for his persistence and unfailing belief in the value of this project. Assistance in securing publishing permissions for the selections was provided by Jack Ucciferri, Jeff MacMillan, and Hamed Faquiryan, and useful comments on the manuscript were provided by Michael Jerryson. Margo Kitts would like to thank her son, Giordan, for his good-natured support; and Mark Juergensmeyer appreciates the patience of his spouse, Sucheng Chan.

In acknowledging their appreciation for the contributions of each other in producing this book, the editors also want to explain how this book came about and what each of them did in producing it. Years ago, Juergensmeyer was one of Kitts's graduate advisers when she did her doctoral work at Berkeley. When Juergensmeyer was approached about doing a book of readings in religion and violence, he realized that the volume would be greatly enhanced by a coeditor who knew well the literary and anthropological material on the subject and he turned to Kitts. Happily, she agreed to collaborate on the project. The book was conceptualized through vast amounts of email between Honolulu and Santa Barbara, and at a crucial meeting in a coffeehouse in Berkeley. The introductory essay of the volume was written together. Juergensmeyer wrote a draft of the introduction to section I and wrote drafts of the paragraphs introducing each of the selections in this section; Kitts drafted the introduction to section II and its selections; and Juergensmeyer drafted the concluding comments. Then they edited and rewrote each other's essays and argued about the whole thing. Surprisingly, they are still friends.

Princeton Readings in Religion and Violence

Introduction

WHY IS RELIGION VIOLENT AND VIOLENCE RELIGIOUS?

VIOLENCE IN THE NAME OF RELIGION, plentiful enough in our time, is an enduring feature of religious life. Rituals of sacrifice and martyrdom and legendary tales of great battles abound within every religious tradition. In most cases the violent images are symbolic, but the reality of religion is clouded with actual events of violence—inquisitions and internal attacks, sacrifices and martyrdoms, wars and conquests. Virtually every religious tradition has left a trail of blood.

Some would argue that the violent images in religion are greatly misunderstood. Religion itself is not violent, these defenders of religion claim, but a voice of peace. Rather, the misuse of religion leads to violence—stealthy activists legitimizing their deeds with religious justifications—and that sullies the purity of religion's reputation.

We agree, in part, for indeed most religious teachings are about peace. They not only preach tolerance and understanding of those who are different but advocate forgiveness and mercy in the face of opposition. The idea of killing is abhorrent to all religious traditions, and even the attempts to coerce and bully are regarded as anathema. We wish that this volume were large enough to include the peaceful sides of religion and to counteract all of the violent passages.

Yet we feel that there is value in having a volume that focuses on the destructive side. After all, these brutal passages exist, and despite the overwhelming peacefulness of religious traditions, the fact remains that they are also filled with the symbols and language of violence. Why is this the case? It may well be, as some will claim, that these images help to alleviate real violence by symbolically displacing violent urges. It also may be true that religious violence is the rare exception rather than the rule. Yet these are precisely what need to be explained—how religious language can embrace violent images and acts, and why, and on what occasions, and how it is possible that symbolic violence can turn to real acts of bloodshed.

The link between religion and violence extends back into the early history of religious traditions. The sword of Islam and the cross of Christianity—an execution device—are only the most obvious indications of ancient associations with bloody images in religious culture. Tales of violence are frequent in the most ancient Western texts, from the Bible through the Assyrian and Hittite royal annals to the earliest Sumerian and Akkadian poetic celebrations of such deities as Ishtar, Ninurta, and Nergal. The violent images in Asian religious traditions are equally ancient. The auspicious acts of destruction undertaken by Vedic gods such as Indra and Rudra are conspicuous in early Indian poetry and epic, and the martial arts traditions associated with Taoism and Buddhism reflect principles based in 2,500-year-old texts—and some would say in the cosmos itself.

Virtually all cultural traditions have contained sacrificial acts and martial metaphors. Some would argue that the rise of religion is intimately related to the origins of sacrifice. But images of warfare are equally ubiquitous and similarly ancient. The Muslim notion of jihad is the most notable example, but even in Buddhist legends great wars are to be found. In Sri Lankan culture, for instance, virtually canonical status is accorded to the legendary history recorded in the Pali Chronicles, the Dipavamsa and the Mahavamsa, that relate the triumphs of battles waged by Buddhist kings. In India, warfare has contributed to the grandeur of the great epics, the Ramayana and the Mahabharata, which are tales of seemingly unending conflict and military intrigue. Arguably, more than the Vedic rituals, these martial epics defined subsequent Hindu culture. In Sikhism, the Dal Khalsa ("army of the faithful") is the term for the Sikh community, denoting a disciplined religious organization. Great passages of the Hebrew Bible are devoted to the military exploits of great kings, their contests reported in gory detail. Though the New Testament did not take up the battle cry, the later history of the church did, supplying Christianity with a bloody record of crusades and religious wars. Protestant Christianity is an example. Although the reformed tradition is strongly pacifist, martial images abound in the rhetoric and symbolism of the faith. Protestant preachers everywhere have encouraged their flocks to wage war against the forces of evil, and their homilies are followed with hymns about "Christian soldiers," fighting "the good fight," and struggling "manfully onward." Given both the antiquity and the persistence of such images, it seems reasonable to conclude that violence is in some way intrinsic to religion.

This is a book of readings that helps us understand this dark attraction between religion and violence. The first section of the book focuses on war and religious language, and contains a collection of writings, including scriptures and ancient texts, that justify military action for religious reasons at special moments in history. This section also includes writings from contemporary religious activists—Christian, Muslim, Jewish, and Buddhist—who justify acts that most observers would regard as terrorism. Included are the last instructions for the hijackers involved in the September 11, 2001, attacks, as well as the theories of those who have formulated the jihadi ideology of global struggle and Christian and Jewish militancy in the contemporary world.

In the second section, sacrifice and theoretical ideas are at the center. This section contains excerpts from such formative thinkers as Émile Durkheim, Karl Marx, and Sigmund Freud up to contemporary theorists like René Girard and Elaine Scarry. Each of them has attempted to make sense of the role of religion in human culture by focusing on what might appear to be religion's most peculiar obsession, violence. They offer thoughts on the essential question: What is it about religious traditions that seems to welcome images of violence? What is it about religion that can lead to violence? Speculation about the link between religion and violence has been launched from a number of different disciplines—history of religions, psychology, sociology, anthropology, and political science, among others. Early theorists pondered religious violence in forms they identified mostly with arcane cults—totemism and blood sacrifice. More recently scholars have questioned the roles that ritualized killing seems to play within broader cultural constructions, such as punitive codes, scapegoating, gang-related activities, terrorism, and war. This section offers ideas from thinkers whose voices continue to resonate in the scholarly world's attempt to make sense of the phenomenon of religious violence.

Is there a relationship between the writings in the first section and those in the second? At first glance, it might appear that they are about different things. The religious apologists in the first section justify and defend the *actual* use of violence in religious contexts. The scholarly essays in the second section are largely ruminating about the *symbolic* images and rituals within the religious imagination. Those who read the selections in this volume may very well conclude that the two kinds of writings have nothing to do with one another, or that—as some theorists argue—real acts of violence are the result of the imperfect application of religious rites and symbols that in their best moments diffuse violent urges rather than promote them.

At the same time there may be a closer connection between real and symbolic acts of violence than one might think. For one thing, symbolic violence is often thought to be the ritual reenactment of ancient but quite real acts of violence. Freud, for example, thought that there was an original conflict that involved fratricide among brothers and patricide of the father. The oldest forms of sacrifice, some scholars argue, were human sacrifices. Even later sacrifices that involved animals were, from the perspective of unwilling sheep, violent events. Similarly the legendary stories of warfare were in many cases actual wars. The Crusades, the Sikh battles against Moghul rule, the warfare between Buddhist and Tamil kings described in Sri Lanka's Pali Chronicles—all these were real battles that later became remembered as legendary ones.

Moreover, contemporary acts of religious violence are often conducted in a ritual way, with intentions that are as symbolic as they are strategic. The martyrs chosen for suicide attacks often carry the hallmarks of a sacrificial victim. The attackers on September 11, 2001, acted as though they were undergoing a sacred rite. One might argue that their act of terrorism was an attempt to redefine public space in religious terms. In many contemporary acts of religious terrorism, the activists appear to be conducting public rites of purification as much as they are making a political statement. To some extent then, acts of religious violence can be seen as religious acts indeed, events that need to be understood and challenged from a religious as well as a political perspective.

For these reasons, we think that it is helpful to include in one volume readings that embrace both the activist writings that justify violence in a religious milieu and the scholarly attempts to understand religious violence in its symbolic forms. Given the incendiary mix of religion and violence that characterizes much of contemporary global conflict, it is helpful to understand this volatile combination from a variety of perspectives—historical and contemporary, scholarly and activist, symbolic and political. The ultimate goal of all understanding, however, is not just to appreciate reality but to change it. In a modest way, we hope that this effort at making sense of religious violence will lead to a new appreciation of the transformative capacity of religion and its ability to lead to tranquillity as well as destruction, and to healing as well as to harm.

Part I

RELIGIOUS JUSTIFICATIONS FOR VIOLENCE

Introduction to Part I

"GOD IS A WARRIOR," proclaims the book of Exodus (15:3). This famous song of Moses extols divine acts of warfare, whereby God smashes the Pharaoh's chariots and drowns the Egyptian leader's handpicked commanders in the depths of the Red Sea. With his "right hand," the book of Exodus exults, God "shatters the enemy" (15:6).

Behind this arresting image is an interesting idea—that God is intimately tied to human relationships, including hostile encounters. God is someone, or something, that can become engaged in human affairs and take sides, favoring one group or another. The divine warrior image suggests a certain theology, but it also implies a theory of religious violence, for this theological image indicates that real acts of violence can have sacred significance. Violence is undertaken by no less a figure than God.

It is this divine mandate for violence that is explored in the first section of the book. Yet, as we will see, there is disagreement in every religious community about whether there can be religious merit in violent acts. Religious thinkers argue over whether violence can sometimes be sanctifying, or whether it is at most a necessary evil. Some argue that religious authority approves of violence only in extraordinary cases, to justify the messy business of the real world, such as defending the innocent. Indeed, the "just war" theory of Christianity—an idea that has its parallels in other religious traditions, including Islam—gives this impression. In these cases religion hesitantly approves of force under certain rare conditions. It appears not so much to gleefully celebrate violence as to be its conscience, applying the brakes on morally sanctioned coercive force before it gets out of hand.

But not all of the religious writings about violence are of this nature. There are also writings within most religious traditions that view some acts of violence as sacred duties. These writings, such as the book of Exodus, portray God as an activist who plays a direct hand in earthly affairs, including warfare. Individuals who participate in these acts as holy warriors are thus fulfilling sacred obligations. They are undertaking a "neglected duty," as Abd al-Salam Faraj, a twentieth-century ideologue for radical Islam, has put it. The same sense of mission motivated Yigal Amir to assassinate a fellow Jew, Israel's Prime Minister Yitzhak Rabin, in 1995 in Tel Aviv. Amir had consulted rabbis for confirmation that his act of political assassination was a rabbinically sanctioned sacred act.

Religion and warfare have been intimately tied together throughout history. Some three thousand years ago, ancient Mesopotamian poems and war chronicles celebrated the deities of battle. The writings portrayed gods marching before armies, championing their favorites and decimating their foes. Gods such as Ashur were made to receive tribute in the form of human carnage, and the gods Ninurta, Nergal, and Ishtar were said to delight in battle frenzy. True, the warring aspects of these deities were often balanced by benign aspects. Yet even the goddess Ishtar, sometimes a tender goddess of love, was alleged to have lethally punished those who spurned her advances, demonstrating the auspicious and destructive power of divine attention.

In ancient texts describing the Vedic divinities in South Asia and the Greek and Norse pantheons in Europe, warfare was also an activity of the gods. When humans engaged in it, they called on the power of warrior gods to support their own militant positions. There is a thin line between mortal and immortal battlefield displays in the ancient Greek epic, the *Iliad*. Mortal fighting is often described with the very same similes, phrases, and precise details as the mythical warfare of the gods. Moreover, Greek gods are described as having impersonated men on the battlefield in order to stir up bellicose passions. A similar tactic was undertaken by gods in ancient India's legendary epic, the Mahabharata.

In the third and fourth centuries B.C.E., new writings emerged in India and China that focused on the human activity of war under divine mandate. These works, the Arthashastra of Kautilya in India, and the *Art of War* by Sun Tzu in China, are similar in several ways. Both are essentially manuals for conducting war. They include advice for the ruthless use of spies and devious trickery in order to achieve a military victory. At the same time, both of them include a role for religion, especially in motivating soldiers into battle. But behind both of these manuals of warfare is the notion that the kind of war that they deem worthy of conducting is carried out for an ultimately moral purpose: to uphold social order.

Other ancient writings, including the Bhagavad Gita and similar sacred scriptures, also follow the theme that warfare is just when it is necessary to uphold social order. In the Hebrew Bible, for instance, warfare is always cast in moral terms. The special covenant that God formed with the Israelite people gave a divine mandate for their protection. In both Exodus and Deuteronomy in the Hebrew Bible, God is portrayed as directly entering into combat on the side of the chosen people to fulfill a moral obligation.

In the Qur'an, the figure of God is never portrayed as anthropomorphic as is the case in the Hebrew Bible, and in the Muslim texts God is not described as a warrior. As in most of the Hebrew Bible and the New Testament, the central message in the Qur'an is about peace and the proscription against killing. Yet in the Qur'an, as in the Hebrew Bible and the New Testament, there are moments when force, even deadly force, is deemed necessary for a righteous cause. Defending the community against obliteration is one of those righteous causes, and in both the Qur'an and the Hebrew Bible one can find approval of killing in defense of the community.

Yet, in a larger sense, it was not just the people in religious communities who were being defended; it was the very idea of civilized society. Early texts of most religious traditions have justified warfare when it was deemed necessary to protect the framework of morality that lies beneath a righteous social order. The Zen instructions of Takuan, for instance, regard the martial arts as essential to upholding a disciplined society. In all of these cases, the alternative to the righteously established communities was thought to be anarchy, chaos, and disorder. To allow one of these enemies to win would be not just a transfer of title from one ruler to another in the control of a territory but also a capitulation to a sea of immoral disarray. In this sense then, war was part of the ultimate moral good, for it protected righteous social order: civilization itself.

This theme was not dominant in early Christianity under the Roman Empire. Congregating in small isolated communities for much of that time, the early Christians tended to be pacifist, in part because they took seriously Jesus's injunction to "turn the other cheek" and avoid violence, and in part because some early Christians regarded the act of joining the Roman army as showing deference to Caesar as a god. But then the early Christians had the luxury of being pacifist because as a minority sect they did not have territory to defend nor law and order to maintain.

All this changed when Christianity became the dominant religion of an empire after the conversion of the Roman emperor Constantine to Christianity in 312 C.E. In the centuries that followed, Christian thinkers tried to make sense of the pacifist mandate in light of the need to morally justify the military actions of the state. They tried to reconcile the nonviolent idealism of the Gospels with the demands of state power and the example of some bellicose images in the Hebrew Bible.

A fourth-century Christian bishop, Augustine, hit upon a solution. Borrowing the concept of "just war" developed by Cicero in Roman jurisprudence, Augustine expanded on this notion and set it in context. Augustine specified the conditions in which a Christian could morally sanction war. This set of prerequisites for warfare was categorized by the medieval Catholic theologian, Thomas Aquinas, and has been refined and expanded by numerous theologians ever since. In general, just war theory allows for military action only as a last resort, when it will lead to less violence rather than more, when it is conducted for a just cause, and when it is authorized by a proper public authority. Islamic thinkers and scholars in other religious traditions have developed similar thinking about the moral criteria that might make warfare permissible.

Contemporary Christian thinking continues to be guided by just war criteria. One of the twentieth century's most influential Protestant thinkers, Reinhold Niebuhr, began his career as a pacifist. The evil powers of Hitler and Stalin persuaded Niebuhr that there were moments when the force of evil had to be countered by righteous military force in order for justice to prevail. In an influential essay, "Why the Christian Church Is Not Pacifist," Niebuhr cited the Christian tradition's defense of justice as more important than pacifism when it came to great encounters in history between evil powers and social order.

A similar line of reasoning has motivated some of religion's more radical activists. The late twentieth and early twenty-first centuries have witnessed a burst of new religious militancy in virtually every religious tradition. These small but vocal groups of extremists—be they Muslim followers of al Qaeda, Jewish supporters of anti-Arab militants, right-wing Christian militia, or Buddhist, Hindu, and Sikh activists—all see their justification of violence based on traditional religious principles. But there are some major differences.

Unlike their predecessors—ancient apologists, just war theorists, and twentieth-century theologians like Niebuhr—the new religious radicals do not affirm the status quo or see the current authorities as legitimate upholders of moral social order. Instead, they imagine themselves to be righteous defenders of an alternative order. In most cases, this new order is not described in any kind of detail, but its proponents think that it will be a more fulfilled realization of morality and religious social life than the secular regimes of the day. Religious law is often thought to be a fundamental necessity for this new order. As one leader of a revolutionary Jewish group in Israel put it in an interview with one of this book's editors, "What we want is not democracy but Torahcracy." In the readings in this book, we find that the Islamic political thinker Abd al-Salam Faraj, the Christian activist Michael Bray, and the Jewish anti-Arab extremist Meir Kahane were all exponents of incorporating religious law—Muslim, Christian, or Jewish, as the case may be—as the basis of a new religious state. Though they speak for only a tiny minority in each of their religious communities, their violent actions create a loud voice.

These recent proponents of violence are religious revolutionaries. Their justifications for the use of violence for a religious cause are not defenses of an existing sociopolitical order, for they see the secular state as deeply flawed. Most of them are, indeed, at war with their own governments. A Christian activist, Timothy McVeigh, bombed the Oklahoma City federal building in his own country, the United States; a Jewish extremist assassinated Israel's prime minister; Egypt's President Anwar Sadat and India's Prime Minister Indira Gandhi were killed by Muslim and Sikh activists in their respective countries; and the nerve gas attack in Japan by the syncretic Buddhist movement Aum Shinrikyo was aimed at a subway stop adjacent to Japan's government buildings in downtown Tokyo. The United States has been a target of Muslim extremists in part because it is seen as the power behind the secular or quasi-secular Muslim governments that they despise in their home countries. As the writings in this section show, these religious revolutionaries are defending a religious society that they have never seen—and perhaps one that has never existed. But they are convinced that the secular governments of the present age are preventing a righteous social order from coming into being.

In many cases this radical hope for a new social order is merged with an apocalyptic vision. Rabbi Meir Kahane expected that his anti-Arab activism would create the conditions in which the Messiah would come on earth and Israel would be established as a wholly religious state. Added to his messianic Zionism was the idea of a catastrophic encounter that would usher in this extraordinary messianic occasion. In order for this extraordinary encounter to happen, Jews had to avenge the humiliation that was suffered by them and by God. An even more radical apocalyptic vision was propagated by the Aum Shinrikyo master Shoko Asahara, who imagined a cataclysmic encounter, one even greater than World War II, that would engulf the world in a firestorm of nuclear, biological, and chemical warfare.

The Aum Shinrikyo idea is only an extreme example of a common theme within the world view of the revolutionary religious movements of the contemporary age: the notion of cosmic war. The idea of cosmic war is that of a grand encounter between the forces of good and evil, religion and irreligion, order and chaos, and it is played out on an epic scale. Real-world social and political confrontations can be swept up into this grand scenario. Conflicts over territory and political control are lifted into the high proscenium of sacred drama. Such extraordinary images of cosmic war are meta-justifications for religious violence. They not only explain why religious violence happens—why religious persons feel victimized by violence and why they need to take revenge—but also provide a large world view, a template of meaning in which religious violence makes sense. In the context of cosmic war, righteous people are impressed into service as soldiers, and great confrontations occur in which noncombatants are killed. But ultimately the righteous will prevail, for cosmic war is, after all, God's war. And God cannot lose.

In this image of God's role in human history, we have come full circle and return to the ancient idea of God as a warrior. In most of the writings by religious revolutionaries, they see themselves as soldiers in an army commanded by God. Interestingly, just like the ancient manuals of warfare, many of the writings of these present-day activists are essentially how-to books for paramilitary actions. Yet their military manuals, like those of their ancient forebears, are also undergirded by a sense of moral imperative. They fight because they imagine it to be their righteous obligation—a neglected religious duty, as the Egyptian activist Abd al-Salam Faraj put it. Such duties are themselves religious responsibilities and lead to the most extreme forms of religious obligation: martyrdom and sacrifice.

With the idea of sacrifice, we have also, in an interesting way, turned to the central subject matter discussed in the writings in the second section of this reader. The very act of engaging in cosmic war can be imagined to be a redemptive religious event. It is for this reason that many volunteer willingly, even eagerly, for suicide missions that will result in their own martyrdom. Their sacrifices are religious in nature. It is no surprise, then, that the last instructions given to the hijackers who attacked the World Trade Center and the Pentagon on September 11, 2001, were overwhelmingly religious. When Mohammad Atta and his colleagues boarded the airplanes on that fateful day, they followed a carefully crafted ritualized plan aimed at purifying themselves and their horrible act, which they committed with the personal assurance that they were following the path of God.

1
KAUTILYA

ANCIENT HINDU JUSTIFICATIONS for undertaking violence in warfare are found in the classic fourth-century B.C.E. text, the Arthashastra. The very name of the volume indicates its religious purpose: it is knowledge (*shastra*) about political and economic issues—*artha*—that are one of the four essential aspects of the Hindu way of life. Similarly, the Dharmashastra shows the proper way to undertake one's *dharma*—one's social obligations. These texts show that fulfilling one's political, economic, and social responsibilities are religious duties, and persons who are in positions of responsibility are expected to live out each of these aspects of life in a skillful and appropriate way.

Responsibility for political life is ultimately in the hands of the rulers, and thus the Arthashastra is largely aimed at how a king should rule, especially when confronted with enemies of the state. The authorship of the multiple-volume work is attributed to a court adviser, Kautilya, and the object of the *Arthashastra* is to give guidance to the king in formulating political and economic policies for the sake of a larger moral and spiritual cause.

The Arthashastra does not encourage kings to wage warfare indiscriminately. In fact, it says nothing about the decision to go to war in the first place. It assumes that this critical moral determination is part of the responsibilities given to a king as an upholder of *rajdharma*—the righteousness of public life. The traditional symbol of the moral responsibility of rulers was the "white umbrella"—the shield of social order that the king was supposed to maintain so that the citizens of a kingdom could fulfill their own *dharma*—their own moral and social obligations.

In this excerpt, the Arthashastra provides advice to a ruler who is at war. A fight may be "open"—waged on a battlefield—or "treacherous." The latter is one conducted in the manner of guerrilla warfare. The text recommends that verses from the classic Hindu text, the Vedas, be recited and rituals performed by priests in order to give blessings to the soldiers as they enter into battle.

"FORMS OF TREACHEROUS FIGHTS," THE ARTHASHASTRA

He who is possessed of a strong army, who has succeeded in his intrigues, and who has applied remedies against dangers may undertake an open fight, if he has secured a position favorable to himself; otherwise a treacherous fight.

He should strike the enemy when the latter's army is under trouble or is furiously attacked; or he who has secured a favorable position may strike the enemy entangled in an unfavorable position. Or he who possesses control over the elements of his own state may, through the aid of the enemy's traitors, enemies and inimical wild tribes, make a false impression of his own defeat on the mind of the enemy who is entrenched in a favorable position, and having thus dragged the enemy into an unfavorable position, he may strike the latter. When the enemy's army is in a compact body, he should break it by means of his elephants; when the enemy has come down from its favorable position, following the false impression of the invader's defeat, the invader may turn back and strike the enemy's army, broken or unbroken. Having struck the front of the enemy's army, he may strike it again by means of his elephants and horses when it has shown its back and is running away. When frontal attack is unfavorable, he should strike it from behind; when attack on the rear is unfavorable, he should strike it in front; when attack on one side is unfavorable, he should strike it on the other.

Or having caused the enemy to fight, with his own army of traitors, enemies and wild tribes, the invader should with his fresh army strike the enemy when tired. Or having through the aid of traitors given to the enemy the impression of defeat, the invader with full confidence in his own strength may allure and strike the over-confident enemy. Or the invader, if he is vigilant, may strike the careless enemy when the latter is deluded with the thought that the invader's merchants, camp and carriers have been destroyed. Or having made his strong force look like a weak force, he may strike the enemy's brave men when falling against him. Or having captured the enemy's cattle or having destroyed the enemy's dogs, he may induce the enemy's brave men to come out and may slay them. Or having made the enemy's men sleepless by harassing them at night, he may strike them during the day, when they are weary from want of sleep and are parched by heat, himself being under the shade. Or with his army of elephants enshrouded with cotton and leather dress, he may offer a night-battle to his enemy. Or he may strike the enemy's men during the afternoon when they are tired by making preparations during the forenoon; or he may strike the whole of the enemy's army when it is facing the sun.

A desert, a dangerous spot, marshy places, mountains, valleys, uneven boats, cows, cart-like array of the army, mist, and night are temptations alluring the enemy against the invader.

The beginning of an attack is the time for treacherous fights.

As to an open or fair fight, a virtuous king should call his army together, and, specifying the place and time of battle, address them thus: "I am a paid servant like yourselves; this country is to be enjoyed (by me) together with you; you have to strike the enemy specified by me."

His minister and priest should encourage the army by saying thus:

"It is declared in the *Vedas* that the goal which is reached by sacrificers after performing the final ablutions in sacrifices in which the priests have been duly paid for is the very goal which brave men are destined to attain." About this there are the two verses:

"Beyond those places which Bráhmans, desirous of getting into heaven, attain together with their sacrificial instruments by performing a number of sacrifices, or by practicing penance are the places which brave men, losing life in good battles, are destined to attain immediately."

"Let not a new vessel filled with water, consecrated and covered over with grass be the acquisition of that man who does not fight in return for the subsistence received by him from his master, and who is therefore destined to go to hell."

Astrologers and other followers of the king should infuse spirit into his army by pointing out the impregnable nature of the array of his army, his power to associate with gods, and his omniscience; and they should at the same time frighten the enemy. The day before the battle, the king should fast and lie down on his chariot with weapons. He should also make oblations into the fire pronouncing the *mantras* of the *Atharvaveda,* and cause prayers to be offered for the good of the victors as well as of those who attain to heaven by dying in the battle-field. He should also submit his person to Bráhmans; he should make the central portion of his army consist of such men as are noted for their bravery, skill, high birth, and loyalty and as are not displeased with the rewards and honors bestowed on them. The place that is to be occupied by the king is that portion of the army which is composed of his father, sons, brothers, and other men, skilled in using weapons, and having no flags and headdress. He should mount an elephant or a chariot, if the army consists mostly of horses; or he may mount that kind of animal, of which the army is mostly composed or which is the most skillfully trained. One who is disguised like the king should attend to the work of arraying the army.

Soothsayers and court bards should describe heaven as the goal for the brave and hell for the timid; and also extol the caste, corporation, family, deeds, and character of his men. The followers of the priest should proclaim the auspicious aspects of the witchcraft performed. Spies, carpenters and astrologers should also declare the success of their own operations and the failure of those of the enemy.

After having pleased the army with rewards and honors, the commander-in-chief should address it and say:

"A hundred thousand for slaying the king (the enemy); fifty thousand for slaying the commander-in-chief, and the heir-apparent; ten thousand for slaying the chief of the brave; five thousand for destroying an elephant, or a chariot; a thousand for killing a horse; a hundred for slaying the chief of the infantry; twenty for bringing a head; and twice the pay in addition to whatever is seized." This information should be made known to the leaders of every group of ten men.

Physicians with surgical instruments, machines, remedial oils, and cloth in their hands; and women with prepared food and beverage should stand behind, uttering encouraging words to fighting men.

The army should be arrayed on a favorable position, facing other than the south quarter, with its back turned to the sun, and capable to rush as it stands. If the array is made on an unfavorable spot, horses should be run. If the army arrayed on an unfavorable position is confined or is made to run away from it (by the enemy), it will be subjugated either as standing or running away; otherwise it will conquer the enemy when standing or running away. The even, uneven, and complex nature of the ground in the front or on the sides or in the rear should be examined. On an even site, staff-like or circular array should be made; and on an uneven ground, arrays of compact movement or of detached bodies should be made.

Having broken the whole army of the enemy, the invader should seek for peace. If the armies are of equal strength, he should make peace when requested for it; and if the enemy's army is inferior, he should attempt to destroy it, but not that which has secured a favorable position and is reckless of life.

When a broken army, reckless of life, resumes its attack, its fury becomes irresistible; hence he should not harass a broken army of the enemy.

2

SUN TZU

———

SAID TO BE THE OLDEST military treatise in the world, *The Art of War* provides a spiritually balanced way of approaching warfare. It was written in the fifth century B.C.E. in ancient China by Sun Tzu, "Master Sun"—which is most likely an honorific name given to a general, Sun Wu. *The Art of War* is a practical manual for fighting that has been applied to martial arts as well as to warfare between states. Like the ancient Indian text, the Arthashastra, *The Art of War* implies that kings in ancient China conduct warfare only if they have a justifiable reason for doing so. Moreover, the manual insists that the conduct of war be consistent with the balanced state of harmony that is advocated in Chinese religious texts.

In this excerpt, Sun Tzu provides the conditions that determine whether a potential fighter is prepared for battle. The five constant factors that determine the outcome of warfare include "the moral law," a state of harmony that unites followers and their rulers and makes certain that warfare is conducted with the consent of the governed. Though, as Sun Tzu states, "all warfare is based on deception," it is also clear that the aim of battle is to restore a state of order and calm, and elsewhere in *The Art of War* Sun Tzu observes that the most favorable outcome is when the context is shifted and the conflict diverted so that no bloodshed is required at all.

"LAYING PLANS," *THE ART OF WAR*

1. Sun Tzu said: The art of war is of vital importance to the State.
2. It is a matter of life and death, a road either to safety or to ruin. Hence it is a subject of inquiry which can on no account be neglected.
3. The art of war, then, is governed by five constant factors, to be taken into account in one's deliberations when seeking to determine the conditions obtaining in the field.
4. These are: (1) The Moral Law; (2) Heaven; (3) Earth; (4) The Commander; (5) Method and Discipline.
5, 6. The Moral Law causes the people to be in complete accord with their ruler, so that they will follow him regardless of their lives, undismayed by any danger.
7. Heaven signifies night and day, cold and heat, times and seasons.

8. Earth comprises distances, great and small; danger and security; open ground and narrow passes; the chances of life and death.

9. The Commander stands for the virtues of wisdom, sincerity, benevolence, courage and strictness.

10. By Method and Discipline are to be understood the marshaling of the army in its proper subdivisions, the graduations of rank among the officers, the maintenance of roads by which supplies may reach the army, and the control of military expenditure.

11. These five heads should be familiar to every general: he who knows them will be victorious; he who knows them not will fail.

12. Therefore, in your deliberations, when seeking to determine the military conditions, let them be made the basis of a comparison, in this wise:

13.

(1) Which of the two sovereigns is imbued with the Moral Law?

(2) Which of the two generals has most ability?

(3) With whom lie the advantages derived from Heaven and Earth?

(4) On which side is discipline most rigorously enforced?

(5) Which army is stronger?

(6) On which side are officers and men more highly trained?

(7) In which army is there the greater constancy both in reward and punishment?

14. By means of these seven considerations I can forecast victory or defeat.

15. The general that hearkens to my counsel and acts upon it will conquer: let such a one be retained in command! The general that hearkens not to my counsel nor acts upon it, will suffer defeat: let such a one be dismissed!

16. While heading the profit of my counsel, avail yourself also of any helpful circumstances over and beyond the ordinary rules.

17. According as circumstances are favorable, one should modify one's plans.

18. All warfare is based on deception.

19. Hence, when able to attack, we must seem unable; when using our forces, we must seem inactive; when we are near, we must make the enemy believe we are far away; when far away, we must make him believe we are near.

20. Hold out baits to entice the enemy. Feign disorder, and crush him.

21. If he is secure at all points, be prepared for him. If he is in superior strength, evade him.

22. If your opponent is of choleric temper, seek to irritate him. Pretend to be weak, that he may grow arrogant.

23. If he is taking his ease, give him no rest. If his forces are united, separate them.

24. Attack him where he is unprepared, appear where you are not expected.

25. These military devices, leading to victory, must not be divulged beforehand.

26. Now the general who wins a battle makes many calculations in his temple ere the battle is fought.

The general who loses a battle makes but few calculations beforehand. Thus do many calculations lead to victory, and few calculations to defeat: how much more no calculation at all! It is by attention to this point that I can foresee who is likely to win or lose.

THE BHAGAVAD GITA

ONE OF THE HINDU TRADITION'S most beloved texts, the Bhagavad Gita, is a sermon delivered in the context of war. It is part of the great epic, the Mahabharata, that comprises a shelf of books that were written down several centuries before the time of Christ. At the heart of the epic is a great battle on the field of Kurukshetra in North India between two sets of cousins, the Kauravas and the Pandavas. As one of the princes, Arjuna, prepares to command his chariot into battle, he reflects out loud about the meaninglessness of warfare. Either he will kill or be killed, he despairs, and either way it will involve taking a life or being destroyed by one of his own cousins.

As luck would have it, his chariot driver overhears Arjuna's lament, and he is no ordinary soldier. The driver is Lord Krishna. The Hindu god turns to Arjuna and patiently explains to him the necessity for entering into battle, which turns out to be an explanation for discovering meaning in life itself. The sermon is known as the Bhagavad Gita—the song (*gita*) of the auspicious one (*bhagavad*).

The passages that follow begin with Arjuna's dilemma about being forced into a conflict where he will either kill or be killed. Everything that follows is part of Lord Krishna's response. He begins by berating Arjuna not only for his cowardice but also for taking the physical body too seriously. Beneath this physical world is a more eternal one, and a more true self, a soul that cannot slay or be slain. Lord Krishna also talks about the reason why people should strive in the world—not for accomplishment but for duty and the virtue of struggle itself.

The last section of the passage is a plea for what has come to be known as "non-attached action," focusing on the purity of an action and not on its goals. Mohandas Gandhi found this section of the Bhagavad Gita to be important as he created his idea of *satyagraha*, a form of fighting that focused on the character of the struggle—the means rather than the ends. Because the Gita maintains that true fighting should focus on the way the battle is waged and not on its outcome, Gandhi suggested that virtuous struggle should always be nonviolent.

THE BHAGAVAD GITA IN THE MAHABHARATA

"Woe! We have resolved to commit a great crime as we stand ready to kill family out of greed for kingship and pleasures! It were healthier for me if the Dhartartastras, weapons in hand, were to kill me, unarmed and defenseless, on the battlefield!"

Having spoken thus, on that field of battle, Arjuna sat down in the chariot pit, letting go of arrows and bow, his heart anguished with grief.

Samjaya said:

Then, to this Arjuna who was so overcome with compassion, despairing, his troubled eyes filled with tears. Madhusudana said:

The Lord said:

Why has this mood come over you at this bad time. Arjuna, this cowardice unseemly to the noble, not leading to heaven, dishonorable? Do not act like a eunuch. Partha, it does not become you! Rid yourself of this vulgar weakness of heart, stand up, enemy-burner!

Arjuna said:

How can I fight back at Bhisma with my arrows in battle, or at Drona, Madhusudana? Both deserve my homage, enemy-slayer!

> It were better that without slaying my gurus
> I went begging instead for alms in this land
> Than that I by slaying my covetous gurus.
> Indulge in the joys that are dipped in their blood.

> And we do not know what is better for us:
> That we defeat them or they defeat us;
> Dhrtarastra's men are positioned before us,
> After killing whom we have nothing to live for.

> My nature afflicted with the vice of despair,
> My mind confused over what is the Law,
> I ask, what is better? Pray tell me for sure,
> Pray guide me, your student who asks for your help!

> There is nothing I see that might dispel
> This sorrow that desiccates my senses,
> If on earth I were to obtain without rivals
> A kingdom, nay even the reign of the Gods!

Samjaya said:

Having spoken thus to Hrskesa, enemy-burner Gudakesa said to Govinda, "I will not fight!" and fell silent. And with a hint of laughter Hrskesa spoke to him who sat forlorn between the two armies. O Bharata—

The Lord said:

You sorrow over men you should not be sorry for, and yet you speak to sage issues. The wise are not sorry for wither the living of the dead.

immortality of the soul

Never was there a time when I did not exist, or you, or these kings, nor shall any of us cease to exist hereafter. Just as creatures with bodies pass through childhood, youth, and old age in their bodies, so there is a passage to another body, and a wise man is not confused about it. The contacts of the senses with their objects, which produce sensations of cold and heat, comfort and discomfort, come and go without staying, Kaunteya. Endure them, Bharata. The wise man whom they do not trouble, for whom happiness and unhappiness are the same, is fit for immortality.

There is no becoming of what did not already exist, there I no unbecoming of what does exist: those who see the principles see the boundary between the two. But know that that on which all this world is strung is imperishable: no one can bring about the destruction of this indestructible. What ends of this unending embodied, indestructible, and immeasurable being is just its bodies—therefore fight, Bharata! He who thinks that this being is a killer and he who imagines that it is killed do neither of them know. It is not killed nor does it kill.

the self

It is never born nor does it die;
Nor once that it is will it ever not be;
Unborn, unending, eternal, and ancient
It is not killed when the body is killed.

The man who knows him for what he is—indestructible, eternal, unborn, without end—how does he kill whom or have whom killed, Partha?

As a man discards his worn-out clothes
And puts on different ones that are new.
So the one in the body discards aged bodies
And joins with other ones that are new.

Swords do not cut him, fire does not burn him, water does not wet him, wind does not parch him. He cannot be cut, he cannot be burned, wetted, or parched, for he is eternal, ubiquitous, stable, unmoving, and forever. He is the unmanifest, beyond thought, he is said to be beyond transformation; therefore if you know him as such, you have no cause for grief.

Or suppose you hold that he is constantly born and constantly dead, you still have no cause to grieve over him, strong-armed prince, for to the born death is assured, and birth is assured to the dead; therefore there is no cause for grief, if the matter is inevitable. Bharata, with creatures their beginnings are unclear, their middle periods are clear, and their ends are unclear—why complain about it?

It is by a rare chance that a man does see him,
It's a rarity too if another proclaims him,
A rare chance that someone else will hear him,
And even if hearing him no one knows him.

This embodied being is in anyone's body forever beyond killing, Bharata; therefore you have no cause to sorrow over any creatures. Look to your Law and do not waver, for there is nothing more salutary for a baron than a war that is lawful. It is an open door to heaven, happily happened upon; and blesses are the warriors, Partha, who find a war like that!

Or suppose you will not engage this lawful war: then you give up your Law and honor, and incur guilt. Creatures will tell of your undying shame, and for one who has been honored dishonor is worse than death. The warriors will think that you shrank from the battle out of fear, and those who once esteemed you highly will hold you of little account. Your ill-wishers will spread many unspeakable tales about you, condemning your skill—and what is more miserable than that?

Either you are killed and will then attain to heaven, or you triumph and will enjoy the earth. Therefore rise up, Kaunteya, resolved upon battle! Holding alike happiness and unhappiness, gain and loss, victory and defeat, yoke yourself to the battle, and so do not incur evil.

This is the spirit according to theory; now hear how this spirit applies in practice, yoked with which you will cut away the bondage of the act. In this there is no forfeiture of effort, nor an obstacle to completion; even very little of *this* Law saves from great peril. This one spirit is defined here as singleness of purpose, scion of Kuru, whereas the spirits of those who are not purposeful are countless and many-branched. This flowering language which the unenlightened expound, they who delight in the disputations on the Veda, holding that there is nothing more, Partha, inspired by desire, set upon heaven—this language that brings on rebirth as the result of acts and abounds in a variety of rituals aimed at the acquisition of pleasures and power, robs those addicted to pleasures and power of their minds; and on them this spirit, this singleness of purpose in concentration, is not enjoined. The domain of the Vedas is the world of the three *gunas*: transcend that domain, Arjuna, beyond the pairs of opposites, always abiding in purity, beyond acquisition and conservation, the master of yourself. As much use as there is in a well when water overflows on all sides, so much use is there in all Vedas for the enlightened Brahmin.

Your entitlement is only to the rite, not ever at all to its fruits. Be not motivated by the fruits of acts, but also do not purposely seek to avoid acting. Abandon self-interest, Dhanamanjaya, and perform the acts while

applying this singlemindedness. Remain equable in success and failure—
this equableness is called the application—for the act as such is far inferior to the application of singleness of purpose to it, Dhanamanjaya. Seek
shelter in this singlemindedness—pitiful are those who are motivated by
fruits! Armed with this singleness of purpose, a man relinquishes here
both good and evil *karman*. Therefore yoke yourself to this application—
this application is the capacity to act. The enlightened who are armed
with this singleness of purpose rid themselves of the fruits that follow
upon acts; and, set free from the bondage of rebirth, go on to a state of
bliss. When you have the desire to crossover this quagmire of delusion,
then you will become disenchanted with what is supposed to be revealed,
and the revealed itself. When your spirit of purposiveness stands unshaken
at cross-purposes with the revealed truth, and immobile in concentration, then you will have achieved the application.

4
SOHO TAKUAN

SOHO TAKUAN WAS an early seventeenth-century Zen master who was associated with the martial arts and the samurai warrior art of swordsmanship. He was one of the leading monks in the Rinzai school of Zen Buddhism and served as the chief abbot of a monastery in Kyoto and Tokyo (then known as Edo). His interests ranged from gardening to art and calligraphy, and his writings were informed with a Zen sensibility about discipline and control in all aspects of life. Takuan wrote a hundred poems and several books, including his best known, *The Unfettered Mind,* which still serves as a reference work for applying Buddhist concepts to all aspects of culture and especially to the martial arts.

In the excerpt from *The Unfettered Mind* that follows, Takuan prescribes the correct attitude for someone engaging in battle and applying the martial arts. He does not raise the issue of whether the conflict is a worthy one or whether one is entering it for just reasons. He seems to assume that the fight is for defensive reasons, not for personal gain. He also seems to assume that there are no nonviolent options available for resolving the conflict. So assuming that a fight is unavoidable and necessary, the question for Takuan is how to conduct himself in a way that is effective and consistent with Buddhist principles.

Takuan does not address the Buddhist requirement of nonviolence directly. Rather, like the Hindu scriptures, the Bhagavad Gita, Takuan observes that the True Self is beyond one's mortal character. Thus, although he advocates avoiding taking life as much as possible, he claims that the True Self neither kills nor is killed in battle. The character of the fighter comes in the quality of the fighting, not in the outcome. Takuan shows that Zen Buddhist practices are able to purify these actions, and—as in many other aspects of Buddhist life—the warrior's strength comes from discipline, concentration, and being free from extraneous thought.

"ANNALS OF THE SWORD TAIA,"
THE UNFETTERED MIND

Presumably, as a martial artist, I do not fight for gain or loss, am not concerned with strength or weakness, and neither advance a step nor retreat a step. The enemy does not see me. I do not see the enemy. Penetrating to a place where heaven and earth have not yet divided, where Ying and Yang have not yet arrived, I quickly and necessarily gain effect.

Presumably indicates something I do not know for sure.

Originally this character was read with the meaning "lid." For example, when a lid is put on a tier of boxes, although we do not know for sure what has been put inside, if we use our imaginations we will hit the mark six or seven times out of ten. Here also I do not know for sure, but figure tentatively that it must be so. Actually, this is a written for we use even about things we do know for sure. We do this to humble ourselves and so as not to seem to be speaking in a knowing manner.

Martial artist is as the character indicates.

Not to fight for gain or loss, not to be concerned with strength or weakness means not vying for victory or worrying about defeat, and not being concerned with the functions of strength or weakness.

Neither advance a step nor retreat a step means taking neither one step forward nor one step to the rear. Victory is gained without stirring from where you are.

The me of "the enemy does not see me" refers to my True Self. It does not mean my perceived self.

People can see the perceived self; it is rare for them to discern the True Self. Thus, I say, "The enemy does not see me."

I do not see the enemy. Because I do not take the personal view of the perceived self, I do not see the martial art of the enemy's perceived self. Although I say, "I do not see the enemy," this does not mean I do not see the enemy right before my very eyes. To be able to see the one without seeing the other is a singular thing.

Well then, the True Self is the self that existed before the division of heaven and earth and before one's father and mother were born. This self is the self within me, the birds and the beasts, the grasses and the trees and all phenomena. It is exactly what is called the Buddha-nature.

This self has no shape or form, has no birth, and has no death. It is not a self that can be seen with the aid of your present physical eye. Only the man who has received enlightenment is able to see this. The man who does see this is said to have seen into his own nature and become a Buddha.

Long ago, the World Honored One went into the Snowy Mountains and after passing six years in suffering, became enlightened. This was the enlightenment of the True Self. The ordinary man has no strength of faith, and does not know the persistence of even three or five years. But those who study the Way are absolutely diligent for ten to twenty, twenty-four hours a day. They muster up great strength of faith, speak with those who have wisdom, and disregard adversity and suffering. Like a parent who has lost a child, they do not retreat a scintilla from their established resolution. They think deeply, adding inquiry to inquiry. In the end, they,

they arrive at the place where even Buddhist doctrine and Buddhist Law melt away, and are naturally able to see "This."

Penetrating to a place where heaven and earth have not yet divided, where Ying and Yang have not yet arrived, I quickly and necessarily gain effect means to set one's eyes on the place that existed before heaven became heaven and earth became earth, before Ying and Yang came into being. It is to use neither thought nor reasoning and to look straight ahead. In this way, the time of gaining great effect will surely arrive.

Well then, the accomplished man uses the sword but does not kill others. He uses the sword and gives other life. When it is necessary to kill, he kills. When it is necessary to give life, he gives life. When killing, he kills in complete concentration; when giving life, he gives life in complete concentration. Without looking at right and wrong, he is able to see right and wrong; without attempting to discriminate, he is able to discriminate well. Treading on water is just like treading on land, and treading on land is just like treading on water. If he is able to gain this freedom, he will not be perplexed by anyone on earth. In all things, he will be beyond companions.

The *accomplished man* means the man accomplished in the martial arts.

He uses the sword, but does not kill others means that even though he does not use the sword to cut other down, when others are confronted by this principle, they cower and become as dead men of their own accord. There is no need to kill them.

He uses the sword and gives others life means that while he deals with his opponents with a sword, he leaves everything to the movements of the other man, and is able to observe him just as he pleases.

When it is necessary to kill, he kills; when it is necessary to give life, he gives life. When killing, he kills in complete concentration; when giving life, he gives life in complete concentration means that in either giving life or taking life, he does so with freedom in a meditative state that is total absorption, and the meditator becomes one with the object of meditation.

Without looking at right and wrong, he is able to see right and wrong; without attempting to discriminate, he is able to discriminate well. This means that concerning his martial art, he does not look at it to say "correct" or "incorrect," but he is able to see which it is. He does not attempt to judge matters, but he is able to do so well.

If one sets up a mirror, the form of whatever happens to be in front of it will be reflected and will be seen. As the mirror does this mindlessly, the various forms are reflected clearly, without any intent to discriminate this from that. Setting up his whole mind like a mirror, the man who employs the martial arts will have no intention of discriminating right from wrong, but according to the brightness of the mirror of his mind, the judgement of right and wrong will be perceived without his giving it any thought.

Treading on water is just like treading on land, and treading on land is just like treading on water. The meaning of this will not be known by anyone unenlightened about the very source of mankind.

If the fool steps on land like he steps on water, when he walks on land, he is going to fall on his face. If he steps on water like he steps on land, when he does step onto water he may think that he can actually walk around. Concerning this matter, the man who forgets about both land and water should arrive at this principle for the first time.

If he is able to gain this freedom, he will not be perplexed by anyone on earth. According to this, the martial artist who is able to gain freedom will not be in a quandary about what to do, regardless of whom on earth he comes up against.

In all things, he will be beyond companions means that as he will be without peer in all the world, he will be just like Shakyamuni, who said, "In Heaven above and Earth below, I alone am the Honored One."

Buddha

Do you want to obtain this? Walking, stopping, sitting or lying down, in speaking and in remaining quiet, during tea and during rice, you must never neglect exertion, you must quickly set your eye on the goal, and investigate thoroughly, both coming and going. Thus should you look straight into things. As months pile up and years pass by, it should seem like a light appearing on its own in the dark. You will receive wisdom without a teacher and will generate mysterious ability without trying to do so. At just such a time, this does not depart from the ordinary, yet it transcends it. By name, I call it "Taia."

Do you want to obtain this? "This" points out what was written about above, so the question is whether you are considering obtaining the meaning of the foregoing.

Walking, stopping, sitting or lying down. The four of these - walking, stopping, sitting, lying down - are called the Four Dignities. All people are involved in them.

In speaking and in remaining silent means while talking about things or without uttering a word.

During tea and during rice means while drinking tea and eating rice.

You must never neglect exertion, you must quickly set your eye on the goal, and investigate thoroughly, both coming and going. Thus should you look straight into things. This means that you should never be careless or negligent in your efforts, and you should constantly come back to yourself. You should quickly fix your eye on the goal and continually investigate these principles in depth. Always go straight ahead, considering what is right to be right, and what is wrong to be wrong, while observing this principle in all things.

As months pile up and years pass by, it should seem like a light appearing on its own in the dark means that, in just that way, you should carry on with your efforts tirelessly. As you advance with the accumulation of months and years, the acquiring you do on your own of the mysterious principle will be just like suddenly encountering the light from a lantern on a dark night.

You will receive wisdom without a teacher means that you will acquire this fundamental wisdom without its ever having been transmitted to you by a teacher.

You will generate mysterious ability without trying to do so. Because the works of the ordinary man all come from his consciousness, they are all actions of the world of created phenomena, and are involved with suffering. At the same time, because actions that are uncreated are generated from this fundamental wisdom, they alone are natural and peaceful.

At just such a time means precisely at such a time. It indicated the time when one receives wisdom without a teacher and generates mysterious ability without trying to do so.

The meaning of *this does not depart from the ordinary, yet it transcends it* is that this uncreated mysterious ability is not generated from the unusual.

Since only actions that are unremarkably everyday in character become the uncreated, this principle never departs, nor does it separate itself, from the ordinary. Which is still to say that the ordinary actions in the world of created phenomena of the everyday ordinary man are entirely different. Thus it is said that "this does not depart from the ordinary, yet it transcends it."

By name, I call it "Taia." Taia is the name of an [ancient Chinese] sword that has no equal under heaven. This famous jewelled sword can freely cut anything, from rigid metal and tempered steel to dense and hardened gems and stones. Under heaven there is nothing that can parry this blade. The person who obtains this uncreated mysterious ability will not be swayed by the commander of huge armies or an enemy force of hundreds of thousands. This is the same as there being nothing that can impede the blade of this famous sword. Thus I call the strength of this mysterious ability the Sword Taia.

THE HEBREW BIBLE

MANY OF THE EARLIEST BOOKS of the Bible refer to warfare. The books of Exodus and Deuteronomy, for instance, testify that battles were carried out not only in God's name but also as a part of a divine action. These books are part of the Torah, a text revered by Jews, Christians, and Muslims and set in the historical context of the founding of ancient Israel. The book of Exodus describes how Moses led the formerly captive people out of bondage in Egypt into the promised land, where twelve tribes came together in a confederated political entity on the west bank of the Jordan River. But they were threatened by competing tribes both north and south of them. Put to writing centuries later, the biblical books remember a series of battles for the very survival of the kingdom of Israel.

For this reason, war was in the background of many of these early books in the Hebrew Bible (known to Christians as the Old Testament). The book of Deuteronomy makes a distinction between required wars and wars of expansion. Wars of expansion were justified not for material gain but for defensive purposes—to preempt the possibility of attack by distant enemies—and required wars were necessary in order to prevent foreign religious influence on the chosen people within the holy land. Defense of the community was the only circumstance in which warfare was required and the only situation of military encounter in which Israelites could be certain that God was on their side.

In these passages from Exodus, God literally enters the fray as an avenging warrior. In the account described in Deuteronomy, God is portrayed as being directly involved in the affairs of battle, identifying enemies, and leading the Israelite forces into combat. The passages from Deuteronomy also allow for armed attacks against those who attempt to lure someone into worship of other gods, even if the tempter is one's own brother, wife, or son. As with enemies of state, no mercy is allowed: they are utterly destroyed. In Deuteronomy, enemies in distant lands who surrender are allowed to live—though as forced laborers—and the scenes of battle are vivid and bloody. In Exodus, God states a willingness to send "terror before you."

Elsewhere in the Hebrew Bible there appears to be a link between warfare and sacrifice—as when conquered soldiers are regarded as sacrificial victims (see Isaiah 34). The authors of the early books in the Bible appear to be aware of rituals involving human sacrifice performed by neighboring peoples, and warn against such practices. The near sacrifice of Isaac by his father Abraham (Genesis 22) has riveted the imaginations of Jews, Christians, and Muslims, who regard the story as a parable of divine testing and ultimate mercy.

In the passages that follow, the violence of military action is tempered with a call for moderation and peace. A military assault is warranted only when an enemy is offered the opportunity for peaceful submission and declines. The innocent should be spared, and strangers should not be oppressed. Though the proscription for warfare is aggressive in these texts, the purpose is ultimately not selfish but is to reject falsehood and fulfill God's plan.

DEUTERONOMY 20

1: "When you go forth to war against your enemies, and see horses and chariots and an army larger than your own, you shall not be afraid of them; for the Lord your God is with you, who brought you up out of the land of Egypt.

2: And when you draw near to the battle, the priest shall come forward and speak to the people,

3: and shall say to them, 'Hear, O Israel, you draw near this day to battle against your enemies: let not your heart faint; do not fear, or tremble, or be in dread of them;

4: for the Lord your God is he that goes with you, to fight for you against your enemies, to give you the victory.'

5: Then the officers shall speak to the people, saying, 'What man is there that has built a new house and has not dedicated it? Let him go back to his house, lest he die in the battle and another man dedicate it.

6: And what man is there that has planted a vineyard and has not enjoyed its fruit? Let him go back to his house, lest he die in the battle and another man enjoy its fruit.

7: And what man is there that has betrothed a wife and has not taken her? Let him go back to his house, lest he die in the battle and another man take her.'

8: And the officers shall speak further to the people, and say, 'What man is there that is fearful and fainthearted? Let him go back to his house, lest the heart of his fellows melt as his heart.'

9: And when the officers have made an end of speaking to the people, then commanders shall be appointed at the head of the people.

10: "When you draw near to a city to fight against it, offer terms of peace to it.

11: And if its answer to you is peace and it opens to you, then all the people who are found in it shall do forced labor for you and shall serve you.

12: But if it makes no peace with you, but makes war against you, then you shall besiege it;

13: and when the Lord your God gives it into your hand you shall put all its males to the sword,

14: but the women and the little ones, the cattle, and everything else in the city, all its spoil, you shall take as booty for yourselves; and you shall enjoy the spoil of your enemies, which the Lord your God has given you.

15: Thus you shall do to all the cities which are very far from you, which are not cities of the nations here.

16: But in the cities of these peoples that the Lord your God gives you for an inheritance, you shall save alive nothing that breathes,

17: but you shall utterly destroy them, the Hittites and the Amorites, the Canaanites and the Per'izzites, the Hivites and the Jeb'usites, as the Lord your God has commanded;

18: that they may not teach you to do according to all their abominable practices which they have done in the service of their gods, and so to sin against the Lord your God.

19: "When you besiege a city for a long time, making war against it in order to take it, you shall not destroy its trees by wielding an axe against them; for you may eat of them, but you shall not cut them down. Are the trees in the field men that they should be besieged by you?

20: Only the trees which you know are not trees for food you may destroy and cut down that you may build siegeworks against the city that makes war with you, until it falls."

EXODUS 23

1: "You shall not utter a false report. You shall not join hands with a wicked man, to be a malicious witness.

2: You shall not follow a multitude to do evil; nor shall you bear witness in a suit, turning aside after a multitude, so as to pervert justice;

3: nor shall you be partial to a poor man in his suit.

4: "If you meet your enemy's ox or his ass going astray, you shall bring it back to him.

5: If you see the ass of one who hates you lying under its burden, you shall refrain from leaving him with it, you shall help him to lift it up.

6: "You shall not pervert the justice due to your poor in his suit.

7: Keep far from a false charge, and do not slay the innocent and righteous, for I will not acquit the wicked.

8: And you shall take no bribe, for a bribe blinds the officials, and subverts the cause of those who are in the right.

9: "You shall not oppress a stranger; you know the heart of a stranger, for you were strangers in the land of Egypt.

10: "For six years you shall sow your land and gather in its yield;

11: but the seventh year you shall let it rest and lie fallow, that the poor of your people may eat; and what they leave the wild beasts may eat. You shall do likewise with your vineyard, and with your olive orchard.

12: "Six days you shall do your work, but on the seventh day you shall rest; that your ox and your ass may have rest, and the son of your bondmaid, and the alien, may be refreshed.

13: Take heed to all that I have said to you; and make no mention of the names of other gods, nor let such be heard out of your mouth.

14: "Three times in the year you shall keep a feast to me.

15: You shall keep the feast of unleavened bread; as I commanded you, you shall eat unleavened bread for seven days at the appointed time in the month of Abib, for in it you came out of Egypt. None shall appear before me empty-handed.

16: You shall keep the feast of harvest, of the first fruits of your labor, of what you sow in the field. You shall keep the feast of in-gathering at the end of the year, when you gather in from the field the fruit of your labor.

17: Three times in the year shall all your males appear before the Lord God.

18: "You shall not offer the blood of my sacrifice with leavened bread, or let the fat of my feast remain until the morning.

19: "The first of the first fruits of your ground you shall bring into the house of the Lord your God. 'You shall not boil a kid in its mother's milk.'

20: "Behold, I send an angel before you, to guard you on the way and to bring you to the place which I have prepared.

21: Give heed to him and hearken to his voice, do not rebel against him, for he will not pardon your transgression; for my name is in him.

22: "But if you hearken attentively to his voice and do all that I say, then I will be an enemy to your enemies and an adversary to your adversaries.

23: "When my angel goes before you, and brings you in to the Amorites, and the Hittites, and the Per'izzites, and the Canaanites, the Hivites, and the Jeb'usites, and I blot them out,

24: you shall not bow down to their gods, nor serve them, nor do according to their works, but you shall utterly overthrow them and break their pillars in pieces.

25: You shall serve the Lord your God, and I will bless your bread and your water; and I will take sickness away from the midst of you.

26: None shall cast her young or be barren in your land; I will fulfil the number of your days.

27: I will send my terror before you, and will throw into confusion all the people against whom you shall come, and I will make all your enemies turn their backs to you.

28: And I will send hornets before you, which shall drive out Hivite, Canaanite, and Hittite from before you.

29: I will not drive them out from before you in one year, lest the land become desolate and the wild beasts multiply against you.

30: Little by little I will drive them out from before you, until you are increased and possess the land.

31: And I will set your bounds from the Red Sea to the sea of the Philistines, and from the wilderness to the Euphra'tes; for I will deliver the inhabitants of the land into your hand, and you shall drive them out before you.

32: You shall make no covenant with them or with their gods.

33: They shall not dwell in your land, lest they make you sin against me; for if you serve their gods, it will surely be a snare to you."

6
THE QUR'AN

WARFARE ALSO APPEARS IN the most sacred scripture of Islam, the Qur'an. The Qur'an (also transliterated as "Koran") is regarded by Muslims as the revealed word of God (Allah). It is thought to have been transmitted in a series of remarkable revelations given to the Prophet Muhammad by the Angel Gabriel in the Arabian cities of Mecca and Medina in the first decades of the seventh century C.E. These were turbulent times for the early Muslim community since the Prophet himself was driven out of his home in Mecca. From nearby Medina he organized a military force, which was eventually able to retake his native city. But threats from other armies in the region persisted and the battles continued. By the end of the Prophet's life in 632, Islam dominated most of the Arabian world. In such a conflict of armed strife, it is not surprising that the Qur'anic revelations mention military struggle.

What is remarkable is how seldom the Qur'an speaks about fighting. The revelations consist of more than six thousand verses, and only a few—a hundred or so, less than 2 percent—refer to warfare. Most of the verses in the Qur'an provide guidance on how to live a moral life, explanations about the nature of the world and divine revelation, and suggestions of how to praise God. Specific historical events are seldom mentioned, and specific rules are not provided. Many references are made to the earlier prophetic traditions, including the stories and sayings in the Hebrew Bible and the New Testament. Christians and Jews are regarded as "people of the book" and therefore have a special place of honor for Muslims.

The section of the Qur'an that appears here is from one of the longest sections of the Qur'an, Surah 2, or "The Cow" (so called because it relates a dialogue between Moses and the ancient Israelites over the sacrifice of a cow). It reflects the diversity that is found in the sacred Muslim writings. It begins with prescriptions for worshiping God and living an ethical life. It also talks about the "law of equality," and the need for equal justice before the law. It urges Muslims to fast during the month of Ramadan, undertake the pilgrimage to Mecca, and be fair in matters of money and social justice.

It also requires Muslims to be fair in times of warfare—to spare innocent people and to allow enemies to peacefully surrender. In the passage that follows, the Qur'an makes clear that military action may be justified to allow people to worship freely. But the Qur'an does not make a judgment about what other battles may be undertaken—most interpreters assume that war is warranted only for defensive reasons, when the Muslim community is under attack, as it frequently was in the Prophet's lifetime. When fighting is necessary, it should be limited and just. Fighting was not undertaken by God himself (as was sometimes the case in the Hebrew Bible and other ancient scriptures), but by angels or humans fighting for the will of God.

SURAH 2 ("THE COW")

177. It is not righteousness that ye turn your faces Towards east or West; but it is righteousness to believe in Allah and the Last Day, and the Angels, and the Book, and the Messengers; to spend of your substance, out of love for Him, for your kin, for orphans, for the needy, for the wayfarer, for those who ask, and for the ransom of slaves; to be steadfast in prayer, and practice regular charity; to fulfill the contracts which ye have made; and to be firm and patient, in pain (or suffering) and adversity, and throughout all periods of panic. Such are the people of truth, the Allah fearing.

178. O ye who believe! the law of equality is prescribed to you in cases of murder: the free for the free, the slave for the slave, the woman for the woman. But if any remission is made by the brother of the slain, then grant any reasonable demand, and compensate him with handsome gratitude, this is a concession and a Mercy from your Lord. After this whoever exceeds the limits shall be in grave penalty.

179. In the Law of Equality there is (saving of) Life to you, o ye men of understanding; that ye may restrain yourselves.

180. It is prescribed, when death approaches any of you, if he leave any goods that he make a bequest to parents and next of kin, according to reasonable usage; this is due from the Allah fearing.

181. If anyone changes the bequest after hearing it, the guilt shall be on those who make the change. For Allah hears and knows (All things).

182. But if anyone fears partiality or wrong-doing on the part of the testator, and makes peace between (The parties concerned), there is no wrong in him: For Allah is Oft-forgiving, Most Merciful.

183. O ye who believe! Fasting is prescribed to you as it was prescribed to those before you, that ye may (learn) self-restraint,—

184. (Fasting) for a fixed number of days; but if any of you is ill, or on a journey, the prescribed number (Should be made up) from days later. For those who can do it (With hardship), is a ransom, the

feeding of one that is indigent. But he that will give more, of his own free will,—it is better for him. And it is better for you that ye fast, if ye only knew.

185. Ramadan is the (month) in which was sent down the Qur'an, as a guide to mankind, also clear (Signs) for guidance and judgment (Between right and wrong). So every one of you who is present (at his home) during that month should spend it in fasting, but if any one is ill, or on a journey, the prescribed period (Should be made up) by days later. Allah intends every facility for you; He does not want to put to difficulties. (He wants you) to complete the prescribed period, and to glorify Him in that He has guided you; and perchance ye shall be grateful.

186. When My servants ask thee concerning Me, I am indeed close (to them): I listen to the prayer of every suppliant when he calleth on Me: Let them also, with a will, Listen to My call, and believe in Me: That they may walk in the right way.

187. Permitted to you, on the night of the fasts, is the approach to your wives. They are your garments and ye are their garments. Allah knoweth what ye used to do secretly among yourselves; but He turned to you and forgave you; so now associate with them, and seek what Allah Hath ordained for you, and eat and drink, until the white thread of dawn appear to you distinct from its black thread; then complete your fast Till the night appears; but do not associate with your wives while ye are in retreat in the mosques. Those are Limits (set by) Allah. Approach not nigh thereto. Thus doth Allah make clear His Signs to men: that they may learn self-restraint.

188. And do not eat up your property among yourselves for vanities, nor use it as bait for the judges, with intent that ye may eat up wrongfully and knowingly a little of (other) people's property.

189. They ask thee concerning the New Moons. Say: They are but signs to mark fixed periods of time in (the affairs of) men, and for Pilgrimage. It is no virtue if ye enter your houses from the back: It is virtue if ye fear Allah. Enter houses through the proper doors: And fear Allah. That ye may prosper.

190. Fight in the cause of Allah those who fight you, but do not transgress limits; for Allah loveth not transgressors.

191. And slay them wherever ye catch them, and turn them out from where they have Turned you out; for tumult and oppression are worse than slaughter; but fight them not at the Sacred Mosque, unless they (first) fight you there; but if they fight you, slay them. Such is the reward of those who suppress faith.

192. But if they cease, Allah is Oft-forgiving, Most Merciful.

193. And fight them on until there is no more Tumult or oppres-

sion, and there prevail justice and faith in Allah. but if they cease,
Let there be no hostility except to those who practise oppression.

194. The prohibited month for the prohibited month,—and so
for all things prohibited,—there is the law of equality. If then any
one transgresses the prohibition against you, Transgress ye likewise
against him. But fear Allah, and know that Allah is with those who
restrain themselves.

195. And spend of your substance in the cause of Allah, and make
not your own hands contribute to (your) destruction; but do good;
for Allah loveth those who do good.

196. And complete the Hajj or umra in the service of Allah. But if
ye are prevented (From completing it), send an offering for sacrifice,
such as ye may find, and do not shave your heads until the offering
reaches the place of sacrifice. And if any of you is ill, or has an ail-
ment in his scalp, (Necessitating shaving), (He should) in compensation either fast, or feed the poor, or offer sacrifice; and when ye are in
peaceful conditions (again), if any one wishes to continue the umra
on to the hajj, He must make an offering, such as he can afford, but
if he cannot afford it, He should fast three days during the hajj and
seven days on his return, Making ten days in all. This is for those
whose household is not in (the precincts of) the Sacred Mosque. And
fear Allah, and know that Allah Is strict in punishment.

197. For Hajj are the months well known. If any one undertakes
that duty therein, Let there be no obscenity, nor wickedness, nor
wrangling in the Hajj. And whatever good ye do, (be sure) Allah
knoweth it. And take a provision (With you) for the journey, but the
best of provisions is right conduct. So fear Me, o ye that are wise.

198. It is no crime in you if ye seek of the bounty of your Lord
(during pilgrimage). Then when ye pour down from (Mount) Arafat,
celebrate the praises of Allah at the Sacred Monument, and celebrate
His praises as He has directed you, even though, before this, ye went
astray.

199. Then pass on at a quick pace from the place whence it is
usual for the multitude so to do, and ask for Allah's forgiveness. For
Allah is Oft-forgiving, Most Merciful.

200. So when ye have accomplished your holy rites, celebrate the
praises of Allah, as ye used to celebrate the praises of your fathers,—
yea, with far more Heart and soul. There are men who say: "Our
Lord! Give us (Thy bounties) in this world!" but they will have no
portion in the Hereafter.

201. And there are men who say: "Our Lord! Give us good in this
world and good in the Hereafter, and defend us from the torment of
the Fire!"

202. To these will be allotted what they have earned; and Allah is quick in account.

203. Celebrate the praises of Allah during the Appointed Days. But if any one hastens to leave in two days, there is no blame on him, and if any one stays on, there is no blame on him, if his aim is to do right. Then fear Allah, and know that ye will surely be gathered unto Him.

204. There is the type of man whose speech about this world's life May dazzle thee, and he calls Allah to witness about what is in his heart; yet is he the most contentious of enemies.

205. When he turns his back, His aim everywhere is to spread mischief through the earth and destroy crops and cattle. But Allah loveth not mischief.

206. When it is said to him, "Fear Allah. He is led by arrogance to (more) crime. Enough for him is Hell;—An evil bed indeed (To lie on)!

207. And there is the type of man who gives his life to earn the pleasure of Allah. And Allah is full of kindness to (His) devotees.

208. O ye who believe! Enter into Islam whole-heartedly; and follow not the footsteps of the evil one; for he is to you an avowed enemy.

209. If ye backslide after the clear (Signs) have come to you, then know that Allah is Exalted in Power, Wise.

210. Will they wait until Allah comes to them in canopies of clouds, with angels (in His train) and the question is (thus) settled? but to Allah do all questions go back (for decision).

211. Ask the Children of Israel how many clear (Signs) We have sent them. But if any one, after Allah's favour has come to him, substitutes (something else), Allah is strict in punishment.

212. The life of this world is alluring to those who reject faith, and they scoff at those who believe. But the righteous will be above them on the Day of Resurrection; for Allah bestows His abundance without measure on whom He will.

213. Mankind was one single nation, and Allah sent Messengers with glad tidings and warnings; and with them He sent the Book in truth, to judge between people in matters wherein they differed; but the People of the Book, after the clear Signs came to them, did not differ among themselves, except through selfish contumacy. Allah by His Grace Guided the believers to the Truth, concerning that wherein they differed. For Allah guided whom He will to a path that is straight.

214. Or do ye think that ye shall enter the Garden (of bliss) without such (trials) as came to those who passed away before you? they

encountered suffering and adversity, and were so shaken in spirit that even the Messenger and those of faith who were with him cried: "When (will come) the help of Allah." Ah! Verily, the help of Allah is (always) near!

215. They ask thee what they should spend (In charity). Say: Whatever ye spend that is good, is for parents and kindred and orphans and those in want and for wayfarers. And whatever ye do that is good,—(Allah) knoweth it well.

✗ 216. Fighting is prescribed for you, and ye dislike it. But it is possible that ye dislike a thing which is good for you, and that ye love a thing which is bad for you. But Allah knoweth, and ye know not.

217. They ask thee concerning fighting in the Prohibited Month. Say: "Fighting therein is a grave (offence); but graver is it in the sight of Allah to prevent access to the path of Allah, to deny Him, to prevent access to the Sacred Mosque, and drive out its members." Tumult and oppression are worse than slaughter. Nor will they cease fighting you until they turn you back from your faith if they can. And if any of you Turn back from their faith and die in unbelief, their works will bear no fruit in this life and in the Hereafter; they will be companions of the Fire and will abide therein.

218. Those who believed and those who suffered exile and fought (and strove and struggled) in the path of Allah,—they have the hope of the Mercy of Allah. And Allah is Oft-forgiving, Most Merciful.

7
THOMAS AQUINAS

THE "JUST WAR" THEORY that has become the foundation of most Christian thought about morally sanctioned violence is based on a compromise. According to the early Christian theologian, Aurelius Augustine, the perfect ethics of peace that Jesus talked about in the New Testament was appropriate to the "city of God," to which we should all aspire. We live, however, in a more mundane realm—the "city of man"—where life is less pleasant, and force is sometimes necessary to keep evil at bay. Reaching back to earlier concepts of just war that extend back at least to the time of Cicero, Augustine specified the conditions in which war could be morally sanctioned. He specifically condemns "the lust for power," which he regards as an inappropriate reason for warfare. These conditions were later refined by the medieval Catholic theologian, Thomas Aquinas, and have become the bedrock of the Christian Church's teaching on the morality of war ever since.

Aquinas, a thirteenth-century Italian Roman Catholic theologian, was a scholar in the Dominican order of Friars who compiled the most comprehensive theological treatise of his time, *Summa Theologica* ("the highest theology"). To this day "Thomistic theology" is required reading in Catholic seminaries, and his systematic categorization of virtues and rules are regarded as normative Christian teaching.

Included in Saint Thomas's systematic treatment of ethics is just war theory. In the excerpt that follows, Aquinas responds to hypothetical questions about warfare. Even though it might first appear that all war is sinful, Aquinas points out that military defense is sometimes necessary to keep evil things from happening. For this reason, war can be justified, but only if three conditions are met: it is approved by a proper authority, it is conducted for a just cause, and the intention is to reduce violence and evil in the world. War should be undertaken only for the purpose of enabling peace.

"WHETHER IT IS ALWAYS SINFUL TO WAGE WAR?" *SUMMA THEOLOGICA*

Objection 1: It would seem that it is always sinful to wage war. Because punishment is not inflicted except for sin. Now those who wage war are threatened by Our Lord with punishment, according to Mt.

obj 1 - Waging war is a sin

26:52: "All that take the sword shall perish with the sword." Therefore all wars are unlawful.

Objection 2: Further, whatever is contrary to a Divine precept is a sin. But war is contrary to a Divine precept, for it is written (Mt. 5:39): "But I say to you not to resist evil"; and (Rm. 12:19): "Not revenging yourselves, my dearly beloved, but give place unto wrath." Therefore war is always sinful.

Objection 3: Further, nothing, except sin, is contrary to an act of virtue. But war is contrary to peace. Therefore war is always a sin.

Objection 4: Further, the exercise of a lawful thing is itself lawful, as is evident in scientific exercises. But warlike exercises which take place in tournaments are forbidden by the Church, since those who are slain in these trials are deprived of ecclesiastical burial. Therefore it seems that war is a sin in itself.

On the contrary, Augustine says in a sermon on the son of the centurion: "If the Christian Religion forbade war altogether, those who sought salutary advice in the Gospel would rather have been counselled to cast aside their arms, and to give up soldiering altogether. On the contrary, they were told: 'Do violence to no man . . . and be content with your pay' [Lk. 3:14]. If he commanded them to be content with their pay, he did not forbid soldiering."

I answer that, In order for a war to be just, three things are necessary. First, the authority of the sovereign by whose command the war is to be waged. For it is not the business of a private individual to declare war, because he can seek for redress of his rights from the tribunal of his superior. Moreover it is not the business of a private individual to summon together the people, which has to be done in wartime. And as the care of the common weal is committed to those who are in authority, it is their business to watch over the common weal of the city, kingdom or province subject to them. And just as it is lawful for them to have recourse to the sword in defending that common weal against internal disturbances, when they punish evil-doers, according to the words of the Apostle (Rm. 13:4): "He beareth not the sword in vain: for he is God's minister, an avenger to execute wrath upon him that doth evil"; so too, it is their business to have recourse to the sword of war in defending the common weal against external enemies. Hence it is said to those who are in authority (Ps. 81:4): "Rescue the poor: and deliver the needy out of the hand of the sinner"; and for this reason Augustine says: "The natural order conducive to peace among mortals demands that the power to declare and counsel war should be in the hands of those who hold the supreme authority."

Secondly, a just cause is required, namely that those who are attacked, should be attacked because they deserve it on account of some fault. Wherefore Augustine says: "A just war is wont to be described as one that avenges wrongs, when a nation or state has to be punished, for refusing to make amends for the wrongs inflicted by its subjects, or to restore what it has seized unjustly."

Thirdly, it is necessary that the belligerents should have a rightful intention, so that they intend the advancement of good, or the avoidance of evil. Hence Augustine says: "True religion looks upon as peaceful those wars that are waged not for motives of aggrandizement, or cruelty, but with the object of securing peace, of punishing evil-doers, and of uplifting the good." For it may happen that the war is declared by the legitimate authority, and for a just cause, and yet be rendered unlawful through a wicked intention. Hence Augustine says: "The passion for inflicting harm, the cruel thirst for vengeance, an unpacific and relentless spirit, the fever of revolt, the lust of power, and such like things, all these are rightly condemned in war."

Reply to Objection 1: As Augustine says: "To take the sword is to arm oneself in order to take the life of anyone, without the command or permission of superior or lawful authority." On the other hand, to have recourse to the sword (as a private person) by the authority of the sovereign or judge, or (as a public person) through zeal for justice, and by the authority, so to speak, of God, is not to "take the sword," but to use it as commissioned by another, wherefore it does not deserve punishment. And yet even those who make sinful use of the sword are not always slain with the sword, yet they always perish with their own sword, because, unless they repent, they are punished eternally for their sinful use of the sword.

Reply to Objection 2: Such like precepts, as Augustine observes, should always be borne in readiness of mind, so that we be ready to obey them, and, if necessary, to refrain from resistance or self-defense. Nevertheless it is necessary sometimes for a man to act otherwise for the common good, or for the good of those with whom he is fighting. Hence Augustine says: "Those whom we have to punish with a kindly severity, it is necessary to handle in many ways against their will. For when we are stripping a man of the lawlessness of sin, it is good for him to be vanquished, since nothing

is more hopeless than the happiness of sinners, whence arises a guilty impunity, and an evil will, like an internal enemy."

Reply to Objection 3: Those who wage war justly aim at peace, and so
they are not opposed to peace, except to the evil peace, which Our Lord
"came not to send upon earth" (Mt. 10:34). Hence Augustine says: "We
do not seek peace in order to be at war, but we go to war that we may
have peace. Be peaceful, therefore, in warring, so that you may vanquish
those whom you war against, and bring them to the prosperity of peace."

Reply to Objection 4: Manly exercises in warlike feats of arms are not
all forbidden, but those which are inordinate and perilous, and end in
slaying or plundering. In olden times warlike exercises presented no such
danger, and hence they were called "exercises of arms" or "bloodless
wars," as Jerome states in an epistle.

REINHOLD NIEBUHR

REINHOLD NIEBUHR (1892–1971), often considered America's greatest Protestant theologian and one of its most influential social critics, created a major impact on twentieth-century political life. As a Christian "realist," he accepted that there were times when violence was necessary to combat injustice and oppression—though military action should always be subject to the rules of a "just war." Born into a German immigrant community in Missouri, Niebuhr became a pastor to a working-class congregation in Detroit during the Depression years and then joined the faculty of Union Theological Seminary in New York City, where he became one of the nation's most articulate voices for social justice.

Deeply influenced by the neo-orthodox theological ideas of Karl Barth, Niebuhr abandoned the romanticism of the Social Gospel and accepted the notion that the moral capacity of humans is limited by original sin. He found in the ideas of Augustine a basis for Christian ethics that took a "realistic" appraisal of human nature. In *Moral Man and Immoral Society* (1932), Niebuhr gave a theological basis for explaining the difference between personal and organizational ethics: because groups are utilitarian and goal-oriented they are by definition incapable of sacrificial acts. This basic insight led to the conclusion that collectivities—especially businesses and governments—can express only self-interest.

Niebuhr scorned "moralism"—altruistic excuses given to justify self-interest. In his two-volume work, *The Nature and Destiny of Man*, he condemned the "sentimentalism" of optimistic views of human nature—including those of Mohandas Gandhi and Karl Marx. He regarded history as characterized by irony rather than progress. He argued that love on a social plane can be realized only in justice.

Early in his life Niebuhr was a committed pacifist. He changed his position after the rise of Stalin and Hitler. In this essay, written at a time when the Nazi threat loomed over Europe, Niebuhr explains why the Christian Church "is not pacifist" but has the moral responsibility to justify a limited amount of strategic violence in order to keep even greater violence and social injustice from occurring.

"WHY THE CHRISTIAN CHURCH IS NOT PACIFIST"

Whenever the actual historical situation sharpens on the issue, the debate whether the Christian Church is, or ought to be, pacifist is carried on with fresh vigor both inside and outside the Christian community. Those who are not pacifists seek to prove that pacifism is a heresy; while the pacifists contend, or at least imply, that the church's failure to espouse pacifism unanimously can only be interpreted as apostasy, and must be attributed to its lack of courage or to its want of faith.

There may be an advantage in stating the thesis, with which we enter this debate, immediately. The thesis is, that the failure of the church to espouse pacifism is not apostasy, but is derived from an understanding of the Christian gospel which refuses simply to equate the Gospel with the "law of love." Christianity is not simply a new law, namely, the law of love. The finality of Christianity cannot be proved by analyses which seek to reveal that the law of love is stated more unambiguously and perfectly in the life and teachings of Christ than anywhere else. Christianity is a religion which measures the total dimension of human existence not only in terms of the final norm of human conduct, which is expressed in the law of love, but also in terms of the fact of sin. It recognizes that the same man who can become his true self only by striving infinitely for self-realization beyond himself is also inevitably involved in the sin of infinitely making his partial and narrow self the true end of existence. It believes, in other words, that though Christ is the true norm (the "second Adam") for every man, every man is also in some sense a crucifier of Christ.

The good news of the gospel is not the law that we ought to love one another. The good news of the gospel is that there is a resource of divine mercy which is able to overcome a contradiction within our souls, which we cannot ourselves overcome. This contradiction is that, though we know we ought to love our neighbor as ourself, there is a "law in our members which wars against the law that is in our mind" (Rom. 7:23), so that, in fact, we love ourselves more than our neighbor.

The grace of God which is revealed in Christ is regarded by Christian faith as, on the one hand, an actual "power of righteousness" which heals the contradiction within our hearts. In that sense Christ defines the actual possibilities of human existence. On the other hand, this grace is conceived as "justification," as pardon rather than power, as the forgiveness of God, which is vouchsafed to man despite the fact that he never achieves the full measure of Christ. In that sense Christ is the "impossible possibility." Loyalty to him means realization in intention, but does not actually mean the full realization of the measure of Christ. In this doctrine of forgiveness and justification, Christianity measures the full seriousness of sin as a permanent factor in human history.

It is rather remarkable that so many modern Christians should believe that Christianity is primarily a "challenge" to man to obey the law of Christ; whereas it is, as a matter of fact, a religion which deals realistically with the problem presented by the violation of this law. Far from believing that the ills of the world could be set right "if only" men obeyed the law of Christ, it has always regarded the problem of achieving justice in a sinful world as a very difficult task. In the profounder versions of the Christian faith the very utopian illusions, which are currently equated with Christianity, have been rigorously disavowed.

The Truth and Heresy of Pacifism

Nevertheless, it is not possible to regard pacifism simply as a heresy. In one of its aspects modern Christian pacifism is simply a version of Christian perfectionism. It expresses a genuine impulse in the heart of Christianity, the impulse to take the law of Christ seriously and not to allow the political strategies, which the sinful character of man makes necessary, to become final norms. In its profounder forms, this Christian perfectionism did not proceed from a simple faith that the "law of love" could be regarded as an alternative to the political strategies by which the world achieves a precarious justice. These strategies invariably involve the balancing of power with power; and they never completely escape the peril of tyranny on the one hand, and the peril of anarchy and warfare on the other.

In medieval ascetic perfectionism and in Protestant sectarian perfectionism (of the type of Meno Simons, for instance) the effort to achieve a standard of perfect love in individual life was not presented as a political alternative. On the contrary, the political problem and task were specifically disavowed. This perfectionism did not give itself to the illusion that it had discovered a method for eliminating the element of conflict from political strategies. On the contrary, it regarded the mystery of evil as beyond its power of solution. It was content to set up the most perfect and unselfish individual life as a symbol of the Kingdom of God. It knew that this could only be done by disavowing the political task and by freeing the individual of all responsibility for social justice.

It is this kind of pacifism which is not a heresy. It is rather a valuable asset for the Christian faith. It is a reminder to the Christian community that the relative norms of social justice, which justify both coercion and resistance to coercion, are not final norms, and that Christians are in constant peril of forgetting their relative and tentative character and of making them too completely normative.

There is thus a Christian pacifism which is not a heresy. Yet most modern forms of Christian pacifism are heretical. Presumably inspired by the

Christian gospel, they have really absorbed the Renaissance faith in the goodness of man, have rejected the Christian doctrine of original sin as an outmoded bit of pessimism, have reinterpreted the cross so that it is made to stand for the absurd idea that perfect love is guaranteed a simple victory over the world, and have rejected all other profound elements of the Christian gospel as "Pauline" accretions which must be stripped from the "simple gospel of Jesus." This form of pacifism is not only heretical when judged by the standards of the total gospel. It is equally heretical when judged by the facts of human existence. There are no historical realities which remotely conform to it. It is important to recognize this lack of conformity to the facts of experience as a criterion of heresy.

All forms of religious faith are principles of interpretation which we use to organize our experience. Some religions may be adequate principles of interpretation at certain levels of experience, but they break down at deeper levels. No religious faith can maintain itself in defiance of the experience which it supposedly interprets. A religious faith which substitutes faith in man for faith in God cannot finally validate itself in experience. If we believe that the only reason men do not love each other perfectly is because the law of love has not been preached persuasively enough, we believe something to which experience does not conform. If we believe that if Britain had only been fortunate enough to have produced 30 percent instead of 2 percent conscientious objectors to military service, Hitler's heart would have been softened and he would not have dared to attack Poland, we hold a faith which no historic reality justifies.

Such a belief has no more justification in the facts of experience than the communist belief that the sole cause of man's sin is the class organization of society and the corollary faith that a "classless" society will be essentially free of human sinfulness. All of these beliefs are pathetic alternatives to the Christian faith. They all come finally to the same thing. They do not believe that man remains a tragic creature who needs the divine mercy as much at the end as at the beginning of his moral endeavors. They believe rather that there is some fairly easy way out of the human situation of "self-alienation." In this connection it is significant that Christian pacifists, rationalists like Bertrand Russell, and mystics like Aldous Huxley, believe essentially the same thing. The Christians make Christ into the symbol of their faith in man. But their faith is really identical with that of Russell or Huxley.

The common element in these various expressions of faith in man is the belief that man is essentially good at some level of his being. They believe that if you can abstract the rational-universal man from what is finite and contingent in human nature, or if you can only cultivate some mystic-universal element in the deeper levels of man's consciousness, you will be able to eliminate human selfishness and the consequent conflict of life with life. These rational or mystical views of man conform neither to the New Testament's view of human nature nor yet to the complex facts of human experience.

The Absolute Ethic of Jesus

In order to elaborate the thesis more fully, that the refusal of the Christian Church to espouse pacifism is not apostasy and that most modern forms of pacifism are heretical, it is necessary first of all to consider the character of the absolute and unqualified demands which Christ makes and to understand the relation of these demands to the gospel.

It is very foolish to deny that the ethic of Jesus is an absolute and uncompromising ethic. It is, in the phrase of Ernst Troeltsch, an ethic of "love universalism and love perfectionism." The injunctions "resist not evil," "love your enemies," "if ye love them that love you what thanks have you?" "be not anxious for your life," and "be ye therefore perfect even as your father in heaven is perfect," are all of one piece, and they are all uncompromising and absolute. Nothing is more futile and pathetic than the effort of some Christian theologians who find it necessary to become involved in the relativities of politics, in resistance to tyranny or in social conflict, to justify themselves by seeking to prove that Christ was involved in the relativities of politics, in resistance to tyranny, or in social conflict, to justify themselves by seeking to prove that Christ was also involved some of these relativities, that he used whips to drive the money-changers out of the Temple, or that he came "not to bring peace but a sword," or that he asked the disciples to sell a cloak and buy a sword. What could be more futile than to build a whole ethical structure upon the exegetical issue whether Jesus accepted the sword with the words: "It is enough," or whether he really meant: "Enough of this" (Luke 22:36)?

Those of us who regard the ethic of Jesus as finally and ultimately normative, but as not immediately applicable to the task of securing justice in a sinful world, are very foolish if we try to reduce the ethic so that it will cover and justify our prudential and relative standards and strategies. To do this is to reduce the ethic to a new legalism. The significance of the law of love is precisely that it is not just another law, but a law which transcends all law. Every law and every standard which falls short of the law of love embodies contingent factors and makes concessions to the fact that sinful man must achieve tentative harmonies of life with life which are less than the best. It is dangerous and confusing to give these tentative and relative standards final and absolute religious sanction.

Curiously enough the pacifists are just as guilty as their less absolutist brethren of diluting the ethic of Jesus for the purpose of justifying their position. They are forced to recognize that an ethic of pure non-resistance can have no immediate relevance to any political situation; for in every political situation it is necessary to achieve justice by resisting pride and power. They therefore declare that the ethic of Jesus is not an ethic of non-resistance, but one of non-violent resistance; that it allows one to resist evil provided the resistance does not involve the destruction of life or property.

There is not the slightest support in Scripture for this doctrine of non-violence. Nothing could be plainer than that the ethic uncompromisingly enjoins non-resistance and not non-violent resistance. Furthermore, it is obvious that the distinction between violent and non-violent resistance is not an absolute distinction. If it is made absolute, we arrive at the morally absurd position of giving moral preference to the non-violent power which Doctor Goebbels wields, over the type of power wielded by a general. This absurdity is really derived from the modern (and yet probably very ancient and very Platonic) heresy of regarding the "physical" as evil and the "spiritual" as good. The reductio ad absurdum of this position is achieved in a book which has become something of a textbook for modern pacifists, Richard Gregg's *The Power of Non-Violence*. In this book, non-violent resistance is commended as the best method of defeating your foe, particularly as the best method of breaking his morale. It is suggested that Christ ended his life on the cross because he had not completely mastered the technique of non-violence, and must for this reason be regarded as a guide who is inferior to Gandhi, but whose significance lies in initiating a movement which culminates in Gandhi.

One may well concede that a wise and decent statesmanship will seek not only to avoid conflict, but to avoid violence in conflict. Parliamentary political controversy is one method of sublimating political struggles in such a way as to avoid violent collisions of interest. But this pragmatic distinction has nothing to do with the more basic disinction has nothing to do with the more basic distinction between the ethic of the "Kingdom of God," in which no concession is made to human sin, and all relative political strategies which, assuming human sinfulness, seek to secure the highest measure of peace and justice among selfish and sinful men.

The Tension between "Be Not Anxious" and "Love Thy Neighbor"

If pacifists were less anxious to dilute the ethic of Christ to make it conform to their particular type of non-violent politics, and if they were less obsessed with the obvious contradiction between the ethic of Christ and the fact of war, they might have noticed that the injunction "resist not evil" is only part and parcel of a total ethic which we violate not only in war-time, but every day of our life, and that overt conflict is but a final vivid revelation of the character of human existence. This total ethic can be summarized most succinctly in the two injunctions "Be not anxious for your life" and "Love thy neighbor as thyself" (cf. Matt. 6:31, 19:19).

In the first of these, attention is called to the fact that the root and source of all undue self-assertion lies in the anxiety which all men have in regard to their existence. The ideal possibility is that perfect trust in God's providence ("for your heavenly father knoweth what things ye have need of") and perfect unconcern for the physical life ("fear not them which are able to kill the body") would create a state of serenity in which one life would not seek to take advantage of another life. But the fact is that anxiety is an inevitable concomitant of human freedom, and is the root of the inevitable sin which expresses itself in every human activity and creativity. Not even the most idealistic preacher who admonishes his congregation to obey the law of Christ is free of the sin which arises from anxiety. He may or may not be anxious for his job, but he is certainly anxious about his prestige. Perhaps he is anxious for his reputation as a righteous man. He may be tempted to preach a perfect ethic the more vehemently in order to hide an unconscious apprehension of the fact that his own life does not conform to it. There is no life which does not violate the injunction "Be not anxious." That is the tragedy of human sin. It is the tragedy of man who is dependent upon God, but seeks to make himself independent and self-sufficing.

In the same way there is no life which is not involved in a violation of the injunction, "Thou shalt love thy neighbor as thyself." No one is so blind as the idealist who tells us that war would be unnecessary "if only" nations obeyed the law of Christ, but who remains unconscious of the fact that even the most saintly life is involved in some measure of contradiction to this law. Have we not all known loving fathers and mothers who, despite a very genuine love for their children, had to be resisted if justice and freedom were to be gained for the children? Do we not know that the sinful will-to-power may be compounded with the most ideal motives and may use the latter as its instruments and vehicles? The collective life of man undoubtedly stands on a lower moral plane than the life of individuals, yet nothing revealed in the life of races and nations is unknown in individual life. The sins of pride and of lust for power and the consequent tyranny and injustice are all present, at least in an inchoate form, in individual life. Even as I write, my little five-year-old boy comes to me with the tale of an attack made upon him by his year-old sister. This tale is concocted to escape paternal judgment for being too rough in playing with his sister. One is reminded of Germany's claim that Poland was the aggressor and the similar Russian charge against Finland.

The Tension between Tyranny and Anarchy

The pacifists do not know human nature well enough to be concerned about the contradictions between the law of love and the sin of man, until sin has conceived and brought forth death. They do not see that sin introduces an element of conflict into the world and that even the most loving relations are not free of it. They are, consequently, unable to appreciate the complexity of the problem of justice. They merely assert that if only men loved one another, all the complex, and sometimes horrible, realties of the political order could be dispensed with. They do not see that their "if" begs the most basic problem of human history. It is because men are sinners that justice can be achieved only by a certain degree of coercion on the one hand, and by resistance to coercion and tyranny on the other hand. The political life of man must constantly steer between the Scylla of anarchy and the Charybdis of tyranny.

Human egotism makes large-scale co-operation upon a purely voluntary basis impossible. Governments must coerce. Yet there is an element of evil in this coercion. It is always in danger of serving the purposes of the coercing power rather than the general weal. We cannot fully trust the motives of any ruling class or power. That is why it is important to maintain democratic checks upon the centers of power. It may also be necessary to resist a ruling class, nation or race, if it violates the standards of relative justice which have been set up for it. Such resistance means war. It need not mean overt conflict or violence. But if those who resist tyranny publish their scruples against violence too publicly, the tyrannical power need only threaten the use of violence against non-violent pressure to persuade the resisters to quiescence. The relation of pacifism to the abortive effort to apply non-violent sanctions against Italy in the Ethiopian dispute is instructive at this point.

The refusal to recognize that sin introduces an element of conflict into the world invariably means that a morally perverse preference is given to tyranny over anarchy (war). If we are told that tyranny would destroy itself, if only we would not challenge it, the obvious answer is that tyranny continues to grow if it is not resisted. If it is to be resisted, the risk of overt conflict must be taken. The thesis that German tyranny must not be challenged by other nations because Germany will throw off this yoke in due time, merely means that an unjustified moral preference is given to civil war over international war, for internal resistance runs the risk of conflict as much as external resistance. Furthermore, no consideration is given to the fact that a tyrannical state may grow too powerful to be successfully resisted by purely internal pressure, and that the injustices which it does to other than its own nationals may rightfully lay the problem of the tyranny upon other nations.

It is not unfair to assert that most pacifists who seek to present their religious absolutism as a political alternative to the claims and counter-claims, the pressures and counter-pressures of the political order, invariably betray themselves into this preference for tyranny. Tyranny is not war. It is peace, but it is a peace which has nothing to do with the peace of the Kingdom of God. It is a peace which results from one will establishing a complete dominion over other wills and reducing them to acquiescence.

One of the most terrible consequences of a confused religious absolutism is that it is forced to condone such tyranny as that of Germany in the nations which it has conquered and now cruelly oppresses. It usually does this by insisting that the tyranny is no worse than that which is practised in the so-called democratic nations. Whatever may be the moral ambiguities of the so-called democratic nations, and however serious may be their failure to conform perfectly to their democratic ideals, it is sheer moral perversity to equate the inconsistencies of a democratic civilization with the brutalities which modern tyrannical states practise. If we cannot make a distinction here, there are no historical distinctions which have any value. All the distinctions upon which the fate of civilization has turned in the history of mankind have been just such relative distinctions.

One is persuaded to thank God in such times as these that the common people maintain a degree of "common sense," that they preserve an uncorrupted ability to react against injustice and the cruelty of racial bigotry. This ability has been lost among some Christian idealists who preach the law of love but forget that they, as well as all other men, are involved in the violation of that law; and who must (in order to obscure this glaring defect in their theory) eliminate all relative distinctions in history and praise the peace of tyranny as if it were nearer to the peace of the Kingdom of God than war. The overt conflicts of human history are periods of judgment when what has been hidden becomes revealed. It is the business of Christian prophecy to anticipate these judgments to some degree at least, to call attention to the fact that when men say "peace and quiet" "destruction will come upon them unaware" (cf. Ps. 35:8, Ez. 7:25), and reveal to what degree this overt destruction is a vivid portrayal of the constant factor of sin in human life. A theology which fails to come to grips with this tragic factor of sin is heretical, both from the standpoint of the gospel and in terms of its blindness to obvious facts of human experience in every realm and on every level of moral goodness.

The Contribution of a True Pacifism

Despite our conviction that most modern pacifism is too filled with secular and moralistic illusions to be of the highest value to the Christian community, we may be grateful for the fact that the Christian church has learned, since the last war, to protect its pacifists and to appreciate their testimony. Even when this testimony is marred by self-righteousness, because it does not proceed from a sufficiently profound understanding of the tragedy of human history, it has its value.

It is a terrible thing to take human life. The conflict between man and man and nation and nation is tragic. If there are men who declare that, no matter what the consequences, they cannot bring themselves to participate in this slaughter, the church ought to be able to say to the general community: We quite understand this scruple and we respect it. It proceeds from the conviction that the true end of man is brotherhood, and that love is the law of life. We who allow ourselves to become engaged in war need this testimony of the absolutist against us, lest we accept the warfare of the world as normative, lest we become callous to the horror of war, and lest we forget the ambiguity of our own actions and motives and the risk we run of achieving no permanent good from this momentary anarchy in which we are involved.

But we have a right to remind the absolutists that their testimony against us would be more effective if it were not corrupted by self-righteousness and were not accompanied by the implicit or explicit accusation of apostasy. A pacifism which really springs from the Christian faith, without secular accretions and corruptions, could not be as certain as modern pacifism is that it possesses an alternative for the conflicts and tensions from which and through which the world must rescue a precarious justice.

A truly Christian pacifism would set each heart under the judgment of God to such a degree that even the pacifist idealist would know that knowledge of the will of God is no guarantee of his ability or willingness to obey it. The idealist would recognize to what degree he is himself involved in rebellion against God, and would know that this rebellion is too serious to be overcome by just one more sermon on love, and one more challenge to man to obey the law of Christ.

9

Michael Bray

MICHAEL BRAY IS A LUTHERAN PASTOR in Bowie, Maryland, where he edits one of the most outspoken anti-abortion newsletters in the country, *Capitol Area Christian News*. He is also one of the leading spokespersons for the extreme wing of the anti-abortion movement that justifies the killing of medical personnel involved in providing abortion services.

Bray's father was a naval officer based in Annapolis, Maryland. Though young Michael also began military training at Annapolis, he left after a year and eventually attended seminary and became an ordained Lutheran minister. Bray then left the official Lutheran organization to form his own Reformation Lutheran Church. It meets in his suburban home, which also provides space for a home-care school taught by Bray and his wife. In 1985 Bray and two other defendants stood trial for destroying seven abortion facilities in Delaware, Maryland, Virginia, and the District of Columbia, with a total of more than one million dollars in damages. He was convicted of these charges and served prison time until May 15, 1989.

Bray has publicly defended several activists who have been accused of murderous assaults on abortion clinic staff members. Bray's friend, Rev. Paul Hill, killed Dr. John Britton and his volunteer escort James Barrett as they drove up to The Ladies Center, a clinic providing abortion services in Pensacola, Florida, in 1994. Hill was captured, sentenced to death, and executed by the State of Florida. Several years earlier another member of Bray's network of associates, Rachelle ("Shelly") Shannon, a housewife from rural Oregon, also confessed to a string of abortion clinic bombings. She was convicted of attempted murder for shooting and wounding Dr. George Tiller as he drove away from his clinic in Wichita, Kansas. When Dr. Tiller was killed in 2009 by another of Bray's colleagues, Scott Roeder, Bray wrote that the killer had acted in "righteousness and mercy." Roeder shot the defenseless doctor while he was attending church on a Sunday morning.

Bray is accused of being the author of the underground manual of the Army of God, which specifies how to undertake terrorist attacks. He is also the author of the definitive book on the ethical justification for anti-abortion violence, *A Time to Kill*, which defends his own acts of terrorism, the murders of abortion clinic doctors, and the attempted murder by Shannon. The book was written during the presidency of Bill Clinton, whom Bray denegrates as an apologist for abortion. In the excerpts from the book that follow, Bray argues that his extreme position—rejected by most Christians—is in keeping with the biblical injunctions regarding war, the ethical stance of the theologian Reinhold Niebuhr, and the just war tradition of the Christian Church. In making this ethical parallel, Bray assumes that the acts of abortion are as evil as those acts perpetrated by Nazi war criminals and the other cruelties and dangers for which just war theory provides a moral warrant to violently oppose.

"A TIME FOR REVOLUTION?" *A TIME TO KILL*

Whenever an abortuary goes up in smoke (or, more recently, when an abortionist is killed) I am confronted in the course of interviews with the question: "Do you advocate this sort of thing?" It may seem to be a political (i.e. disingenuous) reply, but I discriminate between defending the justice of forceful intervention and advocating the same.

It is a fair distinction. As much as we have *advocated* public blockades ("rescues") in this country, we would not necessarily have advocated this tactic in the former Soviet Union. One so acting would have found himself on the discomfiting end of a firing squad or relocated to Siberia forever. Now, to be sure, we would have defended and cheered the dear folks who successfully blocked a state-run abortuary for five minutes before being locked away for five decades of years, but we would not necessarily have advocated the tactic.

Similarly, we would say that it is right and good for a Christian to risk his life and that of his family by becoming a missionary in a dangerous foreign land. We certainly would not criticize William Carey for the deaths of family members or the mental troubles suffered by his wife. These troubles came upon him and his family as a result of his choice to do missionary work in India in the late eighteenth century. He did that which was good and right for the sake of the Truth and the lives of people. But we would not recommend this work for everyone. We defend it as a legitimate service to which a Christian may be called. It is one thing to defend the ethics of a given deed; it is another to advocate that deed in a particular situation.

Apologists of forceful intervention are truly misunderstood. They are a maligned, abused minority, erroneously charged with being rebels. But they are no more advocating revolution than are pacifist blockaders advocating abject servitude to the Clinton (abortion promoting) regime.

There is a bit of irony here. The use of force for the purpose of saving innocent lives is arguably much less rebellious than the public stridency expressed in the sit-ins. The fellow who shoots the abortionist or demolishes his slaughter house doesn't necessarily make any public statement to the government. He does not even address the government. His deed is directed exclusively toward the evil he intends to eradicate; and the children he intends to save. His action suggests that he will not tolerate child killing; his view of government is unknown.

On the contrary, those who block doors spend most of their "rescue" efforts face to face with the governing authorities. After a few minutes of sitting by a street in front of a door, he spends hours being arrested, processing through the local police precinct; he spends a day or two in the court room, a few minutes writing a check to the government, and perhaps a few days, weeks, months, or years in prison. Throughout the process, he is expressing his opposition—albeit respectfully—to the government's unjust prosecution of himself. He voices his objection to baby killing and politely defies the authorities by sitting and remaining seated in forbidden places.

To be sure, the use of godly force in opposition to something which has become dear to a culture may threaten the existing order. That prospect poses more complicated ethical issues. In the case at hand the use of force to stop abortion threatens a social "order." If the new pagan "order" of godless democracy and sexual libertinism is destroyed, is another in the offing to replace it?

Moreover, if the new pagan order is as a foundation only recently poured, is there an urgency to quickly shovel the concrete out before it sets? Whether by shovel now (minimal force) or jackhammer later, it does no good to overthrow one order only to replace it with a worse one.

If forceful attacks against the rite of abortion precipitate—simply put—a hot religious war between pagans and Christians, what result will it bring? The question is well illustrated by Russell Kirk:

> Once I was told by a scholar born in Russia of how he had come to understand through terrible events that order necessarily precedes justice and freedom. He had been a Menshevik, or moderate Socialist, at the time of the Russian Revolution. When the Bolsheviks seized power in St. Petersburg, he fled to Odessa, on the Black Sea, where he found a great city in anarchy. Bands of young men commandeered street-cars and clattered wildly through the heart of Odessa, firing with rifles at any pedestrian, as though they were hunting pigeons. At any moment, one's apartment might be invaded by a casual criminal or fanatic, murdering for the sake of a loaf of bread. In this anarchy, justice and freedom were only words. "Then I learned that before we can know justice and freedom, we must have order," my friend said. "Much though I hated the Communists, I saw then that even the grim order of Communism is

better than no order at all. Many might survive under Communism; no one could survive in general disorder."'

Yes, and on the other hand we may also take heed to the words of abolitionist pastor John Rankin's words of 1826. He argued with his slave-holding brother that the prolonged existence of the present government depended upon the extermination of slavery:

> We are commanded to "do justly and love mercy," and this we ought to do without delay, and leave the consequences attending it to the control of Him who gave the command.

The point here is not to argue for the superiority of one method of "rescue" over another. (Much more could be said about the tactical advantages of either of the two modes.) Rather, we simply point up the fact that the use of force does not constitute a greater degree of rebellion than do various forms of protest. Rather, the opposite may well be the case.

The pre–Civil War debates among anti-slavery forces come alive today, some arguing for "gradualism" and others for immediate "abolition" by any means necessary. Debates shall properly continue regarding the best strategy. And yet, the fact is that when rebellion comes, it appropriates the tool of force. The tool which can be used to prevent a death, cause a death, and punish evil-doers, can also be used to alter or replace governments. We shall briefly discuss the use of force as a tool of constructive change.

The shift in government policy regarding not only abortion but homosexuality has set government in overt opposition to Christian Law. The Clinton administration made itself an opponent of God's standard and therefore an adversary of His people. The regime wasted no time displaying its invidious, anti-Christian animus. Within a day of swearing an oath on the Bible and getting Billy Graham's blessing at his inauguration, William the Apostate, a member in good standing with his Southern Baptist home church in Arkansas, signed several executive orders designed to increase the number of abortions in the land. With a stroke of his executive pen he removed restrictions on fetal tissue "experimentation," removed bans on abortions in military hospitals, removed restrictions on "Title X" tax money for "family planning" (read: Planned Parenthood) agencies. Clinton's socialist national "health" insurance plan called for abortions to be covered. The Commander in Chief of the armed forces of the United States also pledged to remove the ban on sodomites in the military.

The executive branch was a warm brother of the Congress which moved swiftly toward federal legislation designed to codify the doctrine of *Roe v. Wade* (via the Freedom of Choice Act) and to punish blockaders (the FACE bill). This behavior (along with the blameworthy vote-casting of the citizenry) does not bode well for national survival.

Change will come, but not by the way Christian folk might like. Christians pray for revival, but revival involves high cost and radical change. Witness the persecutions which preceded the ascendancy of Christian influence to the seat of power under Constantine. Witness the Thirty Years' War and the emergence of nations in the wake of the Reformation. Witness the American Revolution following the Great Awakening. Witness the abolitionist movement and the Civil War following the Second Great Awakening.

[handwritten margin note: An American tradition!]

The desired change in the civil foundations of society may well come about through revolution. For this reason it is useful to transfer the discussion of the godly use of force to that issue. A thorough discussion of the subject is beyond the scope of this book. However, since apostasy abounds, questions arise in the minds of Christians who find themselves in conflict with the powers that are. Is it right to overthrow a government? Are we right to celebrate the American Revolution? Could the Civil War have been avoided by means of a vigorous pursuit of peaceful, gradual manumission? (Was it really the "War of Northern Aggression"—as southerners would call it?)

What about the ethics of revolution? What is the Christian's role? What do the Scriptures say? What has the church said down through the ages? One thinks not only of the crusades, but the multitude of wars fought through the ages. How many were not opposed, but supported by churches? Were they all wrong? Surely our lamb-carrying Jesus couldn't have been approving them! Could He?

Yes. He could. That is the short answer. This Jesus—the same yesterday, today, and forever (Heb. 13:8)—is the "Man of War" of the Scriptures. He is the God of Israel who wrought calamity upon Israel as well as her enemies. He is not squeamish about destruction and war. The One who uses force and consecrates others to do the same does not have a problem with it.

But we late twentieth-century American Christians definitely have a problem with it. We are at peace. And we like the peace.

Do we also like our God? Do we know Him? In his most popular book *Knowing God*, J. I. Packer points up this current aversion to things wrathful about God:

> The modem habit throughout the Christian church is to play this subject down. Those who still believe in the wrath of God (not all do) say little about it; perhaps they do not think much

about it. To an age which has unashamedly sold itself to the gods of greed, pride, sex, and self-will, the Church mumbles on about God's kindness, but says virtually nothing about His judgment.

· A God of War

The idea of a wrathful and forceful God puts a lot of us off. . . . We are talking about bad "theology proper"—a false view of God. Our God is holy as well as merciful. How has this bad theology influenced our view of revolution?

Indeed, the Christian God, even the Lord Jesus Christ, is a forceful (some would say "violent") God. Problematic though it may be, the words of Isaiah confirm well this truth about our God:

Draw near, O nations, to hear;
and listen, O peoples!
Let the earth and all it contains hear,
and the world and all that springs from it. For the Lord's indigna-
tion is
against all the nations,
And His wrath against all their armies;
He has utterly destroyed them.
He has given them over to slaughter. So their slain will be thrown
out, And their corpses will give off their stench,
And the mountains will be drenched with their blood. And all the
host of heaven will wear away
As a leaf withers from the vine
Or as one withers from the fig tree. For My sword is satiated in
heaven, Behold it shall descend for judgment upon Edom,
And upon the people whom I have devoted to destruction The sword
of the Lord is filled with blood

(Is. 34:1–6).

This is the God who slays His apostate people with pestilence (1 Chron. 21:2–16); the One who smote with tumors those who had taken the Ark (1 Sam. 5:9); the One who commands the slaughter of idol-worshipping Israelites (Ex. 32:26–28); the One who said on one occasion, "Cursed be he that keeps back his hand from blood" (Jer. 48:10); (etc. at 2 Kings 18:17; 19:21–33; Ex. 17:14; 2 Chron. 21:2–16; Is. 10:12, 24–27). This is our Lord Jesus. He has no problem with the use of force and bloodshed. He has a big problem with the shedding of innocent blood, however (Prov. 6:16, 17).

Let us look further at the revelation of our Lord Jesus' character. Yes, this is the preincarnate Jesus. But His nature did not change when He took on flesh. He is the everlasting, unchanging God (Mal. 3:6). He is the "same yesterday. today, and forever" (Heb.13:8). He remains a "consuming fire" (Heb. 12:29).

10
ABD AL-SALAM FARAJ

ABD AL-SALAM FARAJ IS the author of a remarkably influential argument for waging war against those he imagines to be the political enemies of Islam. Though rejected by most Muslim thinkers as being illogical and extreme, the ideas in his pamphlet, *Al-Faridah al-Gha'ibah* (The Neglected Duty), state more clearly than any other contemporary writing the religious justifications for radical Muslim acts. It was published and first circulated in Cairo in the early 1980s. Mainstream Muslims would have nothing to do with what they regarded as his extremist ramblings, but some political activists eagerly accepted it, because it provided the theological justification they needed for their violent acts. This document grounds the activities of Islamic terrorists firmly in Islamic tradition, specifically in the sacred text of the Qur'an and the biographical accounts of the Prophet in the Hadith.

Faraj argued that the Qur'an and the Hadith are fundamentally about warfare. He claims that the concept of jihad, holy war, is meant to be taken literally, not allegorically. According to Faraj, the "duty" that has been profoundly "neglected" is jihad. He states that it calls for "fighting, which means confrontation and blood." Moreover, Faraj regards anyone who deviates from the moral and social requirements of Islamic law to be fit targets for jihad; these targets include apostates and unjust rulers within the Muslim community as well as enemies from outside it.

In this excerpt from Faraj's book, he argues against mainstream Muslims who regard his views as deviant from true Islam. Most Muslims believe that Islam preaches peace, and the idea of jihad refers to the struggle against sin within one's own soul. Real fighting can only be justified if one is under attack. But Faraj argues against the idea that jihad is meant to be metaphorical or for defensive purposes only. He also argues against the common Muslim belief that the violent passages in the Qur'an are superseded by the requirements for forgiveness and mercy, and he rejects the familiar distinction between Medinan passages of the Qur'an—revelations received in a time of conflict—and Meccan passages that advocate more peaceful relationships.

He also makes the distinction between the "near enemy"—such as the nominally Muslim rulers of Egypt—and the "far enemy," such as the U.S. government that supported the Egyptian regime. They are both enemies, though Faraj thought that jihad against the near enemy should receive priority attention. Egypt's president, Anwar Sadat, was presumably one of these "near enemies," because Muslim extremists in sympathy with Faraj's viewpoint were involved in Sadat's assassination. Faraj himself was arrested and executed in 1982 for his role in supporting the conspiracy to kill the president.

FROM *THE NEGLECTED DUTY*

Explanation of Why the Islamic Community Differs from Other Communities as far as Fighting Is Concerned

God-Exalted He is –made it clear that this Community differs from the other (religious) Communities as far as Fighting is concerned. In the case of earlier communities God -- Praised and Exalted He is -- made His punishment come (down upon the infidels and the enemies of His religion by means of natural phenomena like eclipses (of the moon), floods, shouts and storms. . . . With regard to the Community of Muhammad-- God's Peace be upon Him -- this differs, for God-Praised and Exalted He is -- addressed them saying: "Fight them and God will punish them at your hands, will humiliate them and aid you against them, and will bring healing to the breasts of people who are believers" (Qur'an 9.14).

This means that a Muslim has first of all the duty to execute the command to fight with his hands. (Once he has done so) God—Praised and Exalted He is --will then intervene (and change) the laws of nature. In this way victory will be achieved through the hands of the believers by means of God's -- Praised and Exalted He is -- (intervention).

Revolt against the Ruler

[handwritten margin note: Judging the ruler]

. . . Al-Nawawi says in his commentary on this Tradition: "The Qadi `Ayyad says: 'The leading Muslim scholars agree that the (duties of) Leadership (of the Community) can not be given to an infidel, and that when (a Leader) suddenly becomes an unbeliever, his leadership comes to an end. The same is the case when he neglects to perform the prayer ceremonies, or to urge (others to perform) them. The majority (of the scholars) also holds (this to be true) when (this leader introduces) a *bid(ah* (innovation)."

Some of the scholars from Basra say, however, that (the leadership nevertheless) is given to him, and continues because he is (only) guilty of allegorizing.

The Qadi says: "When he suddenly becomes an unbeliever, or changes God's Law, or introduces an innovation *(bid ah),* he has no longer the qualifications needed in a Leader, to obey him is no longer necessary, and the Muslims have the duty to revolt against him and to depose him, and to put a Just Imam in his place when they are able to do so. When this occurs to a group of people, they have the duty to revolt and depose the infidel." (This passage is quoted from the Collection of Traditions entitled) *Al-Sahib*, the Chapter on *Jihad*.

This chapter is also the refutation of those who say that it is only permissible to fight under a Caliph or a Commander *(taht khalrfah aw emir)*.

Ibn Taymiyah says: "Any group of people that rebels against any single prescript of the clear and reliably transmitted prescripts of Islam has to be fought, according to the leading scholars of Islam, even if the members of this group pronounce the Islamic Confession of Faith." (This quotation is taken from) *Al-Fatawa al-Kubra*, the chapter on *jihad, p. 281*.

The Enemy Who Is Near and the Enemy Who Is Far

It is said that the battlefield of *jihad* today is the liberation of Jerusalem since it is (part of) the Holy Land. It is true that the liberation of the Holy Land is a religious command, obligatory for all Muslims, but the Apostle of God --May God's Peace be upon Him-- described the believer as "sagacious and prudent" *(kayyis fatin)*, and this means that a Muslim knows what is useful and what is harmful, and gives priority to radical definitive solutions. This is a point that makes the explanation of the following necessary:

First: To fight an enemy who is near is more important than to fight an enemy who is far.

Second: Muslim blood will be shed in order to realize this victory. Now it must be asked whether this victory will benefit the interests of an Islamic State? Or will this victory benefit the interests of Infidel Rule? It will mean the strengthening of a State which rebels against the Laws of God. ... These Rulers will take advantage of the nationalist ideas of these Muslims in order to realize their un-Islamic aims, even though at the surface (these aims) look Islamic. Fighting has to be done (only) under the Banner of Islam and under Islamic Leadership. About this there is no difference of opinion.

Third: The basis of the existence of Imperialism in the Lands of Islam are (precisely) these Rulers. To begin by putting an end to imperialism is not a laudatory and not a useful act. It is only a waste of time. We must concentrate on our own Islamic situation: we have to establish the Rule of God's Religion in our own country first, and to make the Word of God supreme. ... There is no doubt that the first battlefield for *jihad* is the extermination of these infidel leaders and to replace them by a complete Islamic Order. From here we should start.

The Answer to Those Who Say That in Islam
Jihad is Defensive Only

Concerning this question it is proper that we should refute those who say that *jihad* in Islam is defensive, and that Islam was not spread by the sword. This is a false view, which is (nevertheless) repeated by a great number of those who are prominent in the field of Islamic missionary activities. The right answer comes from the Apostle of God -- God's Peace be upon Him-- when he was asked: "What is *jihad* for God's cause?" He then said: "Whosoever fights in order to make the Word of God supreme is some-one who (really) fights for God's cause." To fight is, in Islam, to make supreme the Word of God in this world, whether it be by attacking or by defending. . . .

Islam spread by the sword, and under the very eyes of these Leaders of Unbelief who conceal it from mankind. After the (removal of these Leaders) nobody has an aversion (to Islam). . . .

It is obligatory for the Muslims to raise their swords under the very eyes of the Leaders who hide the Truth and spread false-hoods. If (the Muslims) do not do this, the Truth will not reach the hearts of Men. . . .

The Verse of the Sword (Qur'an 9.5)

Most Qur'an commentators have said something about a certain verse from the Qur'an which they have named the Verse of the Sword (Qur'an 9.5). This verse runs: "Then when the sacred months have slipped away, slay the polytheists wherever ye find them, seize them, beset them, lie in ambush for them everywhere."

. . . Al-Husayn ibn Fadl says: "This is the verse of the sword. It abrogates every verse in the Qur'an in which suffering the insults of the enemy is mentioned." It is strange indeed that there are those who want to conclude from Qur'an verses that have been abrogated that fighting and *jihad* are to be forsworn. . . .

"So When You Meet Those Who Have Disbelieved, Let There Be Slaughter" (Qur'an 47.4)

. . . The thing that is forgotten is the command to fight, until the time when the Muslims are strong. When, however, the Muslims are weak, the legal ruling is that it is obligatory to endure insults. This weakens a view about which so many are so enthusiastic, namely, that the verse (Qur'an 47.4) on this point is abrogated by the Verse of the Sword (9.5). It is not like that. On the contrary, it is caused to be forgotten. (Al-Suyuti) also said: "Some mention that verses like (Qur'an 2.109 which runs): 'So overlook and pay no attention until God interveneth with His Command' do not address a specific group of people at a specific time and with a specific aim. Hence (the command embodied in this verse) is not abrogated but it is postponed until a certain time." Here ends the quotation from Al-Suyuti.

In spite of Al-Suyuti's disagreement with all the preceding opinions, there is no room for doubt that to adopt the first opinion is correct.

Moreover, whoever thinks that the view that nonabrogation of the verses of pardon and forgiveness (like 2.109) means that we are free to neglect the two duties of *(1) jihad* and (2) urging to what is reputable and prohibiting what is not, is mistaken. . . .

To do away with *jihad* with the argument that it was caused to be forgotten does not only put an end to fighting for this religion but it also puts an end to the intention *(niyah)* of fighting for this religion. The danger of that is apparent from the saying of the Apostle of God-- God's Peace be upon Him: "Someone who does not fight for his religion, or someone whose soul does not talk to him encouraging him to fight for his religion, dies as a pagan." . . .

Muslim Positions on Fighting

Muslim armies in the course of the centuries have been small and ill-prepared, encountering armies double their size. Some argue that this was a prerogative of the Apostle of God -- God's Peace be upon Him -- and His Noble Companions. The refutation of this view is that God promised victory to the Muslims, lasting as long as the Heavens and the Earth last. Maybe you know about what happened (centuries after the days of the Apostle) to Zahir al-Din Babar who faced the Hindu King Rana Sanja with an army of 20,000 while the army of the Hindu King was 200,000. The Muslim Commander was victorious after he repented from drinking wine. . . . There are many others like him.

The Meccan and the Medinan Society

There are those who allege that we live in a Meccan society, thereby endeavoring to obtain for themselves the permission to abandon the waging of *jihad* for God's cause. Whoever puts himself in a Meccan society in order to abandon the religious duty of *jihad,* must also refrain from fasting and prayer (since the Revelations about these duties were only given after the Apostle had emigrated from Mecca to Medina in 622 AD), and he must enrich himself by asking usury since usury was not forbidden until the Medinan period.

The truth of the matter is that (the period in) Mecca is the period of the genesis of the Call (to Islam). The Word of God-Praised and Exalted He is - (Qur'an 5.3): "Today I have perfected your religion for you, and have completed my goodness towards you, and have approved Islam as your religion," abrogates these defeatist ideas that have to be substantiated by the argument that we are Meccans. We are not at the beginning of something, as the Prophet-- God's Peace be upon Him-was at the beginning (of the establishment of Islam), but we (have to) accept the Revelation in its final form.

We do not live in a Meccan society, and neither do we live in a Medinan society. When you wish to know in what kind of society we live, consult the paragraph on "The House in Which We Live".

Fighting Is Now a Duty upon All Muslims

When God-Praised and Exalted He is --made fasting obligatory, He said (Qur'an 2.183): "Fasting is prescribed for you." In regard to fighting He said (Qur'an 2.216): "Fighting is prescribed for you." This refutes the view of whoever says that *jihad* is indeed a duty and then goes on by saying: "When I have fulfilled the duty of engaging in missionary activities for Islam (da'wah), then I have fulfilled the duty (of *jihad*), because (engagement in missionary activities for Islam) is *jihad* too." However, the (real character of this) duty is clearly spelled out in the text of the Qur'an: It is fighting, which means confrontation and blood.

The question now is: When is *jihad* an individual duty? *Jihad* becomes an individual duty in three situations:

First, when two armies meet and their ranks are facing each other, it is forbidden to those who are present to leave, and it becomes an individual duty to remain standing, because God -- Exalted He is -- says: "O ye who have believed, when ye meet a hostile party, stand firm, and call God frequently to mind" (Qur'an 8.45) and also: "O ye who have believed, when ye meet those who have disbelieved moving into battle, turn them not your backs" (Qur'an 8.15).

Second, when the infidels descend upon a country, it becomes an individual duty for its people to fight them and drive them away.

Third, when the Imam calls upon people to fight, they must depart into battle, for GodExalted He is - says (Qur'an 9.38 -39): "O ye who have believed, what is the matter with you? When one says to you: 'March out in the way of God,' ye are weighed down to the ground; are you so satisfied with this nearer life as to neglect the Hereafter? The enjoyment of this nearer life is in comparison with the Hereafter only a little thing. If ye do not march out He will inflict upon you a painful punishment, and will substitute (for you) another people; ye will not injure Him at all; God over everything has power." The Apostle -- God's Peace be upon Him -- says: "When you are called upon to fight, then hasten."

With regard to the lands of Islam, the enemy lives right in the middle of them. The enemy even has got hold of the reins of power, for this enemy is (none other than) these rulers who have (illegally) seized the Leadership of the Muslims. Therefore, waging *jihad* against them is an individual duty, in addition to the fact that Islamic *jihad* today requires a drop of sweat from every Muslim.

Know that when *jihad* is an individual duty, there is no (need to) ask permission of (your) parents to leave to wage *jihad*, as the jurists have said; it is thus similar to prayer and fasting.

The Aspects of Jihad Are Not Successive Phases of Jihad

It is clear that today *jihad* is an individual duty of every Muslim. Nevertheless we find that there are those who argue that they need to educate their own souls, and that *jihad* knows successive phases; and that they are still in the phase of *jihad* against their own soul. They offer as proof the doctrine of Imam Ibn al-Qayyim, who distinguished three aspects in *jihad*:

three forms

1. *Jihad* against one's own soul
2. *Jihad* against the Devil
3. *Jihad* against the infidels and the hypocrites

This argument shows either complete ignorance or excessive cowardice, because Ibn Al-Qayyim (only) distinguished *aspects* in *jihad*, he did not divide it into successive phases. Otherwise we would have to suspend the waging of *jihad* against the Devil until we finished the phase of *jihad* against our own soul. The reality is that the three (aspects) are aspects (only) that follow a straight parallel course. We, in our turn, do not deny that the strongest of us in regard to faith, and the most zealous of us in regard to waging *jihad* against his own soul is the one (of us) who is the most steadfast.

11

Meir Kahane

RABBI MEIR KAHANE WAS THE FOUNDER of Israel's right-wing Kach (Thus) Party, and one of the leading exponents of the religious need to expand Israeli authority over the area held by Palestinian Arabs. Though his ideas were regarded as invalid and extremist by most Israeli Jews, they were appropriated as valid by some radical Israeli settlers on the Palestinian West Bank. They were also consistent with the Jewish justifications for violence expounded by Yigal Amir, who assassinated the Israeli prime minister Yitzhak Rabin, and Dr. Baruch Goldstein who attacked and killed dozens of Muslims as they were worshiping at a mosque at the Shrine of the Patriarchs in the city of Hebron.

A native New Yorker with a long history of political activism, Kahane had helped to establish the Jewish Defense League (JDL) in the 1960s, a movement intended to counter acts of anti-Semitism in the United States. For a time, he also served as an informant to the FBI, turning over information about the radical groups he joined. In 1971 he came to Israel and embraced a messianic vision of Jewish politics, and in 1974 he created the Kach Party, which advocated Israeli control over the West Bank and the removal of Palestinian Arabs who were living there.

His statements about Arabs were compared with those of Hitler about Jews and were found to be surprisingly similar. In the same vein, a biography of the rabbi appearing in the mid-1980s was sardonically titled *Heil Kahane*. In 1984 Kahane was elected to the Israeli parliament, the Knesset, but in 1988, after he served for only one term, his party was banned because of its "racist" and "undemocratic positions."

At the heart of Kahane's thinking was "catastrophic messianism," the idea that the Messiah will come in a time of great conflict in which Jews triumph and praise God through their successes. This was Kahane's understanding of the term kiddush ha-Shem, "the sanctification of God." Anything that humiliated the Jews was not only an embarrassment but a retrograde motion in the world's progress toward salvation. In the following excerpt from Kahane's book, *The Jewish Idea*, he argues that the ancient Jewish scriptures advocate war as much as peace, and that the violent defense of the community was a sacred duty.

"WAR AND PEACE," *THE JEWISH IDEA*

At the end of *Oktzin*, the end of the Talmud, Rabbi Shimon ben Chalafta says, "G-d found no vessel that holds a blessing for Israel other than peace (Ps. 29:11*): 'The L-rd will give strength to His people, the L-rd will bless His people with peace.'"

Our sages also said (*Bamidbar Rabbah* 11:7), "*Great is peace, for G-d's name is Peace*"; (*Vayikra Rabbah* 9:9), "Great is peace, for it includes all blessings"; and (*Tanchuma, Tzav*, 7), "Great is peace, for that is precisely how the priestly blessing concludes."

We also find . . . (*Avot* 1:18), "On three things does the world stand: justice, truth and peace."

No less than four tractates (*Berachot, Yevamot, Nazir,* and *Keritut*) conclude as follows:

> "R[abbi] Elazar said in the name of R[abbi] Chanina, 'Torah scholars increase peace throughout the world, for it says (*Isaiah* 54:13), 'All you children shall be taught by the L-rd, and great shall be the peace of your children.'" (*See: the end of* Berachot)

Likewise, Hillel said (*Avot* 1:12), "Be of Aaron's disciples, loving and pursuing peace."

Peace is so important that "it was said of Rabbi Yochanon ben Zakkai that he greeted everyone, even the non-Jew in the marketplace, before they would greet him" (*Berachot* 17a).

Yet if peace is so important, we must ask why Scripture recorded all the wars of righteous judges and kings. And in general, why is there a *mitzvah* to go to war, i.e., *milchemet mitzvah*, the compulsory war? The answer is provided by King Solomon in *Eccles.* 3:1,8,11: "To every thing there is a season, and a time to every purpose under heaven . . . a time for war and a time for peace. . . He has made everything beautiful in its time."

Peace is surely a magnificent thing, but only when its time comes. As with any other trait, G-d "made everything beautiful - in its time." To apply a trait in an inappropriate time or place is a foul deed. It is just so with war and peace. Each has a time, and that time is learned from the laws of war and peace scattered throughout the Torah. Since peace is limited to its own time, it follows that in wartime all traits associated with love, kindness and mercy are redefined. It is then kind and merciful to go to war against the wicked. Our sages teach (*Kohelet Rabbah* 3:[8]1):

*There is "a time to kill"—during war; "and a time to heal"—
during peace. There is "a time to break down"—during war;
"and a time to build up"—during peace. . . . There is "a time
to seek"—during peace; "and a time to lose"—during war.
There is "a time to rend"—during war; "and a time to sew"—
during peace. . . . There is "a time to love"—during peace;
"and a time to hate"—"during war. There is "a time for war"
—during war; "and a time for peace"—during peace.*

The word of the Living G-d! And how relevant they are to our day:
There is a time for war - during war; and a time for peace—during peace.
We might ask why Scripture must tell us that wartime is a time for war.
Might anyone think otherwise? Our sages were teaching that, in fact,
some might really think so, especially with the insane, alien culture hold-
ing portions of our people captive in its sullied hands.

Above I quoted *Tanchuma, Shoftim* 15:

*"When you go forth to battle against your enemies" (Deut.
20:1) . . . What is meant by "against your enemies"? G-d said,
"Confront them as enemies. Just as they show you no mercy,
so should you not show them mercy."*

We have to realize that the non-Jew who goes to war against Israel is
our enemy and not our friend. How unaware people are nowadays of
this simple yet profound principle! Our sages also said (*Sifri, Shoftim*
192):

*You are going to war against your enemies and not against
your brethren. It is not Judah against Simeon or Simeon
against Judah such that if you fall captive they will have mercy
on you. . . . It is against your ENEMIES that you are waging
war. If you fall into their hands, they will show you no mercy.*

Indeed, a timely war is a *mitzvah*, a duty, a kindness and an everlasting
act of righteousness. Exodus 34:6, which enumerates G-d's attributes,
ends by mentioning "truth": *"The L-rd, the L-rd, Omnipotent, merciful
and kind, slow to anger, with tremendous resources of love and truth."*
There cannot be "mercy, kindness and tremendous resources of love,"
without "truth." We often find the combination of "kindness and truth,"
to teach us that that same Deity Who is "merciful, kind and loving," is
above all else, a G-d of *truth*.

Likewise, G-d is described as follows (Ex. 15:3): "The L-rd is the Master of war, 'Hashem' is His name." Despite His name being "Hashem," a

name indicating mercy, He is still "Master of war." That same Hashem of mercy is also a Master of war against the wicked. Our sages likewise said (*Mechilta, Beshalach, Mesechet Deshira 4*):

> When the typical warrior girds himself in zealous might, he thinks nothing of smiting his closest relative, even his father or mother. G-d is not that way, however. "The L-rd is the Master of war, 'Hashem' is His name." He is "Master of war" - He fought the Egyptians. Yet "Hashem is His name" - He takes pity on His creatures, as it says (Ex. 34:6), "The L-rd, the L-rd, Omnipotent, merciful and kind."

All this is the plain truth. There is a time for war and cruelty and a time for mercy, kindness and clemency. It all depends on G-d's laws, the laws of war by the Master of war. Our sages said (Mechilta, Ibid.):

> "The L-rd is the Master of war, Hashem is His name": R. Ye-huda says, "Such imagery appears throughout Scripture. G-d appeared to Israel with every weapon. He appeared as a warrior with a sword (Ps. 45:4) . . . as a horseman (II Kings 2:12) . . . in armor and helmet (Isaiah 59:17) . . . with bow and arrow (Ps. 45:4) . . . with shield and breastplate (Ps. 35:2) . . . Lest I think G-d needs any of these attributes, it says 'The L-rd is Master of war. Hashem is His name." He fights with His name and needs none of these. Why then did Scripture have to specify each separately? To underscore that G-d fights wars for Israel when they need it, and to inform the nations of the dreadful news that He Whose word created the Universe shall fight them in the future.

We see that G-d has declared war on the wicked and described Himself as Master of war, and that we must emulate Him in war the way we emulate His mercy and kindness, etc. Let death take those pompous individuals who rebel against G-d and against His attributes and principles, who err and mislead others as if they were more righteous than their Creator, pious fools who hypocritically reject the war against evil and evildoers, bleating about peace when we need war, falsifying and distorting G-d's Torah and the laws of compulsory war against the wicked. Of them it says (*Isaiah* 48:22), "The L-rd says to the wicked, 'There is no peace."

Who won the "covenant of peace," the everlasting reward of peace, if not Pinchas? Pinchas acted zealously on G-d's behalf, taking G-d's revenge, and becoming the first *mashuach milchamah*, or *kohen* anointed to lead the nation in *war* (*Deut.* 20:2–4). Yet G-d said (*Num.* 25:12), "Tell him that I have given him My covenant of PEACE."

Here we have a reward well-suited to the deed. Precisely he who gives up his peace and tranquility, devoting himself to G-d's battle and to taking G-d's revenge, merits everlasting peace. And precisely he who rebels against G-d, treating His command to fight and root out evil and evildoers with contempt, will never have peace, for there is no peace to the wicked, those who cast off their yoke.

Today, people have risen up to destroy us who are smitten with the alien culture. Tragically, these include even the Torah scholars and learned Jews who have pronounced that, halachically speaking, there is no state of war between us and the Arabs in our land, hence we are forbidden to treat them as enemies.

They have gone so far as to rule that if an Arab tries to attack or even to kill a Jew with a stone or weapon and then flees, one may not kill him, but may only catch him and deliver him to the authorities, our impoverished regime which is better off ceasing to exist. As our sages said (*Sanhedrin* 98a), "King David's descendent will not come until the impoverished regime ends." Rashi comments, "Until they lack even tenuous control over Israel." In *Tikkunei Zohar* (p. 144), the Jewish kingdom that will exist in the pre-Messianic era is called "the government of the mixed multitude." . . .

If someone renders a *halachic* ruling that there is no state of war between us and the Arabs in our midst, that we are obligated to treat them with mercy, and that it is forbidden to kill one of them even after he tries to attack and kill a Jew, that person is nothing but a *rodef* [one who attacks with intent to kill], who collaborates with gentiles in the killing of Jews. The Torah spoke of such persons in addressing the unsolved murder:

> This is what you must do when a corpse is found fallen in the field in the land that the L-rd your G-d is giving you to occupy, and it is not known who the murderer is. . . . All the elders of the city closest to the corpse shall wash their hands over the decapitated calf at the stream. The elders shall speak up and say, 'Our hands have not spilled this blood, and our eyes have not witnessed it" (*Deut.* 21:1,6–7).

Our sages comment (*Sotah* 46b), "Would we ever think that the city's elders were murderers? Yet, perhaps he approached them and they sent him off without feeding him, or they saw him and let him go without escorting him."

Our sages teach us a great lesson here regarding love for one's fellow Jew and the duty one bears to him: it is not enough for a Jew not to murder. Surely, "Turn away from evil" (Ps. 34:15) applies here, but a much weightier duty applies too: he must do all he can to *save* his fellow Jew from danger, to eradicate every danger and mishap, to defeat every foe who imperils the Jewish people before he can harm them.

12

SHOKO ASAHARA

MASTER SHOKO ASAHARA was the spiritual leader of the Aum Shinrikyo movement in Japan that was associated with a nerve gas attack in the Tokyo subways in 1995 that killed a dozen people and injured thousands. It is the only terrorist act perpetrated by a religious group that has employed a weapon of mass destruction—poisonous sarin gas. Though most Japanese regard him as an odd extremist and many deny that he was really a Buddhist, his teachings are grounded in Buddhist and other religious teachings, and his movement fit into the pattern of prophetic new religious movements that have emerged in Japan in the last decades of the twentieth century.

Asahara was regarded as infallible by his followers, and much of his mystique came from his blindness. He was afflicted with infantile glaucoma shortly after he was born in 1955 in a small village in Japan's southern island of Kyushu. The disease left him completely blind in one eye; in the other he had only limited sight. In a school for the blind, he is said to have gained a great deal of power over the other students, all of whom were sightless, because of his limited vision. Later, after he failed two college entrance examinations, he undertook spiritual lessons on his own. He joined a new religious movement, Agonshu, which was led by a strong, charismatic figure able to prophesy events. By 1984 Asahara had become disenchanted with Agonshu and left it—taking its yoga meditation practices and eclectic Buddhist ideas, along with a dozen of its members, to establish his own group. After a trip to the Himalayas in 1986, where he claimed to have received mystic visions from Hindu masters, he returned to Japan, changed his name to Shoko Asahara from the one given him at birth—Chizuo Matsumoto—and in 1987 created Aum Shinrikyo. Aum is a variant spelling of the Hindu mantra, om, followed by shinri, the Japanese term for "supreme truth," and kyo, for "religious teaching."

Along with meditation practices, Asahara taught an eclectic variety of Buddhist and Hindu concepts. He also prophesied about what he regarded as the coming great catastrophic war, an Armaggedon that would engulf all of humankind. Asahara justified the movement's violent actions as defensive postures necessitated by the evil threats occasioned in the great war. In the excerpts that follow, Asahara states his prophecies about the violence in the great catastrophic war that he thought would erupt in the year 2000. Perhaps it is a coincidence, but the safe location, the Kasumigaseki subway station in central Tokyo that is mentioned in his prophecies, was the destination of the trains in which his followers released the deadly sarin gas in 1995.

DECLARING MYSELF THE CHRIST

The gods have beautiful, clear body; are made of consciousness; eat joy; emit light; fly in the air; and abide in this blissful state for a long long time.

It was just like a mushroom and appeared exactly like a mushroom. It had a color, a smell, and a taste: it had the color of fermented butter or other kinds of butter; and the taste of pure and extremely rare kind of honey.

So the gods began to eat this earth cake. They ate it and lived on it for a very long time.

Then, what is of even grosser quality appeared in their body and they lost their looks even more.

We regard this body of flesh and blood as absolute and the only body we have, but as the scripture says it is not true. For instance, according to esoteric Buddhism, we have what is called five bodies of Dharma; these are subtler kinds of bodies which work in other dimensions. As you become adept with your meditation, you will actually experience your body of manifestation (one of the five bodies of Dharma) slip out of your body.

When we lived in the Heaven of Light and Sound we were made of only light. By our gradual fall, we have eventually come to have this body made of gross substance.

The Devil Means Afflictive Root Poisons

The next key word is the devil. The devil in Christianity is death, in other words, the discontinuity of consciousness caused by afflictive root poisons. In other words, the devil means the afflictive root poisons—this is in perfect accordance with the Buddhist view of the devil. This comes as no surprise because, as we have seen, Buddha Sakyamuni practiced the teachings of the Holy Heaven in his former life. To enter the Holy Heaven and to take rebirth into a higher realm from there to attain Maha Nirvana—this is the goal of Buddhism.

Let us see here why Jesus was crucified and why the crucifixion must be praised. Our consciousness is inherently continuous; our True Self at the heart of our consciousness is imperishable and indestructible. We fear death because our deeper consciousness knows the shock and the successive suffering as a being in a miserable realm through many states of transmigration and rebirths. Jesus was crucified to witness that death is the greatest joy in that life, that is, in the life in which he practiced the teachings of truth.

Why, then, is death the greatest joy? It is because if the being accumulates a lot of merit conducting a lot of virtuous deeds, calms his mind and lives according to the teachings of truth, he will unfailingly take rebirth in a higher world when he leaves this human world full of suffering. Death means suffering for those who do evil, but it is great joy for those who do virtue. Therefore, one should not fear death. Jesus was crucified to give witness to it.

> Since the children have flesh and blood, he too shared in their humanity so that by his death he might destroy him who holds the power of death—that is, the devil—and free those who all their lives were held in slavery by their fear of death. For surely it is not angels he helps, but Abraham's descendants.
>
> For this reason he had to be made like his brothers in every way, in order that he might become a merciful and faithful high priest in service to God, and that he might make atonement for the sins of the people. (Hebrews 2:14–17)

Why did the Great Holy Heaven not try to help angels, in other words, the inhabitants of the Heaven of Degenerate Consciousness (Asuras) or of Playful Degeneration, and instead help Jesus' disciples or other beings in this human realm? This is quite reasonable.

Degenerate Consciousness and Playful Degeneration are both happy worlds. Hence, even if one preached Dharma to the inhabitants in these realms, it would not appeal to them because their lives are happy and long. How about this human realm? As you know, human lifespan in this modern age is eighty to a hundred years. And in this short life, there is more pain than pleasure.

DISASTER COMES TO THE LAND OF THE RISING SUN

The World after the Final War

The Millennium

MASTER: After the Third world War, I imagine that this world will be filled with love. Every person will overcome his or her own suffering and work for the good of others. But each person has a vision of the millennium. Let me ask what your visions are. Mr. Ishitani?

I: As Master always says, we are in the age of Kali Yuga. There are a lot of peculiar situations because people are no longer able to observe precepts. Recently, for example, someone committed suicide as a result of being bullied. Armageddon will occur because of the vice people have accumulated. The world has become like a hell. There is no religion in which the followers strictly observe its precepts, apart from Aum Shinrikyo. Master said in a lecture that during Armageddon many will regret what they have done, and they will begin to observe the precepts. They will be the survivors. The world will be like a heaven and people will be able to live without consuming their merit. We will enter a wonderful new age. This is what I believe.

VI: According to the predictions of Nostradamus, the world population will dramatically decrease, and land formations will drastically change. The land and sea will not have their present shape. Is there anyone who can survive under such circumstances? The bible says that those who have seals impressed on their foreheads will survive. Nostradamus said, "the great Chyren [Christ] will become the ruler of earth. He will be loved and feared, and inspire awe. His esteem and repute is above the gods. The victor will be satisfied with the one title." I imagine that in a world like this, a king will reign as a victor, and those who have the seal will survive.

KN: Today's topics were mainly about the physical aspects and materials used for weapons and defenses. But the fundamental reason Armageddon must occur is that the inhabitants of the present human realm do not recognize that they are fated to die. We can also say that in contemporary society death is concealed from the public eye. However, life and death are closely connected and our life span is short. This is a characteristic of the human world. Therefore, any society that is unaware of death must be corrected. That is why wars happen. I think that in the coming age the survivors of the final war will form a society in which they mindfully face death and stress the importance of the law of karma. People will extinguish their karma, accumulate merit through cooperative lifestyles, and acquire divine powers. Moreover there will be a concrete system of using power of consciousness, especially the subconscious. That system will liberate all people from materialistic ideas. Aum Shinrikyo is currently adopting that system.

TI: Most governments have taken countermeasures against the final war, which I think will mainly be a nuclear war. In Russia subways can be used as shelters. Subways in Japan are approximately 20 meters deep. Russia ones are about 40 meters deep. They constructed the subway system from its inception as a shelter. There is one area in Japan that is similar to the subway in Russia: Kasumigaseki station in Nagata-cho. That is where the Diet Building and other government offices are located. It is said that this underground station is made as a shelter for a nuclear bomb. Those who run into such structures will surely survive. But people should not depend on the government because there are few such facilities in Japan. People should protect themselves from war on their own. Those who acquire the necessary material protection by themselves or from the government will survive the first stage. Then radioactivity and other bad circumstances—poison gas, epidemics, food shortages—will occur. People will have to try to survive these situations too. Those who survive in the end and create the new world must have a much higher wisdom and virtue. I think people with great karma will transcend the worst suffering ever faced by humankind. They will survive and create a new and transcendent human world.

VP: I think what will come will be the opposite of the present world. The world will be completely materially devastated by war. Yet I think that an affluent world of the mind will arise in which the laws of the truth will spread. It will not be an environment in which people lose their virtue and fall to lower worlds. It will be a place where people can jump up to higher worlds. If spirituality is reestablished and virtuous souls come forth, the world will also be materially abundant.

MM: Causes create effects. Since this world is nearly full of vice, the gods will pass judgement on it. Hence the battle will end in the triumph of Ahura Mazda over Griffon. Only those people selected by the gods will survive, and the entire world will become a Shambhala. The present world is connected to the realm of hungry ghosts and hell because vice is being accumulated. I think the future world will be connected to the heavens of the gods through the practice of the truth.

Survive! Ensure a Good Transmigration!

MASTER: How is a saint different from a normal person? A saint sees things that exist as existing, and things that do not exist as not existing. For example, it is a fact that at some point we are going to die. This is something everyone knows. But people are not prepared for death. They make every effort to experience easily obtainable pleasures. The same is true with aging. We are vigorous in our teens. As we reach our thirties, forties, fifties, sixties, and seventies we lose mental and physical strength. As we grow older we lose the ability to do what we want to do. But when we are young, we simply release our energy and do not prepare for old age. The same is true with illness. We get sick from breathing in viruses, poor diet, contagious diseases, and stress. But when we are in good health, we never think about illness.

Like death, aging, and illness, I consider the third world war inevitable.

I am preparing to survive with my disciples gathered here today and all the rest of my disciples who practice the laws of the truth. Some people ask why we must survive. . . . [I]f we are truly saints, why not simply go to heaven when our bodies are destroyed by a nuclear explosion.

In this respect, Buddhist scriptures correctly guide us. They tell us that a spiritual practitioner needs to live long in order to ensure rebirth in a higher realm. Why? Even if we have enough merit to go to heaven, we must fall to the human realm, the realm of hungry ghosts, the animal realm, and hell when we deplete our merit. Therefore, we need time to acquire the ability of transferring our souls to a heaven. More importantly, it is even more difficult to create a cause for practicing in a heaven. So we must live for this purpose.

This is not the only purpose.

How much are we conscious of planet Earth in our everyday lives? We greatly benefit from it. The water we drink comes from rivers. You all know we draw water as it flows from the mountains on its way to the sea. It is not an exaggeration to call the ground upon which we walk the "skin" of the earth. We build our homes and live upon this skin. Forests continuously maintain a certain amount of oxygen in the air with photosynthesis, and we inhale oxygen and exhale carbon dioxide.

What will the earth be like after the third world war? There will be a fusion of nature and souls. Future science will transcend far beyond the present form. What will be the main subjects of scientific research? What is consciousness?, what is the meaning of life?, what is aging?, what is illness?, what is death? These questions will surely be focused on and elucidated in the future.

If we could simply purify the air, if there were a technology that could do this, our life spans would be ten or twenty years longer. If a technique were developed to regulate our biological mechanisms—for example, if a technique that promotes a hormonal balance. . . . Epinephrine is the hormone secreted by the adrenal gland and is especially related to stress. Is this right, Krishnananda?

KN: Yes. That is right.

MASTER: If we could control epinephrine, we would be stronger against exogenous stress. Then it would not be impossible to live on earth to the age of 200, 300, or 1000. The reason this kind of research has never been done is simply because there is no money to be made from it. Japan, and the earth, now exist about halfway within the realm of hungry ghosts.

I am glad the third world war is going to happen because Buddhist scriptures and the Bible say so. I hope we will be able to survive the third world war. There will be some who support, and others who disagree with my latter remarks. You are free to think and express your opinions about them, but try to think deeply. We are fated to die. The third world war will definitely occur, whether or not we want it.

Now what will wise people like yourselves do? Are you going to follow the path of a saint and prepare yourselves? Or are you going to die in agony in the nuclear flash? It is your choice.

13

9/11 CONSPIRATOR

EARLY ON THE MORNING OF SEPTEMBER 11, 2001, nineteen hijackers boarded four commercial flights departing from Boston, Newark, and Washington, D.C., airports. Minutes later, they seized control of all four airplanes. Two were aimed at the twin towers of the World Trade Center in New York City, and approximately an hour after they crashed into the buildings, both towers collapsed, killing thousands. Another plane targeted the Pentagon, the headquarters of the U.S. Defense Department near Washington, D.C., and destroyed one section of the building. The fourth plane was apparently thwarted from its mission—most likely the U.S. Capitol in Washington, D.C.—by passengers on board the plane. It lost control and crashed in a field in Pennsylvania. Most of the hijackers were originally from Saudi Arabia and subscribed to the global jihadi ideology embraced by the al Qaeda network. Though Osama bin Laden was widely regarded in the U.S. news media as being the leader of the global jihadi organization, it was another leader, Khalid Sheikh Muhammad, who, after being captured and placed in U.S. military detention, confessed to being the master organizer of the mission.

Though most Muslims around the world were horrified over the events of 9/11 and regarded the perpetrators as illegitimate Muslims, the writings associated with the hijackers indicate that their actions were undertaken in a religious manner. Shortly after the event, handwritten instructions on how they should comport themselves before and during the terrorist mission were found in the suitcase of one of the hijackers, Mohamed Atta. Other copies of this letter were found at the crash site of United Airlines Flight 93 in Pennsylvania and in a car registered to one of the hijackers on American Flight 77 abandoned at a Dulles International Airport parking lot. No individual was listed as author of the text.

The instructions are reprinted here in their entirety. Although no specific moral or religious justifications are given for the acts of 9/11, the reference to great wars in Muslim history implies that that the perpetrators regarded themselves as soldiers in a great spiritual battle against enemies of Islam. At the same time, the rituals of purification that are specified in the instructions imply that the hijackers were preparing to undertake a religious rite. Some of the references indicate that they should kill their victims in the manner of a religious sacrifice. Mention is made of the rewards that the hijackers would receive in heaven for their suicide missions, but heavenly rewards were clearly not the main point. Rather, the participants were made to feel honored that they were chosen to be on a great spiritual mission.

"LAST INSTRUCTIONS OF 9/11"

The Last Night

He said: one of the Companions said: the Messenger of God ordered us to recite it previous to a raid, and we recited it, took booty and were safe.

1. Mutual swearing of the oath unto death and renewal of [one's] intention. Shave excess hair from the body and apply cologne. Shower.
2. Knowing the plan well—all the angles, together with the [likely] reaction and opposition from the enemy.
3. Reading/recitation of *suras* al-Tawba [9] and al-Anfal [8], and considering their meanings together with Paradise that God has promised to the believers, especially to the martyrs.
4. Reminding the soul of hearing and obedience that night [the "Last Night"] for you will be faced with what will cause it be less than 100% in its hearing and obedience, so spiritually exercise its purification [the soul], understand it, subordinate it and incite it [to good works] at that time. The Most High said: "And obey God and His Apostle and do not quarrel among yourselves lest you lose heart and your strength dissipates. And stand fast, for God is on the side of those who stand fast." [8:46]
5. Staying the night [praying], pressing onward in prayer, divination (*jafr*), strengthening [oneself], [obtaining a] clear victory, and ease of heart that you might not betray us.
6. Much remembrance [of God], and know that the best way of remembrance is to read/recite the Noble Qur'an—according to the consensus of the knowledgeable people so far as I know. It is sufficient that it is the Word of the Creator of heaven and earth—to whom you are going.
7. Purify your heart and cleanse it from all uncleanliness. Forget and become oblivious to that thing called "this world." The time for play is over and the appointed time for seriousness has come. How much of our lives we have wasted! Is it not [right] that we should occupy ourselves

during these hours with advancing in acts pleasing to God and obedience?

8. Let your breast be open, tranquil to the bounty of God because it is only a few minutes before the happy, satisfying life and the eternal Paradise begins in the company of the prophets, the upright people, the martyrs and the righteous, may God have mercy on all of them. We ask God of His bounty. Be optimistic, because [Muhammad] "loved optimism (*fa'l*) in everything he did."

9. You should consider how—if you fall into temptation—you will be able to resist, remain steadfast and recover. You know that whatever happens to you would never detract from you[r spiritual level] and whatever would detract from you would never happen to you. This is nothing but God's test in order to raise the level [of your martyrdom] and to expiate your sins. You can be certain there are only minutes left until the merit will be clear—with God's permission—of that great reward from God. The Most High said: "Or did you suppose that you will enter Paradise, before God has known who were those of you who have struggled, and those who were steadfast." [3:142]

10. Remember the Word of God Most High: "You were yearning for death before you actually met it. Now you have seen it and you are beholding it." [3:143] And also remember: "How many a small band has defeated a large one by God's leave. [God is with the steadfast]." [2:249] And His Word Most High: "If God supports you, no one will overcome you; but if He forsakes you, then who will be able to support you after Him? And in God let the believers put their trust!" [3:160]

11. Remind yourself of the prayers—and [those] of your brothers—and contemplate their meanings (morning and evening devotionals, [the devotional of entering] the town, the devotional of traveling, and the devotional of meeting the enemy [in battle]).

12. The expectoration (from the soul, into a siphon; and the clothes, the knife, your personal belongings, your ID, your passport and all of your papers).

13. Check your weapon before you leave and again before you leave. "Sharpen your knives so as not to cause pain to your sacrifice."

14. Tighten your clothing tightly around you. This is the way
    of the pious forefathers. They would tighten their cloth-
    ing around them previous to a battle. Tighten your shoes
    well. Wear socks so that your feet will fit in the shoes and
    not come out. All of these things are circumstances of
    this present [world]. God suffices for us, and what a
    Guardian!

15. Pray the morning [prayer] in a group, and meditate on its
    merit. Repeat the devotionals after it [the prayer], and do
    not leave your apartment without performing the ritual
    ablutions.

Continue to pray. . . . Read His Word: "Did you, then, think that We
created you in vain and that unto Us you will not be returned?" [23:115]
surat al-mu'minun.

Then you begin the Second Phase

When the taxi is taking you to the a[irport], then recite the devotional of
travel, the devotional of [entering a] town, the devotional of praise and
other devotionals.

When you have arrived and you see the a[irport] and have gotten out
of the taxi, then say the prayer of shelter; every place you go say the
prayer of shelter in it. Smile and be tranquil for this is pleasing to the
believers. Make sure that no one of whom you are unaware is following
you. Then say the prayer: "God, make me strong through your entire
creation," and say: "O God, make me sufficient for what You wish," and
say: "O God, we place you on their [the enemies'] throats, and we take
refuge in You from their evil," and say: "O God, make for us a barrier
before them and one behind them, and then fool them when they are not
looking," and say "God suffices for us; He is the best Guardian" in accordance with His Word Most High: "Those to whom the people said:
'The people have been arrayed against you; so fear them.' But this increased their faith and so they said: 'God is sufficient for us. He is the
best Guardian.'" [3:173]

Then you when you have said it, you will find matters straightened;
and [God's] protection will be around you; no power can penetrate that.
[God] has promised His faithful servants who say this prayer that which
follows:

1. [They will] return with grace [from God] and His bounty
2. Evil will not touch them
3. [They will be in] accordance with the grace of God

The Most High said: "Thus they came back with a grace and bounty from God. No harm touched them; and they complied with God's good pleasure. God's bounty is great." [3:174] All of their devices, their [security] gates and their technology will not save them nor harm [anyone] without God's permission.

The believers will not fear it [death]; only the followers of Satan will fear it—those who at the core are fearful of Satan, and have become his followers. The servitude belongs to God, for fear is mighty servitude towards God, [making certain that one is] turned only towards God—praised is He and Most High—and He alone is worthy of it. Those who said--fearing to perish--the verses: "That indeed is the Devil frightening his followers . . . [3:175] [those] who are impressed by the civilization of the West, those who have drunk of hell; it has given them to drink together with cold water (?), and they have feared its weak and perishing abilities: ". . . but do not fear them and fear Me; if you are true believers!" [3:175] Fear is inside of God's followers, but the believers do not look other than to God, the One and Only, who has everything in His hand and the power of the people. The most certain form of belief is that God will overturn the guile of those unbelievers, for the Most High said: "That was done, so that God might foil the machinations of the unbelievers." [8:18] Then you must remember the most important of all the [possible] remembrances, and that is that it must not be lost upon you to remember the statement "there is no god but God." For if you said it 1000 times none would be able outdo it—even if you were silent[ly praying] or if you were remembering God [out loud]. Of the greatest [remembrances] are the words of [Muhammad] "Whoever says: 'There is no god but God' truly in his heart will enter paradise." Or as he said with the same meaning: "If the seven heavens and the seven earths were placed in one palm and 'there is no god but God' in another palm then 'there is no god but God' would outweigh them all." You should be able to consider the awesomeness of this statement when you fight the "Confederates" (al-ahzab).

The one who considers it will find that there are no pointed letters—this is a sign of perfection and completeness, as the pointed words or letters lessen its power. This is made perfect by the repetition of the word of the unity [of God] with which you affirm to your Lord through fighting under its banner as did the Messenger of God. It is incumbent upon Him to raise them [to Paradise] on the Day of Judgment.

And additionally, do not show outward signs of embarrassment or nervousness, but be joyful and happy, open of heart and calm because you are going towards God's welcome and His favor; then this will be a day—with the permission of God—that you will finish with the houris (women) in Paradise:

Smiling towards the face of the perished one (dead): O youth
You are coming to the Gardens of Eternity

In other words, you are going towards it [paradise], and saying: "We are coming towards you!" with remembrance and prayer: "God is with His servants, the believers, to protect [them], ease [their way], guide [them] and to make certain of the victory in everything."

The Third Phase

When you board the plane, the first step you take as you enter should be to give the prayer and the supplications. Visualize that this is "going out in the morning" in the path of [God] as [Muhammad] said: "Going out in the morning and coming back in the evening in the path of God are better than this world and all that is in it" or whatever he would say. When you place your foot into the p[lane] and take your seat, then say the devotionals, and give the prayers as a good deed to God as we have mentioned previously. Then stay occupied with the remembrance of God—maximizing it. The Most High said: "O believers, if you encounter an enemy host, stand fast and remember God frequently, that perchance you may prosper." [8:45] Then when the p[lane] starts to move toward liftoff, and it begins to advance f[orward?], say the prayer of the traveler, because you are traveling towards God Most High—and how blessed is this journey!

Then you will find it stop and then take off. This is the time of the meeting of the two groups, and so pray to God Most High as the Most High mentioned in His Book: "Lord, fill us with forbearance, enable us to stand fast, and help us against the unbelievers," [2:250] and His Word: "Their only words were: 'Lord, forgive us our sins and our excess in our affairs. Make firm our feet and grant us victory over the unbelieving people," [3:147] and the word of His Prophet: "O God, Revealer of the Book, Mover of the clouds, defeater of the Confederates (*ahzab*); defeat them and grant us victory over them. O God, defeat them and shake them!" Pray for victory for yourself and all of your brothers, and that they might strike their targets. Do not be afraid to ask God that He would grant you [the rank of] martyr, as you advance without retreating, patient and hoping for God's reward.

Then each one of you should prepare to fulfill his part together with the one with whom God is satisfied, and to clench his teeth just as the pious forefathers did previous to entering into battle.

At the beginning of the confrontation, strike in the manner of champions who are not desirous of returning to this world, and shout: *Allahu akbar!* (God is great!), for this shout causes fear to enter into the hearts of the unbelievers. The Most High said: "[And when your Lord revealed to the angels: 'I am with you; so support those who believe. I will cast terror into the hearts of those who disbelieve.] So strike upon the necks and strike every fingertip of theirs." [8:12] You should know that the Gardens [of Paradise] have been decorated for you in the most beautiful way, and that the houris are calling to you: "O friend of God, come," after dressing in their most beautiful clothing.

When God requires one of you to slaughter, go to it as if [the order] came from their father and mother for it is necessary for you. Do not dispute, but listen and obey. When you have slaughtered, loot those whom you have killed—for this is one of the Ways (*sunna*) of the Chosen One [Muhammad]. But he made this conditional upon being certain that no one would be occupied with looting, and consequently abandon that which was more important: watching the enemy—whether [they are occupied with] trickery or attack—this danger is much greater. And if it is thus that they are led according to the necessity of action, and if the group does the opposite to the action of the individual, then forbid him because the action [. . .] the Way [of the Prophet Muhammad] (*sunna*)— and necessity overrides the Way.

Do not take vengeance for yourself, but strike every blow for God Most High. This is in accordance with 'Ali b. Abi Talib who fought one of the unbelievers in [a spirit of] vengeance against the unbeliever and the latter pressed upon 'Ali, and he brandished his sword, and then struck him and then struck [again]. When the battle finished, the Companions [of the Prophet] asked him about this action—why was it that he had not struck [back at] this unbeliever, who had struck him and struck him again. 'Ali said: "This was because I was afraid that I would strike him in vengeance for myself, so I lifted my sword [only in defense]," or whatever he said. Then when he had summoned [correct] intention, he went and struck him [the unbeliever], killing him. "All of this was my religion in the hands of God, seeking to do well to myself before God, so that this action would be for the sake of God alone."

Then follow the law regarding prisoners and pay very close attention to them, fighting them as the Most High said: "It is not up to any prophet to take captives except after too much blood is shed in the land. You desire the fleeting goods of this world, but God desires the Hereafter, and God is Mighty, Wise." [8:67]

When everything is finished according to what is planned complete that which you have begun, striking whoever resists in the c[ockpit] or in the p[lane] and the c[abin], remembering that this action is for God, Exalted and Lifted Up. The brothers should not become gloomy because of what is imposed upon them, but proclaim good news to them, calm them, remind them [of God] and give them courage. How beautiful that the man should read/recite verses from the Qur'an! According to the Word of the Most High: "So let those who sell the present life for the life to come fight in the way of God. [Whoever fights in the way of God and is killed or conquers, We shall accord him a great reward]" [4:74] and His Word Most High: "And do not think those who have been killed in the way of God as dead; [they are rather living with their Lord, well-provided for]" [3:169] and others that are similar, or declaim them just as the pious forefathers would compose poetry in the midst of battles to calm their brothers and to cause tranquility and joy to enter their hearts.

Do not forget to bring a little portion [of food?], a coffee cup or a glass of water for yourself and your brothers to drink so that it is easier for you, as now the True Promise is near and the hour of victory comes.

Open your heart and part your breast as a greeting to death in the path of God; be always remembering [God], and renew your prayer so that it will be easier to follow just before the [sight of the] goal causes one to waver and let your last words be: "There is no god but God and Muhammad is His Messenger."

After that—if God wills—there will be the meeting [with God] and the opening into the mercy of God. When you see the masses of the unbelievers, remember the Confederates (al-ahzab), whose numbers were approximately 10,000 thousand fighters and how God gave victory to His servants the believers [Muslims]. The Most High said: "When the believers saw the Confederates, they said: 'This is what God and His Apostle have promised us, and God and His Apostle are truthful.' And it only increased them in faith and submission." [33:22]

Prayers and peace be upon Muhammad.

Part II
Understanding the Religious Role in Violence

Introduction to Part II

VIOLENCE CAN BE FOUND in seemingly every religious tradition, not only in its holy wars but in its sacred rites. Systematic thinking about the link between acts of destruction and the most exalted of divine offerings has been pondered by a diversity of scholars, ranging from anthropologists to literary theorists. A sample of these writings appears in this section of the book. These writings differ from the ones found in the first section in that they are theoretical in nature, scholarly analyses rather than religious writings and are largely about sacred rites rather than about acts of violence in the broader world. Some of them focus on sacrifice.

But even though there are differences between the writings in the first and second parts, there are also similarities. The writings in this section, like those in the first, are efforts to make sense of the relationship between religion and violence. In many cases what they are trying to understand is not just how religion can tolerate the idea of violence but also how it can, in some cases, encompass it in a spiritual way. Through ritual, for instance, images and acts of violence may be transposed onto a sacred plane. Thus, some of the writings take the position that particular rites of violence are understood by their participants to be therapeutic or redemptive. Those who undertake them are revitalized in some way. Similarly to the activists described in the first section, participants regard themselves as transformed by engaging in violent acts with a religious purpose.

Moreover, just as writings about war have extended back into antiquity, reflections about violent rituals have also reached into the past. More than two thousand years ago, ritualized violence inspired comment by Greek and biblical authors, who questioned the religious purpose of blood sacrifice. Greek Pythagoreans engaged in considerable discussion over the morality and efficacy of sacrificing animals to the gods, and biblical prophets lambasted the practice of human sacrifice, questioning its efficacy and its sanctity (e.g., Jeremiah 7:30-32, 19:5–6; Isaiah 57:5). Yet, as described in part 1, biblical scribes also sensed a connection between sacrifice and war in the rhetoric of the ban, or ḥērem, wherein certain populations were to be offered to God. The East too questioned the morality of violence toward animals and other beings, and nonviolence was endorsed in early Buddhist and Hindu texts. Yet, within these same Eastern traditions, other texts, such as the Mahabharata and the Mahavamsa, justified killing in times of war. Clearly, the subject of religious killing has occupied human imagination for a long time.

Modern commentary on religious violence emerged in Western intellectual thought in the nineteenth century, when the rise of the modern disciplines of the social sciences coincided with the discovery of thriving cultures in non-Western parts of the world. Such discoveries provided fuel for speculation on the evolutionary development of culture, an idea that drew on Charles Darwin's theory of biological evolution. Applying the biological theory to cultural development, a generation of anthropologists, including Lewis Morgan, Edward Tylor, and Herbert Spencer, began to search these newfound cultures for the embryonic elements of contemporary religions. Anthropological fieldwork today provides little support for a single stream of evolutionary religious history; there is no singular progression from savagery to barbarism to civilization, as Morgan would have it. Nonetheless, these early theories of cultural evolution led to a series of important questions about cross-cultural religious patterns. They also led to a fascination with the subject of blood sacrifice.

From this fascination emerged William Robertson Smith's influential theory of totem sacrifice. As Robertson Smith saw it, early human groups felt a sacred bond of kinship with certain animals, or totems, whom they refused to harm except on occasions of ritual sacrifice. Then one or more of these totemic animals would be ceremoniously killed and eaten. The animal flesh—by implication the flesh of kin—would become a kind of mediating substance between the people and their deity. At the same time as the sacrificed totem was eaten by a group of people, it was also imagined to be shared by their god. Hence, the flesh of a totemic animal became a sacred substance that bonded together humans, totems, and gods.

Robertson Smith's theory was taken up in different ways by several thinkers whose writings are represented in this book: Émile Durkheim and his students, Henri Hubert and Marcel Mauss, and Sigmund Freud. Durkheim was particularly influential. He envisioned the totem as the projected collective consciousness of the group, whose members are integrated together around the totem by common cults, rites (including sacrifice), and primary and secondary totemic symbols. This model was applied by Durkheim to society in general, with far-reaching implications.

Hubert and Mauss, on the other hand, disregarded the totemic aspects of Robertson Smith's hypothesis and focused on the communicative aspects. These they explored in the context of Vedic and biblical blood sacrifice. As Hubert and Mauss saw it, the purpose of sacrificial rituals was to make a connection with sacred forces. They thought that the victim does not come to the sacrificial altar already sacred, as Robertson Smith suggested. Rather, the sacrificial victim becomes increasingly holy when entering the sacred sphere of the ritual, which is dedicated to a divinity. The entrance of the victim into this sphere leads to its auspicious death. The victim functions as a mediator, drawing into one sacred circle the divinity, the victim, the one who actually kills the victim, and the one for whom the sacrifice is conducted.

The sacred nature of the victim was addressed also by Freud in an early work, *Totem and Taboo*. Although widely criticized for a number of its presumptions, the book was nonetheless revolutionary in suggesting that the sacrificial themes of the Judeo-Christian tradition were rooted in unconscious urges in human nature. Freud recognized in Judeo-Christian religion the echoes of a primal patricide rooted in the trauma of a ruptured mother-child bond. According to Freud's Oedipal hypothesis, deeply repressed wishes to murder the totem-father and to reclaim a primal bond with the mother are embedded in the Christian worship of the divine father—the totem-god, once slain, devoured, and then mourned. They are also embedded in the secondary devouring of the powerful son, who died to absolve the other sons of patricidal guilt. The Christian ritual of Eucharist (also known as "the Lord's Supper" and "communion") offers a sacred redemption for the patricidal urge through the ritualized ingestion of the sacrificial son. The broader implication is that religious rituals may express and defuse destructive psychological urges.

Although his work is not represented in this book, Adolf Jensen also influenced the thinking of other theorists. Jensen investigated the myth of Hainuwele, a primeval woman venerated by root crop cultivators of Ceram, New Guinea. Hainuwele once offered her people auspicious gifts but was slain and dismembered by primordial men in a mythical time. From the pieces of her body grew the plants essential for survival. As the root crop cultivators saw it, this mythical murder established the foundations for the present order. For Jensen, the slain and dismembered primordial figure has become a culture hero, offering salvation from chaos and violence. Her death is commemorated in sacrificial rituals. Similar to Freud, Jensen pondered the violence at the heart of society's foundational myths: Why should an act of violence rather than, say, birth or initiation, be the magnet for religious imagination? This question led Jensen to contemplate the powerful moments of emotion that might seize audiences who witnessed acts of staged violence.

René Girard too is intrigued by moments of violent epiphany in ritual and the violence at the core of many religious myths. In his view, violence terrifies us because of its implicit anarchism and potential for overwhelming destruction. But it also fascinates us because we see it as an index of power. At some level, societies recognize its danger and its lure. Thus, violence ends up channeled by cultural institutions such as religion. Like Freud, Girard sees the powerful role that ritualized violence can play in symbolically defusing violent impulses. Unlike Freud, he does not see the cause of these impulses to be violent instincts.

Rather, Girard has searched the literature commemorating stories of mythic violence and has proposed a psychosociological disposition—

mimetic rivalry. Mimesis, says Girard, arises from an intrinsic sense of powerlessness and self-doubt about one's true being. This self-doubt gives rise to an urge to imitate one's rival, who appears to have an abundance of power and confidence. Inevitably, the rival feels challenged by the mimicry, responds violently, and a cycle of reciprocal violence is unleashed. Because mimetic rivalry can trigger the cycles of vendetta that destroy societies, societies have developed sacrificial rites and other kinds of staged killings to function as cultural dams for these violent outcomes. Religion is one such cultural dam. It regulates and even authenticates violence in the form of ritualized sacrifice. As did Jensen, Girard sees religion as sanctioning the death of a sacrificial victim in order to stabilize society. This victim, a scapegoat, may function as a cultural hero because his death effectively saves society from violent chaos.

Walter Burkert also is impressed with the fascination inspired by ritualized violence. According to Burkert, "sacrificial killing is the basic experience of the 'sacred.'" In ritualized killing, says Burkert, humans experience a sacred shiver of awe due to a staged confrontation with death. But Burkert adds an evolutionary twist. For Burkert, ritual killing has its roots in the evolution of the human species, originating in our Paleolithic heritage as hunters and gatherers. For millennia, hunting bands experienced a collective exhilaration in tracking and killing large mammals. Yet the killing also induced shock and remorse, because the hunting bands felt an intimate link with the animals dying before their eyes. According to Burkert, over hundreds of centuries these dual experiences of excitement and regret became fused and perpetrated in the institution of domestic animal sacrifice. Sacrificial rituals continue to bind participants together, but they also provide an experience of the sacred. Ritual killing resuscitates the old fascination and remorse of watching the hunted animal die.

A different twist on the same theme is provided by Maurice Bloch, an anthropologist whose wide range of interests has included initiation rituals as expressions of religious violence. In *Prey into Hunter*, Bloch looks at the way that the "rebounding violence" from sacrificial rites can become empowering. In particular, he examines a handful of rituals in which an initiate vicariously takes on the persona of a sacrificial animal but then becomes its victimizer. Bloch observes that in the initiations of the Orokaiva people in Papua New Guinea, the initiate is made to experience a terrifying closeness to a sacrificial pig, who ends up conquered and consumed as meat by the initiate and also by the group with whom the initiate has joined. The initiate thus becomes the predator of the prey with whom he formerly felt a bond. The movement from prey into predator and the dissolution of the identification between them effectively injects a burst of vitality into the new community that eats the prey. The community, thereby revitalized, now may turn its strength outward in the form of aggression against other groups.

A similar closeness to the victim was thought by Georges Bataille to be implicit in the ritual practice of animal sacrifice. In his *Theory of Religion*, Bataille described animal sacrifice as inducing in a sacrificer a sudden awareness of the animal victim as a fellow subject. The animal, belonging initially to the sphere of objects to be used, is lifted from that sphere when the sacrificer is about to kill it. Then, paradoxically, the sacrificer becomes alert to the victim's potential anguish. He also senses the animal's experience of "immanence." Immanence refers to the animal's experience of itself in the world as "like water in water." Although humans can barely grasp that experience of being "like water in water," our sense of a supreme being relies on it. That is, it relies on the suspicion of a continuity of existence that is deeper than our experience of ourselves and everything else as objects. Humans feel a kind of impotent horror, says Bataille, before this profound immanence. It is through ritual sacrifice that a human may perceive that deeper sense of immanence, in his momentary intimacy with the victim that is to be killed. By implication, the intuition of a supreme being is the ironic fruit of an act of animal sacrifice.

Many of the theoretical critiques of religious violence that do not focus on ritual or sacrifice follow the trail established by the nineteenth-century philosopher and activist Karl Marx. Marx saw in all of religion a kind of structural violence, in that religion, from his point of view, was usually a device that dominant classes in society used to manipulate and control the classes that were subjected to them. Marx's famous quote that religion is "an opiate of the people . . . and a sigh of the oppressed" summarizes his view of religious ideology as a form of both manipulation and protest. The Marxist approach to religion was refined by Engels, Adorno, and Habermas, among others, and led to broad critiques of ideological coercion and contemporary consciousness.

The theme of ideological coercion is implicit in Nancy Jay's analysis of religious violence, although she returns to the familiar focus on sacrificial rites. She offers a critique of blood sacrifice that is based on a feminist perspective. Jay finds in diverse agrarian and pastoral societies a persistent pattern in which the intergenerational continuity between fathers and sons is established through sacrificial killing. Sacrificial cults circumvent the biological ties of sons to mothers and exclude daughters from the new community bonds. Sacrificial institutions in all of these societies tend to be reserved for males and to exclude females, especially females of reproductive age. Thus, suggests Jay, sacrificial institutions forge a set of male-to-male relationships that override birth-based lines of descent.

Elaine Scarry's perspective on the coercive effects of religion differs from the feminist or the Marxist point of view. Scarry focuses first on the suffering of victims of torture. Starting with the wordlessness experienced by victims of intense pain, she shows how torturers obliterate their victims' voices and the contents of their consciousness. The deconstruction of the victim's voice and world allows the torturer to replace the victim's reality with that of the victimizer. Perhaps surprisingly, this is the same work that civilizations do: they replace our raw sensory impressions with the layers of language, conceptualization, and imagination that we use to interpret out experiences. Her theory is intricate, involving not just torture but also warfare, the cultural construction of religion, and biblical narratives that depict human bodily wounding by a deity, who, in the Christian tradition, is seen as a wounded—crucified—body.

Ideological coercion was central to the thinking of Jean Baudrillard, and long before 9/11. His understanding of the 9/11 event was tied to his theory of spectacle and media-based simulacra. As he came to see it, bombardment with images, sounds, and ideas from multiple media—the essential experience of postmodernity—has stripped us of our ability to connect with objects. Rather than experience things, we experience a play of signs and mental titillations that saturate our capacity for sensuous contact with the world and yank our attention from one spectacle to another. The collapse of the twin towers in the 9/11 terrorist event was a riveting spectacle with a unique power to arrest our gaze. Its effects radiated beyond the shock of numbers killed to the level of fascination we experience while watching disaster films. We are captivated by the simulated atrocities of disaster films, replaying them over and over in our minds because, like the collapse of those two iconic pillars in Manhattan, they portend the collapse of Western civilization itself. Baudrillard also connected the 9/11 event to the Western push toward globalization and the resulting impoverishment of non-Western cultures. According to Baudrillard, the 9/11 event was not motivated by competing ideologies, despite religious claims. Rather the terrorists were responding blindly to the loss of local cultures and to the hegemonic expansion of the West.

Ashis Nandy, on the other hand, has seen multiple idioms at play in Indian terrorist acts. He explores terrorist incidents from the 1980s and the notions of fair play and duty to protect noncombatants embraced by their Sikh perpetrators. Nandy ponders whether nuanced responses to religious terrorism might help to deflate it, by taking into consideration different layers of the human personality, religious sensibilities, and age-old social relationships. Yet he acknowledges also that today's religious nationalists in India are unlikely to be swayed by traditional virtues. With its complex amalgam of old and new thinking, contemporary Indian society is unpredictable, and its strains of religious nationalism are explosive. According to Nandy, outbreaks of religious violence in India stem in part from the jarring encounter of India's traditional imagination with Western notions, such as secularism and the nation-state.

What unites these various theoretical perspectives from the Greek Pythagoreans to Ashis Nandy is a fascination with the inexorable link between religion and violence. Though many of the theories fasten upon sacrifice as the emblematic form in which killing is tied to the realm of the sacred, it is fair to say that all of these theoretical perspectives are more than attempts to explain a particular kind of ritual behavior. Rather they are efforts to understand a fundamental aspect of the human imagination, the extraordinary link between some of the most violent acts of destruction and the loftiest elements of religious spirit. Beneath this enigmatic connection between violence and the sacred, they find insights into something quite essential, the strange attraction between the destructive and creative sides of the human condition.

14
ÉMILE DURKHEIM

IN 1912 ÉMILE DURKHEIM (1858–1917) reflected on the experience of religious excitement that led to moments of transfiguring exaltation for individuals and to potential outbreaks of violence for a group. According to Durkheim, this "effervescence" tends to occur in conjunction with images, rituals, and other acts in which people experience an emanating religious force. This religious force issues ultimately from the social experience of being part of a clan, said Durkheim. It comes from the collective experience of the group's members but is felt to be autonomous, exterior to individuals and to the collective. Religious symbols—deriving ultimately from the group—are felt to empower individuals but also to compel them. This sense of compulsion is the birth experience of the very idea of the sacred. Effervescence, deriving ultimately from social dynamics, is thus an ineluctable aspect of religion. Insofar as effervescence may culminate in acts of violence, the potential for religious violence is endemic to human groups.

These reflections on effervescence were part of Durkheim's wider study of religious expressions among "totemic" societies. Because they were largely uncontaminated by Western civilization, totemic societies offered Durkheim an opportunity to study the core principles that, he felt, explained social cohesion anywhere. Unlike the British utilitarians of his day, Durkheim saw social experience, not individual choice, as a determining factor in identity formation. Essential to his understanding of social experience were the polar categories of sacred and profane. The central sphere of the "sacred" influenced broad collective identities and seeped into the profane margins of society. Modern societies resemble totemic societies in the way that power reverberates from core symbols out into the social peripheries.

Durkheim is credited with founding the modern discipline of sociology and was also founder of *L'Année Sociologique*, the first journal dedicated to the subject. He came of age as a secular Jew in France during the exciting but also turbulent period around the turn of the twentieth century. His colleagues included many eminent names of the day, such as his professor Fustel de Coulanges, his fellow student Henri Bergson, and his protégés at Sorbonne University, Marcel Mauss and Henri Hubert. Durkheim's major contribution to the study of religion is *Elementary Forms of Religious Life*, an excerpt of which is found here. He also discusses religion in his monograph on suicide, where he compared rates of suicidal deaths among Catholics and Protestants and found social solidarity to be a key factor in the lower rate among Catholics.

FROM *ELEMENTARY FORMS OF THE RELIGIOUS LIFE*

The life of the Australian societies passes alternately through two distinct phases. Sometimes the population is broken up into little groups who wander about independently of one another, in their various occupations; each family lives by itself, hunting and fishing, and in a word, trying to procure its indispensable food by all the means in its power. Sometimes, on the contrary, the population concentrates and gathers at determined points for a length of time varying from several days to several months. This concentration takes place when a clan or a part of the tribe is summoned to the gathering, and on this occasion they celebrate a religious ceremony, or else hold what is called a corrobbori in the usual ethnological language.

These two phases are contrasted with each other in the sharpest way. In the first, economic activity is the preponderating one, and it is generally of a very mediocre intensity. Gathering the grains or herbs that are necessary for food, or hunting and fishing are not occupations to awaken very lively passions. The dispersed condition in which the society finds itself results in making its life uniform, languishing and dull. But when a corrobbori takes place, everything changes. Since the emotional and passional faculties of the primitive are only imperfectly placed under the control of his reason and will, he easily loses control of himself. Any event of some importance puts him quite outside himself. Does he receive good news? There are at once transports of enthusiasm. In the contrary conditions, he is to be seen running here and there like a madman, giving himself up to all sorts of immoderate movements, crying, shrieking, rolling in the dust, throwing it in every direction, biting himself, brandishing his arms in a furious manner, etc. The very fact of the concentration acts as an exceptionally powerful stimulant. When they are once come together, a sort of electricity is formed by their collecting which quickly transports them to an extraordinary degree of exaltation. Every sentiment expressed finds a place without resistance in all the minds, which are very open to outside impressions; each re-echoes the others, and is re-echoed by the others. The initial impulse thus proceeds, growing as its goes, as an avalanche grows in its advance. And as such active passions so free from all control could not fail to burst out, on every side one sees nothing but violent gestures, cries, veritable howls, and deafening noises of every sort, which aid in intensifying still more the state of mind which they manifest. And since a collective sentiment cannot express itself collectively except on the condition of observing a certain order permitting co-operation and movements in unison, these gestures and cries naturally tend to become rhythmic and regular; hence come songs and dances. But in taking a more regular form, they lose nothing of their natural violence; a regulated tumult remains tumult. The human voice is not sufficient for the task; it is reinforced by means of artificial processes; boomerangs are beaten against each other; bull-roarers are whirled. It is probable that these instruments, the use of which is so general in the Australian religious ceremonies, are used primarily to express in a more adequate fashion the agitation felt. But while they express it, they also strengthen it. This effervescence often reaches such a point that it causes un-heard-of actions. The passions released are of such an impetuosity that they can be restrained by nothing. They are so far removed from their ordinary conditions of life, and they are so thoroughly conscious of it, that they feel that they must set themselves outside of and above their ordinary morals. The sexes unite contrarily to the rules governing sexual relations. Men exchange wives with each other. Sometimes even incestuous unions, which in normal times are thought abominable and are severely punished, are now contracted openly and with impunity. If we add to all this that the ceremonies generally take place at night in a darkness pierced here and there by the light of fires, we can easily imagine what effect such scenes ought to produce on the minds of those who participate. They produce such a violent super-excitation of the whole physical and mental life that it cannot be supported very long: the actor taking the principal part finally falls exhausted on the ground.

One can readily conceive how, when arrived at this state of exaltation, a man does not recognize himself any longer. Feeling himself dominated and carried away from some sort of an eternal power which makes him think and act differently than in normal times, he naturally has the impression of being himself no longer. It seems to him that he has become a new being: the decorations he puts on and the masks that cover his face and figure materially in this interior transformation, and to a still greater extent, they aid in determining its nature. And as at the same time all his companions feel themselves transformed in the same way and express this sentiment by their cries, their gestures and their general attitude, everything is just as though he really were transported into a special world, entirely different from the one where he ordinarily lives, and into an environment filled with exceptionally intense forces that take hold of him and metamorphose him. How could such experiences as these, especially when they are repeated every day for weeks, fail to leave in him the conviction that there really exist two heterogeneous and mutually incomparable worlds? One is that where his daily life drags wearily along; but he cannot penetrate into the other without at once entering into relations with extraordinary powers that excite him to the point of frenzy. The first is the profane world, the second, that of sacred things.

So it is in the midst of these effervescent social environments and out of this effervescence itself that the religious idea seems to be born. The theory that this is really its origin is confirmed by the fact that in Australia the really religious activity is almost entirely confined to the moments when these assemblies are held. To be sure, there is no people among whom the great solemnities of the cult are not more or less periodic; but in more advanced societies, there is not, so to speak, a day when some prayer or offering is not addressed to the gods and some ritual act is not performed. But in Australia, on the contrary, apart from the celebrations of the clan and tribe, the time is nearly all filled with lay and profane occupations. Of course there are prohibitions that should be and are preserved even during these periods of temporal activity; it is never permissible to kill or eat freely of the totemic animal, at least in those parts where the interdiction has retained its original vigour; but almost no positive rites are then celebrated, and there are no ceremonies of any importance. These take place only in the midst of assembled groups. The religious life of the Australian passes through successive phases of complete lull and of superexcitation, and the social life oscillates in the same rhythm. . . . By concentrating itself almost entirely in certain determined moments, the collective life has been able to attain its greatest intensity and efficacy, and consequently to give men a more active sentiment of the double existence they lead and of the double nature in which they participate.

But the explanation is still incomplete. We have shown how the clan, by the manner in which it acts upon its members, awakens within them the idea of external forces which dominate them and exalt them; but we must still demand how it happens that these forces are thought of under the form of totems, that is to say, in the shape of an animal or plant.

It is because this animal or plant has given its name to the clan and serves it as emblem. In fact, it is a well-known law that the sentiments aroused in us by something spontaneously attach themselves to the symbol which represents them. For us, black is a sign of mourning; it also suggests sad impressions and ideas. The transference of sentiments comes simply from the fact that the idea of a thing and the idea of its symbol are closely united in our minds; the result is that the emotions provoked by the one extend contagiously to the other. But this contagion, which takes place in every case to a certain degree, is much more complete and more marked when a symbol is something simple, definite and easily representable, while the thing itself, owing to its dimensions, the number of its parts and the complexity of their arrangement, is difficult to hold in the mind. For we are unable to consider an abstract entity, which we can represent only laboriously and confusedly, the source of the strong sentiments which we feel. We cannot explain them to ourselves except by connecting them to some concrete object of whose reality we are vividly aware. Then if the thing itself does not fulfil this condition, it cannot serve as the accepted basis of the sentiments felt, even though it may be what really aroused them. Then some sign takes its place; it is to this that we connect the emotions it excites. It is this which is loved, feared, respected; it is to this that we are grateful; it is for this that we sacrifice ourselves. The soldier who dies for his flag, dies for his country; but as a matter of fact, in his own consciousness, it is the flag that has the first place. It sometimes happens that this even directly determines action. Whether one isolated standard remains in the hands of the enemy or not does not determine the fate of the country, yet the soldier allows himself to be killed to regain it. He loses sight of the fact that the flag is only a sign, and that it has no value in itself, but only brings to mind the reality that it represents; it is treated as if it were this reality itself.

Now the totem is the flag of the clan. It is therefore natural that the impressions aroused by the clan in individual minds – impressions of dependence and of increased vitality – should fix themselves to the idea of the totem rather than that of the clan: for the clan is too complex a reality to be represented clearly in all its complex unity by such rudimentary intelligences. More than that, the primitive does not even see that these impressions come to him from the group. He does not know that the coming together of a number of men associated in the same life results in disengaging new energies, which transform each of them. All that he knows is that he is raised above himself and that he sees a different life from the one he ordinarily leads. However, he must connect these sensations to some external object as their cause. Now what does he see about him? On every side those things which appeal to his senses and strike his imagination are the numerous images of the totem. They are the waninga and the nurtunja, which are symbols of the sacred being. They are churinga and bull-roarers, upon which are generally carved combinations of lines having the same significance. They are the decorations covering the different parts of his body, which are totemic marks. How could this image, repeated everywhere and in all sorts of forms, fail to stand out with exceptional relief in his mind? Placed thus in the centre of the scene, it becomes representative. The sentiments experienced fix themselves upon it, for it is the only concrete object upon which they can fix themselves It continues to bring them to mind and to evoke them even after the assembly has dissolved, for it survives the assembly, being carved upon the instruments of the cult, upon the sides of rocks, upon bucklers, etc. By it, the emotions experienced are perpetually sustained and revived. Everything happens just as if they inspired them directly. It is still more natural to attribute them to it for, since they are common to the group, they can be associated only with something that is equally common to all. Now the totemic emblem is the only thing satisfying this condition. By definition, it is common to all. During the ceremony, it is the center of all regards. While generations change, it remains the same; it is the permanent element of the social life. So it is from it that those mysterious forces seem to emanate with which men feel that they are related, and thus they have been led to represent these forces under the form of the animate or inanimate being whose name the clan bears.

When this point is once established, we are in a position to understand all that is essential in the totemic beliefs.

Since religious force is nothing other than the collective and anonymous force of the clan, and since this can be represented in the mind only in the form of the totem, the totemic emblem is like the visible body of the god. Therefore, it is from it that those kindly and dreadful actions seem to emanate, which the cult seeks to provoke or prevent; consequently, it is to it that the cult is addressed. This is the explanation of why it holds the first place in the series of sacred things.

But the clan, like every other sort of society, can live only in and through the individual consciousnesses that compose it. So if religious force, in so far as it is conceived as incorporated in the totemic emblem, appears to be outside of the individuals and to be endowed with a sort of transcendence over them, it, like the clan of which it is the symbol, can be realized only in and through them; in this sense, it is imminent in them and they necessarily represent it as such. They feel it present and active within them, for it is this which raises them to a superior life. This is why men have believed that they contain within them a principle comparable to the one residing in the totem, and consequently, why they have attributed a sacred character to themselves, but one less marked than that of the emblem. It is because the emblem is the pre-eminent source of the religious life; the man participates in it only indirectly, as he is well aware; he takes into account the fact that the force that transports him into the world of sacred things is not inherent in him, but comes to him from the outside.

But for still another reason, the animals or vegetables of the totemic species should have the same character and even to a higher degree. If the totemic principle is nothing else than the clan, it is the clan thought of under the material form of the totemic emblem; now this form is also that of the concrete beings whose name the clan bears. Owing to this resemblance, they could not fail to evoke sentiments analogous to those aroused by the emblem itself. Since the latter is the object of a religious respect, they too should inspire respect of the same sort and appear to be sacred. Having external forms so nearly identical, it would be impossible for the native not to attribute to them forces of the same nature. It is therefore forbidden to kill or eat the totemic animal, since its flesh is believed to have the positive virtues resulting from the rites; it is because it resembles the emblem of the clan, that is to say, it is in its own image. And since the animal naturally resembles the emblem more than the man does, it is placed on a superior rank in the hierarchy of sacred things. Between these two beings there is undoubtedly a close relationship, for they both partake of the same essence: both incarnate something of the totemic principle. However, since the principle itself is conceived under an animal form, the animal seems to incarnate it more fully than the man. Therefore, if men consider it and treat it as a brother, it is at least as an elder brother.

But even if the totemic principle has its preferred seat in a determined species of animal or vegetable, it cannot remain localized there. A sacred character is to a high degree contagious; it therefore spreads out from the totemic being to everything that is closely or remotely connected with it. The religious sentiments inspired by the animal are communicated to the substances upon which it is nourished and which serve to make or remake its flesh and blood, to the things that resemble it, and to the different beings with which it has constant relations. Thus, little by little, subtotems are attached to the totems and from the cosmological systems expressed by the primitive classifications. At last, the whole world is divided up among the totemic principles of each tribe.

We are now able to explain the origin of the ambiguity of religious forces as they appear in history, and how they are physical as well as human, moral as well as material. They are moral powers because they are made up entirely of the impressions this moral being, the group, arouses in those other moral beings, its individual members; they do not translate the manner in which physical beings affect our senses, but the way in which the collective consciousness acts upon individual consciousnesses. Their authority is only one form of the moral ascendancy of society over its members. But, on the other hand, since they are conceived of under material forms, they could not fail to be regarded as closely related to material things. Therefore they dominate the two worlds. Their residence is in men, but at the same time they are the vital principles of things. They animate minds and discipline them, but it is also they who make plants grow and animals reproduce. It is this double nature which has enabled religion to be like the womb from which come all the leading germs of human civilization. Since it has been made to embrace all of reality, the physical world as well as the moral one, the forces that move bodies as well as those that move minds have been conceived in a religious form. That is how the most diverse methods and practices, both those that make possible the continuation of the moral life (law, morals, beaux-arts) and those serving the material life (the natural, technical and practical sciences), are either directly or indirectly derived from religion.

15

HENRI HUBERT AND MARCEL MAUSS

THE FOLLOWING EXCERPT by Henri Hubert (1872–1927) and Marcel Mauss (1872–1950) outlines the way that religious rituals can engage and also conciliate powers that are felt to be dangerous and destructive. Analyzing the sacrifices described in Vedic documents from ancient India, Hubert and Mauss point to a fundamental enigma: how is it that a sacrificial victim, whose role in the ritual is to die, can offer a pathway to divinity and immortality? They argue that through a complex process of substitution, sacrificial victims die in the place of *sacrifiers* (those for whose benefit the sacrifice is conducted), redeeming them from stain, error, and death, and empowering them with super vitality. The substitution is necessary because traditional societies regard the world of the sacrificer and the world of the divine as intrinsically separate. They must be kept apart lest divine power—inherently too hot to touch—contact the *sacrifiers* and destroy them. Helping to alleviate this danger of destruction are rites of entry and exit, which consecrate and then deconsecrate not only the victim but also the one for whom the victim dies. The whole process is hallowed by a series of ritual actions, which gradually heighten the sacred character of the victim that is to be killed, in order to boost also the vitality of the sacrificer who survives.

Hubert and Mauss were both students of Émile Durkheim. Mauss was Durkheim's nephew and eventually became editor of the sociological journal that Durkheim founded, *L'Année Sociologique*, for which Mauss and Hubert collaborated on a number of contributions. Mauss was trained as a Sanskritist, and Hubert published extensively on the Celts, but both were entrenched also in theoretical debates about the nature of religion. Together they published *Sacrifice: Its Nature and Function* in 1898 and *Outline of a General Theory of Magic* in 1904. The publication of *Sacrifice* preceded that of Durkheim's *Elementary Forms of the Religious Life* by fourteen years, but Hubert and Mauss clearly were influenced by the ideas of their eminent teacher.

In the excerpt, Hubert and Mauss rely on the polar concepts of sacred and profane as described initially by Durkheim. In describing the tension between profane and sacred spheres, Hubert and Mauss laid the foundations for a trend that became known in the later twentieth century as the phenomenology of religious experience.

FROM *SACRIFICE: ITS NATURE AND FUNCTION*

It can now be seen more clearly of what in our opinion the unity of the sacrificial system consists. It does not come, as Smith believed, from the fact that all the possible kinds of sacrifice have emerged from one primitive, simple form. Such a sacrifice does not exist. Of all the procedures of sacrifice, the most general, the least rich in particular elements, that we have been able to distinguish, are those of sacralization and desacralization. Now actually in any sacrifice of desacralization, however pure it may be, we always find a sacralization of the victim. Conversely, in any sacrifice of sacralization, even the most clearly marked, a desacralization is necessarily implied, for otherwise the remains of the victim could not be used. The two elements are thus so closely interdependent that the one cannot exist without the other.

Moreover, these two kinds of sacrifice are still only abstract types. Every sacrifice takes place in certain given circumstances and with a view to certain determined ends. From the diversity of the ends which may be pursued in this way arise varying procedures, of which we have given a few examples. Now there is no religion in which these procedures do not coexist in greater or lesser number; all the sacrificial rituals we know of display a great complexity. Moreover, there is no special rite that is not complex in itself, for either it pursues several ends at the same time, or, to attain one end, it sets in motion several forces. We have seen that sacrifices of desacralization and even expiatory sacrifices proper become entangled with communion sacrifices. But many other examples of complexity might be given. The Amazulu, to bring on rain, assemble a herd of black bullocks, kill one and eat it in silence, and then burn its bones outside the village; which constitutes three different themes in one operation.

In the Hindu animal sacrifice this complexity is even more marked. We have found shares of the animal attributed for expiation purposes to evil spirits, divine shares put on one side, shares for communion that were enjoyed by the sacrifier [one to whom the benefits of sacrifice accrue], shares for the priests that were consumed by them. The victim serves equally for bringing down imprecations on the enemy, for divination, and for vows. In one of its aspects sacrifice belongs to the theriomorphic cults, for the soul of the animal is dispatched to heaven to join the archetypes of the animals and maintain the species in perpetuity. It is also a rite of consumption, for the sacrifier who has laid the fire may not eat meat until he has made such a sacrifice. Lastly it is a sacrifice of redemption, for the sacrifier is consecrated: he is in the power of the divinity, and redeems himself by substituting the victim in his place. All this is mixed up and confused in one and the same system, which, despite its diversity, remains none the less harmonious. This is all the more the case with a rite of immense purport like the sacrifice to Soma, in which, over and above what we have just described, is realized the case of the sacrifice of the god. In a word, just like a magic ceremony or prayer, which can serve at the same time as an act of thanksgiving, a vow, and a propitiation, sacrifice can fulfil a great variety of concurrent functions.

But if sacrifice is so complex, whence comes its unity? It is because, fundamentally, beneath the diverse forms it takes, it always consists in one same procedure, which may be used for the most widely differing purposes. This procedure consists in establishing a means of communication between the sacred and the profane worlds through the mediation of a victim, that is, of a thing that in the course of the ceremony is destroyed. Now, contrary to what Smith believed, the victim does not necessarily come to the sacrifice with a religious nature already perfected and clearly defined: it is the sacrifice itself that confers this upon it. Sacrifice can therefore impart to the victim most varied powers and thereby make it suitable for fulfilling the most varied functions, either by different rites of during the same rite. The victim can also pass on a sacred character of the religious world to the profane world, or vice versa. It remains indifferent to the direction of the current that passes through it. At the same time the spirit that has been released from the victim can be entrusted with the task of bearing a prayer to the heavenly powers, it can be used to foretell the future, to redeem oneself from the wrath of the gods by making over one's portion of the victim to them, and, lastly, enjoying the sacred flesh that remains. On the other hand, once the victim has been set apart, it has a certain autonomy, no matter what may be done. It is the focus of energy from which are released effects that surpass the narrow purpose that the sacrifier [one for whom the sacrifice is conducted] has assigned to the rite. An animal is sacrificed to redeem a *dikshita*; an immediate consequence is that the freed spirit departs to nourish the eternal life of the species. Thus sacrifice naturally exceeds the narrow aims that the most elementary theologies assign to it. This is because it is not made up solely of a series of individual actions. The rite sets in motion the whole complex of sacred things to which it is addressed. From the very beginning of this study sacrifice has appeared as a particular ramification of the system of consecration.

There is no need to explain at length why the profane thus enters into a relationship with the divine: it is because it sees in it the very source of life. It therefore has every interest in drawing closer to it, since it is there that the very conditions for its existence are to be found. But how is it that the profane only draws nearer by remaining at a distance from it? How does it come about that the profane only communicates with the sacred through an intermediary? The destructive consequences of the rite partly explain this strange procedure. If the religious forces are the very principle of the forces of life, they are in themselves of such a nature that contact with them is a fearful thing for the ordinary man. Above all, when they reach a certain level of intensity, they cannot be concentrated in a profane object without destroying it. However much need he has of them, the sacrifier cannot approach them save with the utmost prudence. That is why between these powers and himself he interposes intermediaries, of whom the principal is the victim. If he involved himself in the rite to the very end, he would find death, not life. The victim takes his place. It alone penetrates into the perilous domain of sacrifice, it dies there, and indeed it is there in order to die. The sacrifier remains protected: the gods take the victim instead of him. The victim redeems him. Moses had not circumcised his son, and Yahweh came to "wrestle" with him in a hostelry. Moses was on the point of death when his wife savagely cut off the child's foreskin and, casting it at Yahweh's feet, said to him: "Thou art for me a husband of blood." The destruction of the foreskin satisfied the god: he did not destroy Moses, who was redeemed. There is no sacrifice into which some idea of redemption does not enter.

But this first explanation is not sufficiently general, for in the case of the offering, communication is also effected through an intermediary, and yet no destruction occurs. This is because too powerful a consecration has grave drawbacks, even when it is not destructive. All that is too deeply involved in the religious sphere is by that very fact removed from the sphere of the profane. The more a being is imbued with religious feeling, the more he is charged with prohibitions that render him isolated. The sacredness of the Nazir paralyses him. On the other hand, all that enters into a too-intimate contact with sacred things takes on their nature and becomes sacred like them. Now sacrifice is carried out by the profane. The action that it exerts upon people and things is destined to enable them to fulfil their role in temporal life. None can therefore enter with advantage upon sacrifice save on condition of being able to emerge from it. The rites of exit partly serve this purpose. They weaken the force of the consecration. But by themselves alone they could not weaken it sufficiently if it had been too intense. It is therefore important that the sacrifier or the object of sacrifice receive the consecration only when its force has been blunted, that is to say, indirectly. This is the purpose of the intermediary. Thanks to it, the two worlds that are present can interpenetrate and yet remain distinct.

In this way is to be explained a very particular characteristic of religious sacrifice. In any sacrifice there is an act of abnegation since the sacrifier deprives himself and gives. Often this abnegation is even imposed upon him as a duty. For sacrifice is not always optional; the gods demand it. As the Hebrew ritual declares, worship and service is owed them; as the Hindus say, their share is owed them. But this abnegation and submission are not without their selfish aspect. The sacrifier gives up something of himself but he does not give himself. Prudently, he sets himself aside. This is because if he gives, it is partly in order to receive. Thus sacrifice shows itself in a dual light; it is a useful act and it is an obligation. Disinterestedness is mingled with self-interest. That is why it has so frequently been conceived of as a form of contract. Fundamentally there is perhaps no sacrifice that has not some contractual element. The two parties present exchange their services and each gets his due. For the gods too have need of the profane. If nothing were set aside from the harvest, the god of the corn would die; in order that Dionysus may be reborn, Dionysus' goat must be sacrificed at the grape-harvest; it is the *soma* that men give the gods to drink that fortifies them against evil spirits. In order that the sacred may subsist, its share must be given to it, and it is from the share of the profane that this apportionment is made. This ambiguity is inherent in the very nature of sacrifice. It is dependent, in fact, on the presence of the intermediary, and we know that with no intermediary there is no sacrifice. Because the victim is distinct from the sacrifier and the god, it separates them while uniting them: they draw close to each other, without giving themselves to each other entirely.

There is, however, one case from which all selfish calculation is absent. This is the case of the sacrifice of the god, for the god who sacrifices himself gives himself irrevocably. This time all intermediaries have disappeared. The god, who is at the same time the sacrifier, is one with the victim and sometimes even with the sacrificer [the one who conducts the actual sacrifice on behalf of the sacrifier]. All the differing elements which enter into ordinary sacrifice here enter into each other and become mixed together. But such mixing is possible only for mythical, that is, ideal beings. This is how the concept of a god sacrificing himself for the world could be realized, and has become, even for the most civilized peoples, the highest expression and, as it were, the ideal limit of abnegation, in which no apportionment occurs.

But in the same way as the sacrifice of the god does not emerge from the imaginary sphere of religion, so it might likewise be believed that the whole system is merely a play of images. The powers to whom the devotee sacrifices his most precious possession seem to have no positive element. The unbeliever sees in these rites only vain and costly illusions, and is astounded that all mankind has so eagerly dissipated its strength for phantom gods. But there are perhaps true realities to which it is possible to attach the institution in its entirety. Religious ideas, because they are believed, exist; they exist objectively, as social facts. The sacred things in relation to which sacrifice functions, are social things. And this is enough to explain sacrifice. For sacrifice to be truly justified, two conditions are necessary. First of all, there must exist outside the sacrifier things which *debt* cause him to go outside himself, and to which he owes what he sacrifices. *economy* Next, these things must be close to him so that he can enter into relation- *and* ship with them, find in them the strength and assurance he needs, and *cycle* obtain from contact with them the benefits that he expects from his rites. Now this character of intimate penetration and separation, of immanence and transcendence, is distinctive of social matters to the highest degree. They also exist at the same time both within and outside the individual, according to one's viewpoint. We understand then what the function of sacrifice can be, leaving aside the symbols whereby the believer expresses it to himself. It is a social function because sacrifice is concerned with social matters.

On the one hand, this personal renunciation of their property by individuals or groups nourishes social forces. Not, doubtless, that society has need of the things which are the materials of sacrifice. Here everything occurs in the world of ideas, and it is mental and moral energies that are in question. But the act of abnegation implicit in every sacrifice, by recalling frequently to the consciousness of the individual the presence of collective forces, in fact sustains their ideal existence. These expiations and general purifications, communions and sacralizations of groups, these creations of the spirits of the cities give—or renew periodically for the community, represented by its gods—that character, good, strong, grave, and terrible, which is one of the essential traits of any social entity. Moreover, individuals find their own advantage in this same act. They confer upon each other, upon themselves, and upon those things they hold dear, the whole strength of society. They invest with the authority of society their vows, their oaths, their marriages. They surround, as if with a protective sanctity, the fields they have ploughed and the houses they have built. At the same time they find in sacrifice the means of redressing equilibriums that have been upset: by expiation they redeem themselves from social obloquy, the consequence of error, and re-enter the community; by the apportionments they make of those things whose use society has reserved for itself, they acquire the right to enjoy them. The social norm is thus maintained without danger to themselves, without diminution for the group. Thus the social function of sacrifice is fulfilled, both for the individuals and for the community. And as society is made up not only of men, but also of things and events, we perceive how sacrifice can follow and at the same time reproduce the rhythms of human life and of nature; how it has been able to become both periodical by the use of natural phenomena, and occasional, as are the momentary needs of men, and in short to adapt itself to a thousand purposes.

Moreover we have been able to see, as we have proceeded, how many beliefs and social practices not strictly religious are linked to sacrifice. We have dealt in turn with questions of contract, of redemption, of penalties, of gifts, of abnegation, with ideas relating to the soul and to immortality which are still at the basis of common morality. This indicates the importance of sacrifice for sociology. But in this study we have not had to follow it in its development or all its ramifications. We have given ourselves only the task of attempting to put it in its place.

Sigmund Freud

THE PIONEERING PSYCHOLOGIST SIGMUND FREUD (1856–1939) reflected upon the social and psychological roles of religion in his studies of the Oedipal complex, neurotic ritualism, and the drive toward *thanatos*—a death-instinct at continuous war with the impulses of civilization. But it was his early work on the Oedipal complex—the name he gave for the psychological predispositions reflected in the Greek myth of Oedipus— that directly linked a propensity for violence to religious symbols and rituals.

Freud's Oedipal thesis arose from his investigation of the deep-seated and interrelated emotions of taboo and ambivalence, especially concerning the dead. On the basis of case studies of neurotics and nineteenth-century speculation about fear of ghosts, Freud believed that he had uncovered an unconscious but universal suspicion that death derived from a crime. Rather than a natural and inevitable part of life, death is most deeply perceived to be the result of a tear in life's fabric. We instinctively respond to this tear with feelings of horror and guilt.

In the Oedipal complex, horror and guilt are expressed in the ambivalence a boy feels for his father, whom he admires and simultaneously longs to kill. The boy's deep envy and hostility for his father reproduce emotions that brothers once felt in the primal horde, where a desire for sexual intimacy with the mother led the boys to rise up and slay the powerful father. There, a combination of feelings and events—jealous hatred, murder, then guilt, horror, and the atoning sacrifice of one of the brothers—led eventually to an apologetic worship of the father as a god and to an incest taboo regarding the mother. For Freud, the urge to commit the primal crime continues to influence the processes of male psychological maturation. Men long to destroy authorities and make gods of themselves, but religion checks this urge by imposing a supernatural father figure onto human awareness. Thus, religion defuses our violent impulses into socially acceptable rituals and symbolizations, such as we see in the Christian reverence for the father god, the chaste mother, and the sacrificial son.

This dark side of Freud's thinking may seem out of place in the progress-oriented place and time in which he thrived, Vienna in the early twentieth century. Yet it was also prophetic for the turmoil of World War II. As a Jew, Freud himself was forced to flee Nazi persecution in 1938. He died in England the next year.

FROM *TOTEM AND TABOO*

Let us now envisage the scene of such a totem meal and let us embellish it further with a few probable features which could not be adequately considered before. Thus we have the clan, which on a solemn occasion kills its totem in a cruel manner and eats it raw, blood, flesh, and bones. At the same time the members of the clan disguised in imitation of the totem, mimic it in sound and movement as if they wanted to emphasize their common identity. There is also the conscious realization that an action is being carried out which is forbidden to each individual and which can only be justified through the participation of all, so that no one is allowed to exclude himself from the killing and the feast. After the act is accomplished the murdered animal is bewailed and lamented. The death lamentation is compulsive, being enforced by the fear of a threatening retribution, and its main purpose is, as Robertson Smith remarks on an analogous occasion, to exculpate oneself from responsibility for the slaying.

But after this mourning there follows loud festival gaiety accompanied by the unchaining of every impulse and the permission of every gratification. Here we find an easy insight into the nature of the *holiday*.

A holiday is a permitted, or rather a prescribed excess, a solemn violation of a prohibition. People do not commit the excesses which at all times have characterized holidays, as a result of an order to be in a holiday mood, but because in the very nature of a holiday there is excess; the holiday mood is brought about by the release of what is otherwise forbidden.

But what has mourning over the death of the totem animal to do with the introduction of this holiday spirit? If men are happy over the slaying of the totem, which is otherwise forbidden to them, why do they also mourn it?

We have heard that members of a clan become holy through the consumption of the totem and thereby also strengthen their identification with it and with each other. The fact that they have absorbed the holy life with which the substance of the totem is charged may explain the holiday mood and everything that results from it.

Psychoanalysis has revealed to us that the totem animal is really a substitute for the father, and this really explains the contradiction that it is usually forbidden to kill the totem animal, that the killing of it results in a holiday and that the animal is killed and yet mourned. The ambivalent emotional attitude which to-day still marks the father complex in our children and so often continues into adult life also extended to the father substitute of the totem animal.

But if we associate the translation of the totem as given by psychoanalysis, with the totem feast and the Darwinian hypothesis about the primal state of human society, a deeper understanding becomes possible and a hypothesis is offered which may seem fantastic but which has the advantage of establishing an unexpected unity among a series of hitherto separated phenomena.

The Darwinian conception of the primal horde does not, of course, allow for the beginning of totemism. There is only a violent, jealous father who keeps all the females for himself and drives away the growing sons. This primal state of society has nowhere been observed. The most primitive organization we know, which today is still in force with certain tribes, is *associations of men* consisting of members with equal rights, subject to the restrictions of the totemic system, and founded on matriarchy, or descent through the mother. Can the one have resulted from the other, and how was this possible?

By basing our argument upon the celebration of the totem we are in a position to give an answer: One day the expelled brothers joined forces, slew and ate the father, and thus put an end to the father horde. Together they dared and accomplished what would have remained impossible for them singly. Perhaps some advance in culture, like the use of a new weapon, had given them the feeling of superiority. Of course these cannibalistic savages ate their victim. This violent primal father had surely been the envied and feared model for each of the brothers. Now they accomplished their identification with him by devouring him and each acquired a part of his strength. The totem feast, which is perhaps mankind's first celebration, would be the repetition and commemoration of this memorable, criminal act with which so many things began, social organization, moral restrictions and religion.

In order to find these results acceptable, quite aside from our supposition, we need only assume that the group of brothers banded together were dominated by the same contradictory feelings towards the father which we can demonstrate as the content of ambivalence of the father complex in all our children and in neurotics. They hated the father who stood so powerfully in the way of their sexual demands and their desire for power, but they also loved and admired him. After they had satisfied their hate by his removal and had carried out their wish for identification with him, the suppressed tender impulses had to assert themselves. This took place in the form of remorse, a sense of guilt was formed which coincided here with the remorse generally felt. The dead now became stronger than the living had been, even as we observe it to-day in the destinies of men. What the father's presence had formerly prevented they themselves now prohibited in the psychic situation of "subsequent obedience" which we know so well from psychoanalysis. They undid their deed by declaring that the killing of the father substitute, the totem, was not allowed, and renounced the fruits of their deed by denying themselves the liberated women. Thus they created the two fundamental taboos of totemism out of the *sense of guilt of the son*, and for this very reason these had to correspond with the two repressed wishes of the Oedipus complex. Whoever disobeyed became guilty of the only two crimes which troubled primitive society.

The two taboos of totemism with which the morality of man begins are psychologically not of equal value. One of them, the sparing of the totem animal, rests entirely upon emotional motives; the father had been removed and nothing in reality could make up for this. But the other, the incest prohibition, had, besides, a strong practical foundation. Sexual need does not unite men, it separates them. Though the brothers had joined forces in order to overcome the father, each was the other's rival among the women. Each one wanted to have them all to himself like the father, and in the fight of each against the other the new organization would have perished. For there was no longer any one stronger than all the rest who could have successfully assumed the role of the father. Thus there was nothing left for the brothers, if they wanted to live together, but to erect the incest prohibition—perhaps after many difficult experiences—through which they all equally renounced the women whom they desired, and on account of whom they had removed the father in the first place. Thus they saved the organization which had made them strong and which could be based upon the homosexual feelings and activities which probably manifested themselves among them during the time of their banishment. Perhaps this situation also formed the germ of the institution of the mother right discovered by Bachofen, which was then abrogated by the patriarchal family arrangement.

On the other hand the claim of totemism to be considered the first attempt at a religion is connected with the other taboo which protects the life of the totem animal. The feelings of the sons found a natural and appropriate substitute for the father in the animal, but their compulsory treatment of it expressed more than the need of showing remorse. The surrogate for the father was perhaps used in the attempt to assuage the burning sense of guilt, and to bring about a kind of reconciliation with the father. The totemic system was a kind of agreement with the father in which the latter granted everything that the child's fantasy could expect from him, protection, care, and forbearance, in return for which the pledge was given to honor his life, that is to say, not to repeat the act against the totem through which the real father had perished. Totemism also contained an attempt at justification. "If the father had treated us like the totem we should never have been tempted to kill him." Thus totemism helped to gloss over the real state of affairs and to make one forget the event to which it owed its origin.

In this connection some features were formed which henceforth determined the character of every religion. The totem religion had issued from the sense of guilt of the sons as an attempt to palliate this feeling and to conciliate the injured father through subsequent obedience. All later religions prove to be attempts to solve the same problem, varying only in accordance with the stage of culture in which they are attempted and according to the paths which they take; they are all, however, reactions aiming at the same great event with which culture began and which ever since has not let mankind come to rest.

There is still another characteristic faithfully preserved in religion which already appeared in totemism at this time. The ambivalent strain was probably too great to be adjusted by any arrangement, or else the psychological conditions are entirely unfavorable to any kind of settlement of these contradictory feelings. It is certainly noticeable that the ambivalence attached to the father complex also continues in totemism and in religions in general. The religion of totemism included not only manifestations of remorse and attempts at reconciliation, but also serves to commemorate the triumph over the father. The gratification obtained thereby creates the commemorative celebration of the totem feast at which the restrictions of subsequent obedience are suspended, and makes it a duty to repeat the crime of parricide through the sacrifice of the totem animal as often as the benefits of this deed, namely, the appropriation of the father's properties, threaten to disappear as a result of the changed influences of life. We shall not be surprised to find that a part of the son's defiance also reappears, often in the most remarkable disguises and inversions, in the formation of later religions.

If thus far we have followed, in religion and moral precepts—but little differentiated in totemism—the consequences of the tender impulses towards the father as they are changed into remorse, we must not overlook the fact that for the most part the tendencies which have impelled to parricide have retained the victory. The social and fraternal feelings on which this great change is based, henceforth for long periods exercises the greatest influence upon the development of society. They find expression in the sanctification of the common blood and in the emphasis upon the solidarity of life within the clan. In thus ensuring each other's lives the brothers express the fact that no one of them is to be treated by the other as they all treated the father. They preclude a repetition of the fate of the father. The socially established prohibition against fratricide is now added to the prohibition against killing the totem, which is based on religious grounds. It will still be a long time before the commandment discards the restriction to members of the tribe and assumes the simple phraseology: Thou shalt not kill. At first the *brother clan* has taken the place of the *father horde* and was guaranteed by the blood bond.

Society is now based on complicity in the common crime, religion on the sense of guilt and the consequent remorse, while morality is based partly on the necessities of society and partly on the expiation which this sense of guilt demands.

———————

Thus psychoanalysis, contrary to the newer conceptions of the totemic system and more in accord with older conceptions, bids us argue for an intimate connection between totemism and exogamy as well as for their simultaneous origin.

I am under the influence of many strong motives which restrain me from the attempt to discuss the further development of religions from their beginning in totemism up to their present state. I shall follow out only two threads as I see them appearing in the weft with especial distinctness: the motive of the totem sacrifice and the relation of the son to the father.

Robertson Smith has shown us that the old totem feast returns in the original form of sacrifice. The meaning of the rite is the same: sanctification through participation in the common meal. The sense of guilt, which can only be allayed through the solidarity of all the participants, has also been retained. In addition to this there is the tribal deity in whose supposed presence the sacrifice takes place, who takes part in the meal like a member of the tribe, and with whom identification is effected by the act of eating the sacrifice. How does the god come into this situation which originally was foreign to him?

The answer might be that the idea of god had meanwhile appeared,—no one knows whence—and had dominated the whole religious life, and that the totem feast, like everything else that wished to survive, had been forced to fit itself into the new system. However, psychoanalytic investigation of the individual teaches with especial emphasis that god is in every case modelled after the father and that our personal relation to god is dependent upon our relation to our physical father, fluctuating and changing with him, and that god at bottom is nothing but an exalted father. Here also, as in the case of totemism, psychoanalysis advises us to believe the faithful, who call god father just as they called the totem their ancestor. If psychoanalysis deserves any consideration at all, then the share of the father in the idea of a god must be very important, quite aside from all the other origins and meanings of god upon which psychoanalysis can throw no light. But then the father would be represented twice in primitive sacrifice, first as god, and secondly as the totem-animal-sacrifice, and we must ask, with all due regard for the limited number of solutions which psychoanalysis offers, whether this is possible and what the meaning of it may be.

We know that there are a number of relations of the god to the holy animal (the totem and the sacrificial animal): 1. Usually one animal is sacred to every god, sometimes even several animals. 2. In certain, especially holy, sacrifices, the so-called "mystical" sacrifices, the very animal which had been sanctified through the god was sacrificed to him. 3. The god was often revered in the form of an animal, or from another point of view, animals enjoyed a godlike reverence long after the period of totemism. 4. In myths the god is frequently transformed into an animal, often into the animal that is sacred to him. From this the assumption was obvious that the god himself was the animal, and that he had evolved from the totem animal at a later stage of religious feeling. But the reflection that the totem itself is nothing but a substitute for the father relieves us of all further discussion. Thus the totem may have been the first form of the father substitute and the god a later one in which the father regained his human form. Such a new creation from the root of all religious evolution, namely, the longing for the father, might become possible if in the course of time an essential change had taken place in the relation to the father and perhaps also to the animal.

Such changes are easily divined even if we disregard the beginning of a psychic estrangement from the animal as well as the disintegration of totemism through animal domestication. The situation created by the removal of the father contained an element which in the course of time must have brought about an extraordinary increase of longing for the father. For the brothers who had joined forces to kill the father had each been animated by the wish to become like the father and had given expression to this wish by incorporating parts of the substitute for him in the totem feast. In consequence of the pressure which the bonds of the brother clan exercised upon each member, this wish had to remain unfulfilled. No one could or was allowed to attain the father's perfection of power, which was the thing they had all sought. Thus the bitter feeling against the father which had incited to the deed could subside in the course of time, while the longing for him grew, and an ideal could arise having as a content the fullness of power and the freedom from restriction of the conquered primal father, as well as the willingness to subject themselves to him. The original democratic equality of each member of the tribe could no longer be retained on account of the interference of cultural changes; in consequence of which there arose a tendency to revive the old father ideal in the creation of gods through the veneration of those individuals who had distinguished themselves above the rest. That a man should become a god and that a god should die, which to-day seems to us an outrageous presumption, was still by no means offensive to the conceptions of classical antiquity. But the deification of the murdered father from whom the tribe now derived its origin was a much more serious attempt at expiation than the former covenant with the totem.

In this evolution I am at a loss to indicate the place of the great maternal deities who perhaps everywhere preceded the paternal deities. But it seems certain that the change in the relation to the father was not restricted to religion but logically extended to the other side of human life influenced by the removal of the father, namely, the social organization. With the institution of paternal deities the fatherless society gradually changed into a patriarchal one. The family was a reconstruction of the former primal horde and also restored a great part of their former rights to the fathers. Now there were patriarchs again but the social achievements of the brother clan had not been given up and the actual difference between the new family patriarchs and the unrestricted primal father was great enough to insure the continuation of the religious need, the preservation of the unsatisfied longing for the father.

The father therefore really appears twice in the scene of sacrifice before the tribal god, once as the god and again as the totem-sacrificial-animal. But in attempting to understand this situation we must beware of interpretations which superficially seek to translate it as an allegory, and which forget the historical stages in the process. The twofold presence of the father corresponds to the two successive meanings of the scene. The ambivalent attitude towards the father as well as the victory of the son's tender emotional feelings over his hostile ones, have here found plastic expression. The scene of vanquishing the father, his greatest degradation, furnishes here the material to represent his highest triumph. The meaning which sacrifice has quite generally acquired is found in the fact that in the very same action which continues the memory of this misdeed it offers satisfaction to the father for the ignominy put upon him.

In the further development the animal loses its sacredness and the sacrifice its relation to the celebration of the totem; the rite becomes a simple offering to the deity, a self-deprivation in favor of the god. God himself is now so exalted above man that he can be communicated with only through a priest as intermediary. At the same time the social order produces godlike kings who transfer the patriarchal system to the state. It must be said that the revenge of the deposed and reinstated father has been very cruel; it culminated in the dominance of authority. The subjugated sons have used the new relation to disburden themselves still more of their sense of guilt. Sacrifice, as it is now constituted, is entirely beyond their responsibility. God himself has demanded and ordained it. Myths in which the god himself kills the animal that is sacred to him, which he himself really is, belong to this phase. This is the greatest possible denial of the great misdeed with which society and the sense of guilt began.

There is an unmistakable second meaning in this sacrificial demonstration. It expresses satisfaction at the fact that the earlier father substitute has been abandoned in favor of the higher conception of god. The superficial allegorical translation of the scene here roughly corresponds with its psychoanalytic interpretation by saying that the god is represented as overcoming the animal part of his nature.

But it would be erroneous to believe that in this period of renewed patriarchal authority the hostile impulses which belong to the father complex had entirely subsided. On the contrary, the first phases in the domination of the two new substitutive formations for the father, those of gods and kings, plainly show the most energetic expression of that ambivalence which is characteristic of religion.

In his great work, *The Golden Bough*, Frazer has expressed the conjecture that the first kings of the Latin tribes were strangers who played the part of a deity and were solemnly sacrificed in this role on specified holidays. The yearly sacrifice (self-sacrifice is a variant) of a god seems to have been an important feature of Semitic religions. The ceremony of human sacrifice in various parts of the inhabited world makes it certain that these human beings ended their lives as representatives of the deity. This sacrificial custom can still be traced in later times in the substitution of an inanimate imitation (doll) for the living person. The theanthropic god sacrifice into which unfortunately I cannot enter with the same thoroughness with which the animal sacrifice has been treated throws the clearest light upon the meaning of the older forms of sacrifice. It acknowledges with unsurpassable candor that the object of the sacrificial action has always been the same, being identical with what is now revered as a god, namely with the father. The question as to the relation of animal to human sacrifice can now be easily solved. The original animal sacrifice was already a substitute for a human sacrifice, for the solemn killing of the father, and when the father substitute regained its human form, the animal substitute could also be retransformed into a human sacrifice.

Thus the memory of that first great act of sacrifice had proved to be indestructible despite all attempts to forget it, and just at the moment when men strove to get as far away as possible from its motives, the undistorted repetition of it had to appear in the form of the god sacrifice. I need not fully indicate here the developments of religious thought which made this return possible in the form of rationalizations. Robertson Smith who is, of course, far removed from the idea of tracing sacrifice back to this great event of man's primal history, says that the ceremony of the festivals in which the old Semites celebrated the death of a deity were interpreted as a "commemoration of a mythical tragedy" and that the attendant lament was not characterized by spontaneous sympathy, but displayed a compulsive character, something that was imposed by the fear of a divine wrath. We are in a position to acknowledge that this interpretation was correct, the feelings of the celebrants being well explained by the basic situation.

We may now accept it as a fact that in the further development of religions these two inciting factors, the son's sense of guilt and his defiance, were never again extinguished. Every attempted solution of the religious problem and every kind of reconciliation of the two opposing psychic forces gradually falls to the ground, probably under the combined influence of cultural changes, historical events, and inner psychic transformations.

The endeavor of the son to put himself in place of the father god, appeared with greater and greater distinctness. With the introduction of agriculture the importance of the son in the patriarchal family increased. He was emboldened to give new expression to his incestuous libido which found symbolic satisfaction in laboring over mother earth. There came into existence figures of gods like Attis, Adonis, Tammuz, and others, spirits of vegetation as well as youthful divinities who enjoyed the favors of maternal deities and committed incest with the mother in defiance of the father. But the sense of guilt which was not allayed through these creations, was expressed in myths which visited these youthful lovers of the maternal goddesses with short life and punishment through castration or through the wrath of the father god appearing in animal form. Adonis was killed by the boar, the sacred animal of Aphrodite; Attis, the lover of Kybele, died of castration. The lamentation for these gods and the joy at their resurrection have gone over into the ritual of another son which divinity was destined to survive long.

When Christianity began its entry into the ancient world it met with the competition of the religion of Mithras and for a long time it was doubtful which deity was to be the victor.

The bright figure of the youthful Persian god has eluded our understanding. Perhaps we may conclude from the illustrations of Mithras slaying the steers that he represented the son who carried out the sacrifice of the father by himself and thus released the brothers from their oppressing complicity in the deed. There was another way of allaying this sense of guilt and this is the one that Christ took. He sacrificed his own life and thereby redeemed the brothers from primal sin.

The theory of primal sin is of Orphic origin; it was preserved in the mysteries and thence penetrated into the philosophic schools of Greek antiquity. Men were the descendants of Titans, who had killed and dismembered the young Dionysos-Zagreus; the weight of this crime oppressed them. A fragment of Anaximander says that the unity of the world was destroyed by a primordial crime and everything that issued from it must carry on the punishment for this crime. Although the features of banding together, killing, and dismembering as expressed in the deed of the Titans very clearly recall the totem sacrifice described by St. Nilus—as also many other myths of antiquity, for example, the death of Orpheus himself—we are nevertheless disturbed here by the variation according to which a youthful god was murdered.

In the Christian myth man's original sin is undoubtedly an offense against God the Father, and if Christ redeems mankind from the weight of original sin by sacrificing his own life, he forces us to the conclusion that this sin was murder. According to the law of retaliation which is deeply rooted in human feeling, a murder can be atoned only by the sacrifice of another life; the self-sacrifice points to a blood-guilt. And if this sacrifice of one's own life brings about a reconciliation with god, the father, then the crime which must be expiated can only have been the murder of the father.

Thus in the Christian doctrine mankind most unreservedly acknowledges the guilty deed of primordial times because it now has found the most complete expiation for this deed in the sacrificial death of the son. The reconciliation with the father is the more thorough because simultaneously with this sacrifice there follows the complete renunciation of woman, for whose sake mankind rebelled against the father. But now also the psychological fatality of ambivalence demands its rights. In the same deed which offers the greatest possible expiation to the father, the son also attains the goal of his wishes against the father. He becomes a god himself beside or rather in place of his father. The religion of the son succeeds the religion of the father. As a sign of this substitution the old totem feast is revived again in the form of communion in which the band of brothers now eats the flesh and blood of the son and no longer that of the father, the sons thereby identifying themselves with him and becoming holy themselves. Thus through the ages we see the identity of the totem feast with the animal sacrifice, the theanthropic human sacrifice, and the Christian eucharist, and in all these solemn occasions we recognize the after-effects of that crime which so oppressed men but of which they must have been so proud. At bottom, however, the Christian communion is a new setting aside of the father, a repetition of the crime that must be expiated. We see how well justified is Frazer's dictum that "the Christian communion has absorbed within itself a sacrament which is doubtless far older than Christianity."

A process like the removal of the primal father by the band of brothers must have left ineradicable traces in the history of mankind and must have expressed itself the more frequently in numerous substitutive formations the less it itself was to be remembered. I am avoiding the temptation of pointing out these traces in mythology, where they are not hard to find, and am turning to another field in following a hint of S. Reinach in his suggestive treatment of the death of Orpheus.

There is a situation in the history of Greek art which is strikingly familiar even if profoundly divergent, to the scene of a totem feast discovered by Robertson Smith. It is the situation of the oldest Greek tragedy. A group of persons, all of the same name and dressed in the same way, surround a single figure upon whose words and actions they are dependent, to represent the chorus and the original single impersonator of the hero. Later developments created a second and a third actor in order to represent opponents in playing, and off-shoots of the hero, but the character of the hero as well as his relation to the chorus remains unchanged. The hero of the tragedy had to suffer, this is to-day still the essential content of a tragedy. He had taken upon himself the so-called "tragic guilt," which is not always easy to explain; it is often not a guilt in the ordinary sense. Almost always it consisted of a rebellion against a divine or human authority and the chorus accompanied the hero with their sympathies, trying to restrain and warn him, and lamented his fate after he had met with what was considered fitting punishment for his daring attempt.

But why did the hero of the tragedy have to suffer, and what was the meaning of his "tragic" guilt? We will cut short the discussion by a prompt answer. He had to suffer because he was the primal father, the hero of that primordial tragedy the repetition of which here serves a certain tendency, and the tragic guilt is the guilt which he had to take upon himself in order to free the chorus of theirs. The scene upon the stage came into being through purposive distortion of the historical scene or, one is tempted to say, it was the result of refined hypocrisy. Actually, in the old situation, it was the members of the chorus themselves who had caused the suffering of the hero; here, on the other hand, they exhaust themselves in sympathy and regret, and the hero himself is to blame for his suffering. The crime foisted upon him, namely, presumption and rebellion against a great authority, is the same as that which in the past oppressed the colleagues of the chorus, namely, the band of brothers. Thus the tragic hero, though still against his will, is made the redeemer of the chorus.

17
RENÉ GIRARD

FRENCH LITERARY THEORIST AND STANFORD PROFESSOR René Girard (1923–) understands sacrificial rituals as symbolic diversions that keep violence from occurring within communities. He developed a form of analysis of ritual and mythology known as "mimetic theory" that has been both admired and challenged.

As Girard sees it, mimetic desire is born between two or more individuals when one, the "disciple," desires the fullness of being that the other, the "model," seems to possess. The disciple may believe that she or he desires the model's objects, but mimetic desire in fact is deeper. It emanates from a fundamental insecurity about one's intrinsic self-worth. Because it is the model's very existence, not objects, that inspires mimetic rivalry in the disciple, mimetic desire is inevitable in group dynamics. It pervades societies. Without a social diversion, mimetic desire ends in violence because models react against the desires of the disciples, who react in turn to the models. The cycle of reactions explodes into reciprocal violence. By themselves, humans have no internal braking mechanism against reciprocal violence, Girard argues. Hence, reciprocal violence leads to cycles of revenge and ultimately to social chaos. This is where religious myths and rituals enter situations of social tension and provide symbolic acts of violence that redirect the feelings of hostility away from their original targets.

In this excerpt, Girard discusses a key part of this theory, which he calls generative scapegoating. In order to deflect chaotic violence, mimetic rivals redirect their animosity onto a third party, a scapegoat, who is abused and ultimately killed, thereby absorbing the animosities of the rivals. Societies sanction this scapegoating by inventing rituals and mythologies that serve to redirect the vengeful and violent behavior of rivals onto a sacrificial victim. To be effective in absorbing social tensions, the sacrificial victims must fit various criteria. They must resemble an actual target of mimetic rivalry—for whom they act as surrogates—and they must be vulnerable and socially situated so that their deaths are unlikely to elicit a cycle of revenge. Their ultimate purpose is to draw the urges for reciprocal violence from individual members of a society into one collective act of violence against themselves. When the collective violence, or "violent unanimity," subsides, a temporary calm prevails. Then, through a mythological ploy, religion may construe the collective murder as foundational and redemptive for society.

According to Girard, the functions of religion's sacrificial institutions and the penal institutions of the justice system overlap. In addition to their claimed purposes, both in fact express and divert the violent impulses that otherwise would destroy societies.

"SACRIFICE," *VIOLENCE AND THE SACRED*

In many rituals the sacrificial act assumes two opposing aspects, appearing at times as a sacred obligation to be neglected at grave peril, at other times as a sort of criminal activity entailing perils of equal gravity.

To account for this dual aspect of ritual sacrifice–the legitimate and the illegitimate, the public and the all but covert–Henri Hubert and Marcel Mauss, in their "Essay on the Nature and Function of Sacrifice," adduce the sacred character of the victim. Because the victim is sacred, it is criminal to kill him–but the victim is sacred only because he is to be killed. Here is a circular line of reasoning that at a somewhat later date would be dignified by the sonorous term *ambivalence*.

If sacrifice resembles criminal violence, we may say that there is, inversely, hardly any form of violence that cannot be described in terms of sacrifice–as Greek tragedy clearly reveals. It has often been observed that the tragic poets cast a glimmering veil of rhetoric over the sordid realities of life. True enough–but sacrifice and murder would not lend themselves to this game of reciprocal substitution if they were not in some way related. Although it is so obvious that it may hardly seem worth mentioning, where sacrifice is concerned first appearances count for little, are quickly brushed aside–and should therefore receive special attention. Once one has made up one's mind that sacrifice is an institution essentially if not entirely symbolic, one can say anything whatsoever about it. It is a subject that lends itself to insubstantial theorizing.

Recent studies suggest that the physiology of violence varies little from one individual to another, even from one culture to another. According to Anthony Storr, nothing resembles an angry cat or man so much as another angry cat or man. If violence did indeed play a role in sacrifice, at least at one particular stage of the ritual, we would have a significant clue to the whole subject. Here would be a factor to some extent independent of those cultural variables that are often unknown to us, or only dimly known, or perhaps less familiar than we like to think.

Once aroused, the urge to violence triggers certain physical changes that prepare men's bodies for battle. This set toward violence lingers on; it should not be regarded as a simple reflex that ceases with the removal of the initial stimulus. Storr remarks that it is more difficult to quell an impulse toward violence than to rouse it, especially within the normal framework of social behavior.

Violence is frequently called irrational. It has its reasons, however, and can marshal some rather convincing ones when the need arises. Yet these reasons cannot be taken seriously, no matter how valid they may appear. Violence itself will discard them if the initial object remains persistently out of reach and continues to provoke hostility. When unappeased, violence seeks and always finds a surrogate victim. The creature that excited its fury is abruptly replaced by another, chosen only because it is vulnerable and close at hand.

There are many indications that this tendency to seek out surrogate objects is not limited to human violence. Konrad Lorenz makes reference to a species of fish that, if deprived of its natural enemies (the male rivals with whom it habitually disputes territorial rights), turns its aggression against the members of its own family and destroys them. Joseph de Maistre discusses the choice of animal victims that display human characteristics—an attempt, as it were, to deceive the violent impulse: "The sacrificial animals were always those most prized for their usefulness: the gentlest, most innocent creatures, whose habits and instincts brought them most closely into harmony with man. . . . From the animal realm were chosen as victims those who were, if we might use the phrase, the most *human* in nature."

Modern ethnology offers many examples of this sort of intuitive behavior. In some pastoral communities where sacrifice is practiced, the cattle are intimately associated with the daily life of the inhabitants. Two peoples of the Upper Nile, for example—the Nuers, observed by E. E. Evans-Pritchard, and the Dinka, studied at a somewhat later date by Godfrey Lienhardt—maintain a bovine society in their midst that parallels their own and is structured in the same fashion.

The Nuer vocabulary is rich in words describing the ways of cattle and covering the economic and practical, as well as the poetic and ritualistic, aspects of these beasts. This wealth of expression makes possible a precise and finely nuanced relationship between the cattle, on the one hand, and the human community on the other. The animals' color, the shape of their horns, their age, sex, and lineage are all duly noted and remembered, sometimes as far back as five generations. The cattle are thereby differentiated in such a way as to create a scale of values that approximates human distinctions and represents a virtual duplicate of human society. Among the names bestowed on each man is one that also belongs to the animal whose place in the herd is most similar to the place the man occupies in the tribe.

The quarrels between various subgroups of the tribes frequently involve cattle. All fines and interest payments are computed in terms of head of cattle, and dowries are apportioned in herds. In fact, Evans-Pritchard maintains that in order to understand the Nuer, one must *"chercher la vache"*–"look to the cows." A sort of "symbiosis" (the term is also Evans-Pritchard's) exists between this tribe and their cattle, offering an extreme and almost grotesque example of the closeness that characteristically prevails between pastoral peoples and their flocks.

Fieldwork and subsequent theoretical speculation lead us back to the hypothesis of substitution as the basis for the practice of sacrifice. This notion pervades ancient literature on the subject,which may be one reason, in fact, why many modern theorists reject the concept out of hand or give it only scant attention. Hubert and Mauss, for instance, view the idea with suspicion, undoubtedly because they feel that it introduces into the discussion religious and moral values that are incompatible with true scientific inquiry. And to be sure, Joseph de Maistre takes the view that the ritual victim is an "innocent" creature who pays a debt for the "guilty" party. I propose an hypothesis that does away with this moral distinction. As I see it, the relationship between the potential victim and the actual victim cannot be defined in terms of innocence or guilt. There is no question of "expiation." Rather, society is seeking to deflect upon a relatively indifferent victim, a "sacrificeable" victim, the violence that would otherwise be vented on its own members, the people it most desires to protect.

The qualities that lend violence its particular terror–its blind brutality, the fundamental absurdity of its manifestations–have a reverse side. With these qualities goes the strange propensity to seize upon surrogate victims, to actually conspire with the enemy and at the right moment toss him a morsel that will serve to satisfy his raging hunger. The fairy tales of childhood in which the wolf, ogre, or dragon gobbles up a large stone in place of a small child could well be said to have a sacrificial cast.

Violence is not to be denied, but it can be diverted to another object, something it can sink its teeth into. Such, perhaps, is one of the meanings of the story of Cain and Abel. The Bible offers us no background on the two brothers except the bare fact that Cain is a tiller of the soil who gives the fruits of his labor to God, whereas Abel is a shepherd who regularly sacrifices the first-born of his herds. One of the brothers kills the other, and the murderer is the one who does not have the violence-outlet of animal sacrifice at his disposal. This difference between sacrificial and nonsacrificial cults determines, in effect, God's judgment in favor of Abel. To say that God accedes to Abel's sacrificial offerings but rejects the offerings of Cain is simply another way of saying–from the viewpoint of the divinity–that Cain is a murderer, whereas his brother is not.

A frequent motif in the Old Testament, as well as Greek myth, is that of brothers at odds with one another. Their fatal penchant for violence can only be diverted by the intervention of a third party, the sacrificial victim or victims. Cain's "jealousy" of his brother is only another term for his one characteristic trait: his lack of a sacrificial outlet.

According to the Moslem tradition, God delivered to Abraham the ram previously sacrificed by Abel. This ram was to take the place of Abraham's son Isaac; having already saved on human life, the same animal would now save another. What we have here is no mystical hocus-pocus, but an intuitive insight into the essential function of sacrifice, gleaned exclusively from the scant references in the Bible.

Another familiar biblical scene takes on new meaning in the light of our theory of sacrificial substitution, and it can serve in turn to illuminate some aspects of the theory. The scene is that in which Jacob receives the blessing of his father Isaac.

Isaac is an old man. He senses the approach of death and summons his eldest son, Esau, on whom he intends to bestow his final blessing. First, however, he instructs Esau to bring back some venison from the hunt, so as to make a "savory meat." This request is overheard by the younger brother, Jacob, who hastens to report it to his mother, Rebekah. Rebekah takes two kids from the family flock, slaughters them, and prepares the savory meat dish, which Jacob, in the guise of his elder brother, then presents to his father.

Isaac is blind. Nevertheless Jacob fears he will be recognized, for he is a "smooth man," while his brother Esau is a "hairy man." "My father peradventure will feel me, and I shall seem to him as a deceiver; and I shall bring a curse upon me, not a blessing." Rebekah has the idea of covering Jacob's hands and the back of his neck with the skins of the slaughtered goats, and when the old man runs his hands over his younger son, he is completely taken in by the imposture. Jacob receives the blessing that Isaac had intended for Esau.

The kids serve in two different ways to dupe the father–or, in other terms, to divert from the son the violence directed toward him. In order to receive his father's blessing rather than his curse, Jacob must present to Isaac the freshly slaughtered kids made into a "savory meat." Then the son must seek refuge, literally, in the skins of the sacrificed animals. The animals thus interpose themselves between father and son. They serve as a sort of insulation, preventing the direct contact that could lead only to violence.

Two sorts of substitution are telescoped here: that of one brother for another, and that of an animal for a man. Only the first receives explicit recognition in the text; however, this first one serves as a screen upon which the shadow of the second is projected.

Once we have focused attention on the sacrificial victim, the object originally singled out for violence fades from view. Sacrificial substitution implies a degree of misunderstanding. Its vitality as an institution depends on its ability to conceal the displacement upon which the rite is based. It must never lose sight entirely, however, of the original object, or cease to be aware of the act of transference from that object to the surrogate victim; without that awareness no substitution can take place and the sacrifice loses all efficacy. The biblical passage discussed above meets both requirements. The narrative does not refer directly to the strange deception underlying the sacrificial substitution, nor does it allow this deception to pass entirely unnoticed. Rather, it mixes the act of substitution with another act of substitution, permitting us a fleeting, sidelong glimpse of the process. The narrative itself, then, might be said to partake of a sacrificial quality; it claims to reveal one act of substitution while employing this first substitution to half-conceal another. There is reason to believe that the narrative touches upon the mythic origins of the sacrificial system.

The figure of Jacob has long been linked with the devious character of sacrificial violence. In Greek culture Odysseus plays a similar role. The story of Jacob's benediction can be compared to the episode of the Cyclops in the *Odyssey*, where a splendidly executed ruse enables the hero to escape the clutches of a monster.

Odysseus and his shipmates are shut up in the Cyclops' cave. Every day the giant devours one of the crew; the survivors finally manage to blind their tormentor with a flaming stake. Mad with pain and anger, the Cyclops bars the entrance of the cave to prevent the men from escaping. However, he lets pass his flock of sheep, which go out daily to pasture. In a gesture reminiscent of the blind Isaac, the Cyclops runs his hands over the back of each sheep as it leaves the cave to make sure that it carries no passenger. Odysseus, however, has outwitted his captor, and he rides to freedom by clinging to the thick wool on the underside of one of the rams.

A comparison of the two scenes, one from Genesis and the other from the *Odyssey*, lends credence to the theory of their sacrificial origins. In each case an animal intervenes at the crucial moment to prevent violence from attaining its designated victim. The two texts are mutually revealing: the Cyclops of the *Odyssey* underlines the fearful menace that hangs over the hero (and that remains obscure in the Genesis story); and the slaughter of the kids in Genesis, along with the offering of the "savory meat," clearly implies the sacrificial character of the flock, an aspect that might go unnoticed in the *Odyssey*.

Sacrifice has often been described as an act of mediation between a sacrificer and a "deity." Because the very concept of a deity, much less a deity who receives blood sacrifices, has little reality in this day and age, the entire institution of sacrifice is relegated by most modern theorists to the realm of the imagination. . . .

The two ancient narratives examined above make unmistakable reference to the act of sacrifice, but neither makes so much as a passing mention of a deity. If a god had intervened in either incident, its significance would have been diminished rather than increased, and the reader would have been led to conclude, in accordance with the beliefs common to late antiquity and to the modern world, that sacrifice has no real function in society. Divine intervention would have meant the elimination of the pervasive aura of dread, along with its firmly structured economy of violence. We would have then been thrown back upon a formalistic critical approach that would in no way further our understanding.

As we have seen, the sacrificial practice requires a certain degree of *misunderstanding*. The celebrants do not and must not comprehend the true role of the sacrificial act.

We have remarked that all victims, even the animal ones, bear a certain *resemblance* to the object they replace; otherwise the violent impulse would remain unsatisfied. But this resemblance must not be carried to the extreme of complete assimilation, or it would lead to disastrous confusion. In the case of animal victims the difference is always clear, and no such confusion is possible. Although they do their best to empathize with their cattle, the Nuers never quite manage to mistake a man for a cow—the proof being that they always sacrifice the latter, never the former. I am not lapsing into the trap of Lévy Bruhl's "primitive mentality." I am not saying that primitive man is less capable of making distinctions than we moderns.

In order for a species or category of living creature, human or animal, to appear suitable for sacrifice, it must bear a sharp resemblance to the human categories excluded from the ranks of the "sacrificeable," while still maintaining a degree of difference that forbids all possible confusion. As I have said, no mistake is possible in the case of animal sacrifice. But it is quite another case with human victims. If we look at the extremely wide spectrum of human victims sacrificed by various societies, the list seems heterogeneous, to say the least. It includes prisoners of war, slaves, small children, unmarried adolescents, and the handicapped; it ranges from the very dregs of society, such as the Greek pharmakos, to the king himself.

Is it possible to detect a unifying factor in this disparate group? We notice at first glance beings who are either outside or on the fringes of society: prisoners of war, slaves, pharmakos. In many primitive societies children who have not yet undergone the rites of initiation have no proper place in the community; their rights and duties are almost non-existent. What we are dealing with, therefore, are exterior or marginal individuals, incapable of establishing or sharing the social bonds that link the rest of the inhabitants. Their status as foreigners or enemies, their servile condition, or simply their age prevents these future victims from fully integrating themselves into the community.

But what about the king? Is he not at the very heart of the community? Undoubtedly–but it is precisely his position at the centre that serves to isolate him from his fellow men, to render him casteless. He escapes from society, so to speak, via the roof, just as the pharmakos escapes through the cellar. The king has a sort of foil, however, in the person of his fool. The fool shares his master's status as an outsider – an isolation whose literal truth is often of greater significance than the easily reversible symbolic values often attributed to it. From every point of view the fool is eminently "sacrificeable," and the king can use him to vent his own anger. But it sometimes happens that the king himself is sacrificed, and that (among certain African societies) in a thoroughly regulated and highly ritualistic manner.

It is clearly legitimate to define the difference between sacrificeable and nonsacrificeable individuals in terms of their degree of integration, but such a definition is not yet sufficient. In many cultures women are not considered full-fledged members of society; yet women are never, or rarely, selected as sacrificial victims. There may be a simple explanation for this fact. The married woman retains her ties with her parents' clan even after she has become in some respects the property of her husband and his family. To kill her would be to run the risk of one of the two groups' interpreting her sacrifice as an act of murder committing it to a reciprocal act of revenge. The notion of vengeance casts a new light on the matter. All our sacrificial victims, whether chosen from one of the human categories enumerated above or, *a fortiori*, from the animal realm, are invariably distinguishable from the nonsacrificeable beings by one essential characteristic: between these victims and the community a crucial social link is missing, so they can be exposed to violence without fear of reprisal. Their death does not automatically entail an act of vengeance.

The considerable importance this freedom from reprisal has for the sacrificial process makes us understand that sacrifice is primarily an act of violence without risk of vengeance. We also understand the paradox–not without its comic aspects on occasion--of the frequent references to vengeance in the course of sacrificial rites, the veritable obsession with vengeance when no chance of vengeance exists:

> For the act they were about to commit elaborate excuses were offered; they shuddered at the prospect of the sheep's death, they wept over it as though they were its parents. Before the blow was struck, they implored the beast's forgiveness. They then addressed themselves to the species to which the beast belonged, as if addressing a large family clan, beseeching it not to seek vengeance for the act that was about to be inflicted on one of its members. In the same vein the actual murderer was punished in some manner, either beaten or sent into exile.

It is the entire species *considered as a large family clan* that the sacrificers beseech not to seek vengeance. By incorporating the element of reprisal into the ceremony, the participants are hinting broadly at the true function of the rite, the kind of action it was designed to circumvent and the criteria that determined the choice of victim. The desire to commit an act of violence on those near us cannot be suppressed without a conflict; we must divert that impulse, therefore, toward the sacrificial victim, the creature we can strike down without fear of reprisal, since he lacks a champion.

Like everything that touches on the essential nature of the sacrificial act, the true distinction between the sacrificeable and the nonsacrificeable is never clearly articulated. Oddities and inexplicable anomalies confuse the picture. For instance, some animal species will be formally excluded from sacrifice, but the exclusion of members of the community is never mentioned. In constantly drawing attention to the truly maniacal aspects of sacrifice, modern theorists only serve to perpetuate an old misunderstanding in new terms. Men can dispose of their violence more efficiently if they regard the process not as something emanating from within themselves, but as a necessity imposed from without, a divine decree whose least infraction calls down terrible punishment. When they banish sacrificial practices from the "real," everyday world, modern theorists continue to misrepresent the violence of sacrifice.

The function of sacrifice is to quell violence within the community and to prevent conflicts from erupting. Yet societies like our own, which do not, strictly speaking, practice sacrificial rites, seem to get along without them. Violence undoubtedly exists within our society, but not to such an extent that the society itself is threatened with extinction. The simple fact that sacrificial practices, and other rites as well, can disappear without catastrophic results should in part explain the failure of ethnology and theology to come to grips with these cultural phenomena, and explain as well our modern reluctance to attribute a real function to them. After all, it is hard to maintain that institutions for which, as it seems, we have no needs are actually indispensable.

It may be that a basic difference exists between a society like ours and societies imbued with religion–a difference that is partially hidden from us by rites, particularly by rites of sacrifice, that play a compensatory role. This difference would help explain why the actual function of sacrifice still eludes us.

When internal strife, previously sublimated by means of sacrificial practices, rises to the surface, it manifests itself in interfamily vendettas and blood feuds. This kind of violence is virtually nonexistent in our own culture. And perhaps it is here that we should look for the fundamental difference between primitive societies and our own; we should examine the specific ailments to which we are immune and which sacrifice manages to control, if not to eliminate.

Why does the spirit of revenge, wherever it breaks out, constitute such an intolerable menace? Perhaps because the only satisfactory revenge for spilt blood is spilling the blood of the killer; and in the blood feud there is no clear distinction between the act for which the killer is being punished and the punishment itself. Vengeance professes to be an act of reprisal, and every reprisal calls for another reprisal. The crime to which the act of vengeance addresses itself is almost never an unprecedented offense; in almost every case it has been committed in revenge for some prior crime.

Vengeance, then, is an interminable, infinitely repetitive process. Every time it turns up in some part of the community, it threatens to involve the whole social body. There is the risk that the act of vengeance will initiate a chain reaction whose consequences will quickly prove fatal to any society of modest size. The multiplication of reprisals instantaneously puts the very existence of a society in jeopardy, and that is why it is universally proscribed.

Curiously enough, it is the very communities where the proscription is most strictly enforced that vengeance seems to hold sway. Even when it remains in the background, its role in the community unacknowledged, the specter of vengeance plays an important role in shaping the relationships among individuals. That is not to say that the prohibition against acts of vengeance is taken lightly. Precisely because murder inspires horror and because men must be forcibly restrained from murder, vengeance is inflicted on all those who commit it. The obligation never to shed blood cannot be distinguished from the obligation to exact vengeance on those who shed it. If men wish to prevent an interminable outbreak of vengeance (just as today we wish to prevent nuclear war), it is not enough to convince their fellows that violence is detestable—for it is precisely because they detest violence that men make a duty of vengeance. . . .

Vengeance is a vicious circle whose effect on primitive societies can only be surmised. For us the circle has been broken. We owe our good fortune to one of our social institutions above all: our judicial system, which serves to deflect the menace of vengeance. The system does not suppress vengeance; rather, it effectively limits it to a single act of reprisal, enacted by a sovereign authority specializing in this particular function. The decisions of the judiciary are invariably presented as the final word on vengeance.

Vocabulary is perhaps more revealing here than judicial theories. Once the concept of interminable revenge has been formally rejected, it is referred to as *private* vengeance. The term implies the existence of a *public* vengeance, a counterpart never made explicit. By definition, primitive societies have only private vengeance. Thus, public vengeance is the exclusive property of well-policed societies, and our society calls it the judicial system.

Our penal system operates according to the principles of justice that are in no real conflict with the concept of revenge. The same principle is at work in all systems of violent retribution.

Either the principle is just, and justice is therefore inherent in the idea of vengeance, or there is no justice to be found anywhere. He who exacts his own vengeance is said to "take the law into his own hands." There is no difference of principle between private and public vengeance; but on the social level, the difference is enormous. Under the public system, an act of vengeance is no longer avenged; the process is terminated, the danger of escalation averted.

The absence of a judicial system in primitive societies has been confirmed by ethnologists.

———

If primitive societies have no tried and true remedies for dealing with an outbreak of violence, no certain cure once the social equilibrium has been upset, we can assume that *preventive* measures will play an essential role. Here again I return to the concept of sacrifice as I earlier defined it: an instrument of prevention in the struggle against violence.

In a universe where the slightest dispute can lead to disaster—just as a slight cut can prove fatal to a hemophiliac—the rites of sacrifice serve to polarize the community's aggressive impulses and redirect them toward victims that may be actual or figurative, animate or inanimate, but that are always incapable of propagating further vengeance. The sacrificial process furnishes an outlet for those violent impulses that cannot be mastered by self-restraint; a partial outlet, to be sure, but always renewable, and one whose efficacy has been attested by an impressive number of reliable witnesses. The sacrificial process prevents the spread of violence by keeping vengeance in check.

———————

Our original proposition stands: ritual in general, and sacrificial rites in particular, assume essential roles in societies that lack a firm judicial system. It must not be assumed, however, that sacrifice simply "replaces" a judicial system. One can scarcely speak of replacing something that never existed to begin with. Then, too, a judicial system is ultimately irreplaceable, short of a unanimous and entirely voluntary renunciation of all violent actions.

When we minimize the dangers implicit in vengeance we risk losing sight of the true function of sacrifice. Because revenge is rarely encountered in our society, we seldom have occasion to consider how societies lacking a judicial system of punishment manage to hold it in check.

———————

In primitive societies the risk of unleashed violence is so great and the cure so problematic that the emphasis naturally falls on prevention. The preventive measures naturally fall within the domain of religion, where they can on occasion assume a violent character. Violence and the sacred are inseparable. But the covert appropriation by sacrifice of certain properties of violence–particularly the ability of violence to move from one object to another–is hidden from sight by the awesome machinery of ritual.

Primitive societies are not given over to violence. Nor are they necessarily less violent or less "hypocritical" than our own society. Of course, to be truly comprehensive we ought to take into consideration *all* forms of violence, more or less ritualized, that divert a menace from nearby objects to more distant objects. We ought, for instance, to consider war. War is clearly not restricted to one particular type of society. Yet the multiplication of new weapons and techniques does not constitute a fundamental difference between primitive and modern warfare. On the other hand, if we compare societies that adhere to a judicial system with societies that practice sacrificial rites, the difference between the two is such that we can indeed consider the absence or presence of these institutions as a basis for distinguishing primitive societies from "civilized" ones. These are the institutions we must scrutinize in order to arrive, not at some sort of value judgement, but at an objective knowledge of the respective societies to which they belong.

Religion invariably tries to subdue violence, to keep it from running wild. Paradoxically, the religious and moral authorities in a community attempt to instill nonviolence, as an active force into daily life and as a mediating force into ritual life, through the application of violence. Sacrificial rites serve to connect the moral and religious aspects of daily life, but only by means of a lengthy and hazardous detour. Moreover, it must be kept in mind that the efficacy of the rites depends on their being performed in the spirit of *pietas*, which marks all aspects of religious life. We are beginning to understand why the sacrificial act appears as both sinful and saintly, an illegal as well as a legitimate exercise of violence. However, we are still far from a full understanding of the act itself.

Primitive religion tames, trains, arms, and directs violent impulses as a defensive force against those forms of violence that society regards as inadmissible. It postulates a strange mixture of violence and nonviolence. The same can perhaps be said of our own judicial system of control.

There may be a certain connection between all the various methods employed by man since the beginning of time to avoid being caught up in an interminable round of revenge. They can be grouped into three general categories: (1) preventive measures in which sacrificial rites divert the spirit of revenge into other channels; (2) the harnessing or hobbling of vengeance by means of compensatory measures, trials by combat, etc., whose curative effects remain precarious; (3) the establishment of a judicial system—the most efficient of all curative procedures.

We have listed the methods in ascending order of effectiveness. The evolution from preventive to curative procedures is reflected in the course of history or, at any rate, in the course of the history of the Western world. The initial curative procedures mark an intermediary stage between a purely religious orientation and the recognition of a judicial system's superior efficiency. These methods are inherently ritualistic in character, and are often associated with sacrificial practices.

The curative procedures employed by primitive societies appear rudimentary to us. We tend to regard them as fumbling efforts to improvise a judicial system. Certainly their pragmatic aspects are clearly visible, oriented as they are not toward the guilty parties, but toward the victims—since it is the latter who pose the most immediate threat. The injured parties must be accorded a careful measure of satisfaction, just enough to appease their own desire for revenge but not so much as to awaken the desire elsewhere. It is not a question of codifying good and evil or of inspiring respect for some abstract concept of justice; rather, it is a question of securing the safety of the group by checking the impulse for revenge. The preferred method involves a reconciliation between parties based on some sort of mutual compensation. If reconciliation is impossible, however, an armed encounter can be arranged in such a manner that the violence is wholly self-contained. This encounter can take place within an enclosed space and can involve prescribed regulations and specifically designated combatants. Its purpose is to cut violence short.

To be sure, all these curative measures are steps in the direction of a legal system. But the evolution, if indeed evolution is the proper term, is not continuous. The break comes at the moment when the intervention of an independent legal authority becomes *constraining*. Only then are men freed from the terrible obligations of vengeance. Retribution in its judicial guise loses its terrible urgency. Its meaning remains the same, but this meaning becomes increasingly indistinct or even fades from view. In fact, the system functions best when everyone concerned is least aware that it involves retribution. The system can–and as soon as it can it will– reorganize itself around the accused and the concept of guilt. In fact, retribution still holds sway, but forged into a principle of abstract justice that all men are obliged to uphold and respect.

We have seen that the "curative" measures, ostensibly designed to temper the impulse toward vengeance, becomes increasingly mysterious in their workings as they progress in efficiency. As the focal point of the system shifts away from religion and the preventive approach is translated into judicial retribution, the aura of misunderstanding that has always formed a protective veil around the institution of sacrifice shifts as well, and becomes associated in turn with the machinery of the law.

The procedures that keep men's violence in bounds have one thing in common: they are no strangers to the ways of violence. There is reason to believe that they are all rooted in religion. As we have seen, the various forms of prevention go hand in hand with religious practices. The curative procedures are also imbued with religious concepts–both the rudimentary sacrificial rites and the more advanced judicial forms. *Religion* in is broadest sense, then, must be another term for that obscurity that surrounds man's efforts to defend himself by curative or preventative means against his own violence. It is that enigmatic quality that pervades the judicial system when that system replaces sacrifice. This obscurity coincides with the transcendental effectiveness of a violence that is holy, legal, and legitimate successfully opposed to a violence that is unjust, illegal, and illegitimate.

WALTER BURKERT

THE SWISS SCHOLAR of classical studies, Walter Burkert (1931–), has explored a range of expressions of religious violence, from prehistoric finger sacrifices to animal sacrifices in ancient Near Eastern and Greek literature. In *Homo Necans*, he described the exhilaration and the dread elicited by sacrificial killing as a primordial drama of life and death. Embedded within ancient sacrificial narratives, says Burkert, is evidence of two vestiges inherited from our previous millennia as hunter-gatherers: the lingering thrill and simultaneous discomfort with killing large mammals, and the social bonding of the male hunting band (the *Männerbund*). He saw these two vestiges persisting into religious rituals long after such bands ceased to hunt for their food.

The excerpt that follows summarizes his evolutionary hypothesis about the origins of sacrifice. The success of the earliest hominids, "the hunting ape," was due to the ability of males to move between the sphere of the family and the sphere of the *Männerbund*. The first was a sphere of love, domesticity, and security, while the second was a sphere of adventure, aggression, and death. The tension between those spheres was never easy. Sacrifice, which occurs in the domestic sphere, is essentially a tamed ritualization of the hunt and allows the aggressive features of the *Männerbund* to express themselves within the domestic sphere. In historical times, the dangerous aggression of the *Männerbund* has not entirely dissipated but continues to express itself in religious sacrifice and in war.

FROM *HOMO NECANS*

Sacrifice as an Act of Killing

Aggression and human violence have marked the progress of our civilization and appear, indeed, to have grown so during its course that they have become a central problem of the present. Analyses that attempt to locate the roots of the evil often set out with short-sighted assumptions, as though the failure of our upbringing or the faulty development of a particular national tradition or economic system were to blame. More can be said for the thesis that all orders and forms of authority in human society are founded on institutionalized violence. This at least corresponds to the fundamental role played in biology by intraspecific aggression, as described by Konrad Lorenz. Those, however, who turn to religion for salvation from this "so-called evil" of aggression are confronted with murder at the very core of Christianity—the death of God's innocent son; still earlier, the Old Testament covenant could come about only after Abraham had decided to sacrifice his child. Thus, blood and violence lurk fascinatingly at the very heart of religion.

From a classicizing perspective, Greek religion appeared and still appears to some as bright and harmlessly cheerful. Yet those who maintain that the skandalon of the Cross (1 Cor. 1:23) is on another level altogether overlook the deeper dimension that accompanies the easy life of the gods as portrayed by Homer. If a man is able to draw near to the gods, as the priest Chryses with Apollo or as Hektor or Odysseus with Zeus, he can do so because he has "burnt many thigh-pieces of bulls" (*Il*.1.40, 22.170; *Od*. 1.66), for this is the act of piety: bloodshed, slaughter—and eating. It makes no difference if there is no temple or cult-statue, as often occurs in the cult of Zeus. The god is present at his place of sacrifice, a place distinguished by the heap of ashes left from "sacred" offerings burnt there over long periods of time, or by the horns and skulls of slaughtered rams and bulls, or by the altar-stone where the blood must be sprinkled. The worshipper experiences the god most powerfully not just in pious conduct or in prayer, song, and dance, but in the deadly blow of the axe, the gush of blood and the burning of thigh-pieces. The realm of the gods is sacred, but the "sacred" act done at the "sacred" place by the "consecrating" actor consists of slaughtering sacrificial animals, ἱερεύειν τὰ ἱερεῖα. It was no different in Israel up to the destruction of the temple. It is prescribed that daily "burnt offering shall be on the hearth upon the altar," "all night until the morning" (Lev. 6:2); these offerings, the remnants of two one-year-old lambs cut into pieces, are "a pleasing odor to the Lord." Thus the principal sin of Antiochus Epiphanes against Jerusalem was that he ordered that "the continual burnt offering [be] taken away" (Dan. 8:11). Augustus built an altar to celebrate the establishment of world peace and, together with his family, appears on the reliefs of this Ara Pacis as a sacrificer, proceeded by servants carrying the sacrificial axe. Thus, the most refined Augustan art provides a framework for the bloody sacrifices at the center.

Sacrificial killing is the basic experience of the "sacred." *Homo religiosus* acts and attains self-awareness as *homo necans*. Indeed, this is what it means "to act," ῥέζειν, *operari* (whence "sacrifice" is *Opfer* in German)— the name merely covers up the heart of the action with a euphemism. The bliss of encountering divinity finds expression in words, and yet the strange and extraordinary events that the participant in sacrifice is forced to witness are all the more intense because they are left undiscussed.

Thanks to the descriptions in Homer and tragedy, we can reconstruct the course of an ordinary Greek sacrifice to the Olympian gods almost in its entirety. The path that leads to the center of the sacred experience is complex. The preparations include bathing and dressing in clean clothes, putting on ornaments and wreaths; often sexual abstinence is a requirement. At the start, a procession (πομπή), even if still a small one, is formed. The festival participants depart from the everyday world, moving to a single rhythm and singing. The sacrificial animal is led along with them, likewise decorated and transformed—bound with fillets, its horns covered with gold. Generally it is hoped that the animal will follow the procession compliantly or even willingly. Legends often tell of animals that offered themselves up for sacrifice, apparently evidence of a higher will that commands assent. The final goal is the sacrificial stone, the altar "set up" long ago, which is to be sprinkled with blood. Usually a fire is already ablaze on top of it. Often a censer is used to impregnate the atmosphere with the scent of the extraordinary, and there is music, usually that of a flute. A virgin leads the way, "carrying the basket" (κανηφόρος), that is, an untouched girl holding a covered container. . . . A water jug must be there as well.

First of all, after arriving at the sacred place, the participants mark off a circle; the sacrificial basket and water jug are carried around the assembly, thus marking off the sacred realm from the profane. The first communal act is washing one's hands as the beginning of that which is to take place. The animal is also sprinkled with water. "Shake yourself," says Trygaios in Aristophanes, for the animal's movement is taken to signify a "willing nod," a "yes" to the sacrificial act. The bull is watered again, so that he will bow his head. The animal thus becomes the center of attention. The participants now take unground barley grains (οὐλαί), the most ancient agricultural product, from the basket. These, however, are not meant for grinding or to be made into food: after a brief silence, the solemn εὐφημεῖν, followed by a prayer out loud—in a way, more self-affirmation than prayer—the participants fling the barley grains away onto the sacrificial animal, the altar, and the earth. They are after another kind of food. The act of throwing simultaneously as a group is an aggressive gesture, like beginning a fight, even if the most harmless projectiles are chosen. Indeed, in some ancient rituals stones were used. Hidden beneath the grains in the basket was the knife, which now lies uncovered. The leader in this incipient drama, the ἱερεύς, steps toward the sacrificial animal, carrying the knife still covered so that the animal cannot see it. A swift cut, and a few hairs from the brow are shorn and thrown into the fire. This is another, though more serious, act of beginning (ἄρχεσθαι), just as the water and the barley grains were a beginning. Blood has not yet been spilled and no pain whatsoever has been inflicted, but the inviolability of the sacrificial animal has been abolished irreversibly.

Now comes the death blow. The women raise a piercing scream:

whether in fear or triumph or both at once, the "Greek custom of the sacrificial scream" marks the emotional climax of the event, drowning out the death-rattle. The blood flowing out is treated with special care. It may not spill on the ground; rather, it must hit the altar, the hearth, or the sacrificial pit. If the animal is small it is raised over the altar; otherwise the blood is caught in a bowl and sprinkled on the altar-stone. This object alone may, and must again and again, drip blood.

The "act" is over; its consequences are the next concern. The animal is carved up and disemboweled. Its inner organs are now the main focus, lying revealed, an alien, bizarre, and uncanny sight, and yet common in the same form to men as well, as is known from seeing wounded soldiers. The tradition specifies precisely what must be done with each piece. First of all, the heart, sometimes still beating, is put on the altar. A seer is present to interpret the lobes of the liver. In general, however, the σπλάγχνα—the collective term for the organs—are quickly roasted in the fire from the altar and eaten at once. Thus the inner circle of active participants is brought together in a communal meal, transforming horror into pleasure. Only the bile is inedible and has to be disposed of. Likewise, the bones are not to be used for the subsequent meal, so they are "consecrated" beforehand. The bones, above all the thigh-bones (μηρία) and the pelvis with the tail (ὀσφύς), are put on the altar "in the proper order." From the bones, one can still see exactly how the parts of the living animal fit together: its basic form is restored and consecrated. In Homer, a "beginning," i.e., a first offering, consisting of raw pieces of flesh from every limb, is put on the bones as well, indicating the entirety of the slaughtered animal. The purifying fire then consumes all these remains. The skulls of bulls and rams and goat-horns are preserved in the sacred place as permanent evidence of the act of consecration. The flow of blood is now replaced in its turn by the offerings of the planter, pouring libations of wine into the fire and burning cakes. As the alcohol causes the flames to flare up, a higher reality seems present. Then, as the fire dies down, the pleasing feast gradually gives way to everyday life. The skin of the sacrificial victim is generally sold to benefit the sanctuary, to purchase new votive offerings and new victims: in this way, the cult insures its own continuance.

This rite is objectionable, and was already felt to be so early one, because it so clearly and directly benefits man. Is the god "to whom" the sacrifice is made any more than a transparent excuse for festive feasting? All he gets are the bones, the fat, and the gall bladders. Hesiod says that the crafty Prometheus, the friend of mankind, caused this to be so in order to deceive the gods, and the burning of bones became a standard joke in Greek comedy. Criticism that damned the bloody act per se was far more penetrating. Zarathustra's curse applies to all who lust for blood and slaughter cattle. "I have had enough of burnt offering of rams and the fat of fed beasts; I do not delight in the blood of bulls or of lambs or of he-goats," says the Lord through Isaiah. In the Greek world, the Pythagoreans and Orphics demanded that the lives of all creatures with souls be spared, and Empedokles was the most vehement of all in attacking the cannibalistic madness of the traditional sacrificial meal, as also in expressing the desire for a realm of non-violent love on the path toward "purification." Philosophy then took up the criticism of blood-sacrifice—above all, Theophrastus, in his influential book *On Piety*. This book explained animal-sacrifice as having replaced cannibalism, which, in turn, had been forced on men because of difficult times. After this, a theoretical defense of sacrificial custom was virtually hopeless. Both Varro and Seneca were convinced that gods do not demand blood-sacrifice. Judaism in the Diaspora spread more easily because cult practices had become concentrated in one temple in Jerusalem, thus virtually making Judaism outside Jerusalem a religion without animal-sacrifice. This also helped form Christian practice, which could thus take up the traditions of Greek philosophy. On the other hand, it gave the idea of sacrifice a central significance and raised it to a higher status than ever before. The death of God's son is the one-time and perfect sacrifice, although it is still repeated in the celebration of the Lord's Supper, in breaking the bread and drinking the wine.

Folk custom, however, managed to defy even Christianization and was subdued only by modern technological civilization. The German expression *geschmückt wie ein Pfingstochse* ("decked out like an ox at Pentecost") preserves the memory of the ritual slaughter of an ox at the church festival. . . . In Soviet Armenia the slaughter of a sheep in front of the church is still a feature of regular Sunday service. Isolated Greek communities in Cappadocia celebrated the ancient sacrificial ritual well into the twentieth century: opposite the conventional altar in the chapel of the saint would be a sacrificial altarstone, upon which incense was burned when candles were lit; during prayers, it would be decked with wreaths. The sacrificer would bring the animal—a goat or a sheep—into the chapel, leading it three times around the sacrificial stone while children threw grass and flowers onto it. As the priest stood at the altar, the keeper of the animal would make a sign of the cross with his knife three times and then slaughter the animal while praying. The blood was supposed to sprinkle the stone. After this, outside the chapel, the animal would be carved up and the feast prepared. The priest, like his ancient counterpart, received the animal's thigh and skin, as well as its head and feet. Christianity is here no more than a transparent cover for the ancient form that underlies it: that is to say, for the sacred act of blood-sacrifice.

Animal-sacrifice was an all-pervasive reality in the ancient world. The Greeks did not perceive much difference between the substance of their own customs and those of the Egyptians and Phoenicians, Babylonians and Persians, Etruscans and Romans, though ritual details varied greatly among the Greeks themselves. One peculiarity of Greek sacrifice presents a problem for the modern historian: the combination of a fire-altar and a blood-rite, of burning and eating, corresponds directly only with burnt offerings (*zebah, šelamim*) of the Old Testament—although the details of Ugaritic and Phoenician sacrificial cults are uncertain—and these differ markedly from Egyptian and Mesopotamian, as well as Minoan-Mycenaean, rites, all of which have no altars for burning whole animals or bones. And yet, whatever complexities, layers, and changes in cultural tradition underlie the individual peculiarities, it is astounding, details aside, to observe the similarity of action and experience from Athens to Jerusalem and on to Babylon. A detailed Babylonian text of which several copies were made describes the sacrifice of a bull whose skin was used as the membrane of a tympanum in the temple: an untouched black bull would be chosen for the secret ceremony, which took place in a room enclosed on all sides by curtains. The complicated preparations include scattering grain, offering breads and libations, and sacrificing a sheep. The bull stood chained on a rush mat until it was time for its mouth to be washed. After this, incantations would be whispered into both its ears, after which it was sprinkled with water, purified with a torch, and surrounded by a circle of grain. Following prayer and song, the bull was killed, the heart burned at once, and the skin and left shoulder sinew removed to string the tympanum. After further libations and offerings, the priest would bend down to the severed head and say, "This deed was done by all the gods; I did not do it." One version of the text says that the cadaver would be buried, an older one forbids at least the head priest from eating the meat. Fifteen days later, in a largely parallel ceremony, with preparatory and closing rites, the newly covered tympanum was brought into the center in place of the bull, thus inaugurating it into its function.

Not even the religious revolution in the Near East, i.e., the emergence of Islam, could eliminate animal-sacrifice. The high point in the life of a Moslem is the pilgrimage to Mecca which still today draws hundreds of thousands of worshippers annually. The central point occurs on the ninth day of the holy month, in the journey from Mecca to Mount Arafat, where the pilgrims stay from noon till sundown praying "before God." This is followed by the Day of Sacrifice. On the tenth day, in Mina, the pilgrim must thrown seven pebbles at an old stone monument and then slaughter—usually with his own hands—a sacrificial animal—a sheep, a goat, or even a camel—which is driven up and sold to him by Bedouins. He eats some of the animal, though usually giving most of it away or simply leaving it. Saudi Arabia has resorted to bulldozers to remove the carcasses. After this, the pilgrim is allowed to cut his hair again and remove his pilgrim's robes. Likewise, sexual abstinence ends after his return from Mecca. It is the consecrated man who kills and the act of killing is made sacred. "In the name of Allah" and "Allah is merciful" are the Moslem formulas that accompany even profane slaughter.

Daily routine inevitably made the sacrificial ritual an empty formality. Therefore, in order to stress its importance, especially in the ancient Near East, ordinances were created stipulating countless observances. The Greeks seem to have given most care to the "beginning" stages (ἄρχεσθαι), as if trying to distract attention from the central point, which nonetheless remained permanently fixed. Hubert and Mauss aptly characterized the structure of sacrificial ritual with the concepts of "sacralization" and "desacralization"; that is to say, preliminary rites, on the one hand, and closing rites, on the other, framing a central action clearly marked as the emotional climax by a piercing scream, the "Ololygé." This act, however, is the act of killing, the experience of death. Thus, a threefold rhythm becomes evident in the course of the sacrifice, moving from an inhibited, labyrinthine beginning, through a terrifying midpoint, to a scrupulously tidy conclusion. Vegetable offerings frequently come at the beginning and again at the end of the ceremony, when libations are also especially characteristic. But the offerings can overlap and multiply, enlarging the pattern until a triad of sacrificial festivals emerges which yet adheres to the same unchangeable rhythm: the preliminary sacrifice, the terrifying sacrifice, and the victorious, affirming sacrifice. The core is always the experience of death brought about by human violence, which, in turn, is here subject to predetermined laws. And this is nearly always connected with another human—all too human—action, namely, eating: the festive meal of those who share in the sacred.

The Evolutionary Explanation: Primitive Man as Hunter

Karl Meuli's great essay on "Griechische Opferbräuche" (1946) added a new dimension to our understanding of sacrifice. He noted striking similarities in the details of Greek sacrifice and the customs of hunting and herding societies, mostly in Siberia. Moreover, he pointed out prehistoric discoveries that seemed to attest to similar customs by Middle Palaeolithic times. This powerful step backward about 50,000 years in time admittedly seems to explain *obscurum per obscurius*. Whether the prehistoric evidence may be taken to indicate belief in a supreme being—a kind of primordial monotheism—is a moot question. It seemed less risky to state: "Sacrifice is the oldest form of religious action." But much of the oldest evidence remains controversial.

These customs are more than mere curiosities, for the hunt of the Palaeolithic hunter is not just one activity among many. The transition to the hunt is, rather, one of the most decisive ecological changes between man and the other primates. Man can virtually be defined as "the hunting ape" (even if "the naked ape" makes a more appealing title). The statement leads to a second indisputable fact, namely, that the age of the hunter, the Palaeolithic, comprises by far the largest part of human history. No matter that estimates range between 95 and 99 percent: it is clear that man's biological evolution was accomplished during this time. By comparison, the period since the invention of agriculture—10,000 years, at most—is a drop in the bucket. From this perspective, then, we can understand man's terrifying violence as deriving from the behavior of the predatory animal, whose characteristics he came to acquire in the course of becoming man.

Our conception of primitive man and his society will always be a tentative construct; still, there are some social and psychological preconditions that cannot have been absent from the situation of the early hunters. The primate's biological makeup was not fit for this new way of life. Man had to compensate for this deficiency by a tour de force of ingenious technology and institutions, that is to say, by his culture, although that culture itself quickly became a means of selection. Of primary importance was the use of weapons, without which man poses virtually no threat to beasts. The earliest weapon that was effective at a distance was the wooden spear hardened by fire. This presupposes the use of fire; earlier, bones had served as clubs. Man's upright posture facilitated the use of weapons. But perhaps more important than all this was the development of a social order leading to sharp sexual differentiation, which has even become a part of our inherited biological constitution. Among human beings, hunting is man's work—in contrast to all animal predators—requiring both speed and strength; hence the male's long, slender thighs. By contrast, since women must bear children with ever larger skulls, they develop round, soft forms. Man's extraordinarily protracted youth, his *neoteny*, which permits the development of the mind through learning and the transmission of a complicated culture, requires long years of security. This is basically provided by the mother at home. The man assumes the role of the family breadwinner—an institution universal to human civilizations but contrary to the behavior of all other mammals.

The success of the "hunting ape" was due to his ability to work cooperatively, to unite with other men in a communal hunt. Thus, man ever since the development of hunting has belonged to two overlapping social structures, the family and the *Männerbund*; his world falls into pairs of categories: indoors and out, security and adventure, women's work and men's work, love and death. At the core of this new type of male community, which is biologically analogous to a pack of wolves, are the acts of killing and eating. The men must constantly move between the two realms, and their male children must one day take the difficult step from the women's world to the world of men. Fathers must accept their sons, educating them and looking after them—this, too, has no parallel among mammals. When a boy finally enters the world of men, he does so by confronting death.

What an experience it must have been when man, the relative of the chimpanzee, succeeded in seizing the power of his deadly enemy, the leopard, in assuming the traits of the wolf, forsaking the role of the hunted for that of the hunter! But success brought its own dangers. The earliest technology created the tools for killing. Even the wooden spear and wedge provided man with weapons more dangerous than his instincts could cope with. His rudimentary killing inhibitions were insufficient as soon as he could kill at a distance; and males were even educated to suppress these inhibitions for the sake of the hunt. Moreover, it is as easy, or even easier, to kill a man as it is to kill a fleeing beast, so from earliest times men slipped repeatedly into cannibalism. Thus, from the very start, self-destruction was a threat to the human race.

If man nonetheless survived and with unprecedented success even enlarged his sphere of influence, it was because in place of his natural instincts he developed the rules of cultural tradition, thus artificially forming and differentiating his basic inborn behavior. Biological selection rather than conscious planning determined the educational processes that helped form man, so that he could best adapt himself to his role. A man had to be courageous to take part in the hunt; therefore, courage is always included in the conception of an ideal man. A man had to be reliable, able to wait, to resist a momentary impulse for the sake of a long-range goal. He had to have endurance and keep to his word. In these matters men developed behavior patterns that were lacking in anthropoid apes and were more closely analogous to the behavior of beasts of prey. Above all, the use of weapons was controlled by the strictest—if also artificial—rules: what was allowed and necessary in one realm was absolutely forbidden in the other. A brilliant accomplishment in one was murder in the other. The decisive point is the very possibility that man may submit to laws curbing his individual intelligence and adaptability for the sake of societal predictability. The educative power of tradition attempts to bind him in an irreversible process analogous to biological "imprinting."

On a psychological level, hunting behavior was mainly determined by the peculiar interplay of the aggressive and sexual complexes, which thus gave form to some of the foundations of human society. Whereas research on biological behavior, at least in predatory animals, carefully distinguishes intraspecific aggression from the behavior of hunting and eating, this distinction obviously does not hold for man. Rather, these two became superimposed at the time when men unexpectedly assumed the behavior of predatory animals. Man had to outdo himself in his transition to the hunt, a transition requiring implementation of all his spiritual reserves. And because this sort of behavior became specific to the male sex, that is to say, "men's work," males could more easily adapt themselves to the intraspecific aggression programmed for courtship fights and the impulses of sexual frustration.

Because the hunter's activity was reinforced by behavior aimed originally at a human partner—that is, through intraspecific aggression—in place of a biologically fixed relationship of beast and quarry, something curious occurred: the quarry became a quasi-human adversary, experienced as human and treated accordingly. Hunting concentrated on the great mammals, which conspicuously resembled men in their body structure and movements, their eyes and their "faces," their breath and voices, in fleeing and in fear, in attacking and in rage. Most of all, this similarity with man was to be recognized in killing and slaughtering: the flesh was like flesh, bones like bones, phallus like phallus, and heart like heart, and, most important of all, the warm running blood was the same. One could, perhaps, most clearly grasp the animal's resemblance to man when it died. Thus, the quarry turned into a sacrificial victim. Many observers have told of the almost brotherly bond that hunters felt for their game, and the exchangeability of man and animal in sacrifice recurs as a mythological theme in many cultures besides the Greek.

In the shock caused by the sight of flowing blood we clearly experience the remnant of a biological, life-preserving inhibition. But that is precisely what must be overcome, for men, at least, could not afford "to see no blood," and they were educated accordingly. Feelings of fear and guilt are the necessary consequences of overstepping one's inhibitions; yet human tradition, in the form of religion, clearly does not aim at removing or settling these tensions. On the contrary, they are purposefully heightened. Peace must reign within the group, for what is called for outside, offends within. Order has to be observed inside, the extraordinary finds release without. Outside, something utterly different, beyond the norm, frightening but fascinating, confronts the ordinary citizen living within the limits of the everyday world. It is surrounded by barriers to be broken down in a complicated, set way, corresponding to the ambivalence of the event: sacralization and desacralization around a central point where weapons, blood, and death establish a sense of human com-

munity. The irreversible event becomes a formative experience for all
participants, provoking feelings of fear and guilt and increasing desire to
make reparation, the groping attempt at restoration. For the barriers that
had been broken before are now all the more willingly recognized. The
rules are confirmed precisely in their antithetical tension. As an order
embracing its opposite, always endangered yet capable of adaptation and
development, this fluctuating balance entered the tradition of human culture. The power to kill and respect for life illuminate each other.

With remarkable consistency, myths tell of the origins of man in a fall,
a crime that is often a bloody act of violence. The Greeks speculated that
this was preceded by a golden age of modest vegetarianism, ending in the
"murder" of the plow-ox. Accordingly, anthropologists once saw the
peaceful gatherers, or even the planters, as the original norm of human
civilization. The study of prehistory has changed this picture: man became man through the hunt, through the act of killing. "The greatest
danger to life is the fact that man's food consists entirely of souls," said
an Eskimo shaman, just as Porphyrios characterized the state of mankind, divorced from the gods and dependent on food, by quoting Empedokles: "Such as the conflicts and groanings from which you have been
born." As one of the Old Testament myths seems to tell us, men are the
children of Cain. Yet killing, if it was a crime, was salvation at the same
time. "You saved us by shedding blood," the Mithraists address their
savior-god, Mithras the bull-slayer. What has become a mystic paradox
had been just fact in the beginning.

19

MAURICE BLOCH

THE ANTHROPOLOGIST MAURICE BLOCH (1939–) has observed a cultural pattern of "rebounding violence" in which threatened violence against an initiate is internalized, consolidated, and eventually harnessed for outward aggression by the group with whom the initiate joins. The initiate thus is transformed from "prey into hunter," which is the title of his book on sacrifice.

Bloch uses as his model the initiating rituals of the Orokaiva people of Papua New Guinea. In these rituals, he discerns an intricate process of weakening, conquering, and revitalizing, based upon initiates' identification with sacrificial victims (symbolic prey) and then with their killers (symbolic hunters). Children are initiated into the group by vicariously experiencing the death of pigs, with whom they have enjoyed a special bond. Ultimately the children enter a stage of the initiation ritual that is described as "beyond death," from which they emerge as victorious killers who hunt, kill, and eat pigs. Their emergence entails a symbolic incarnation as birdlike ancestral spirits who hunt, kill, and consume pigs and who have just hunted, killed, and consumed the children. The net effect of this complex process is to inject a powerful vitality into the community when the initiated children finally join it.

Because of his breadth of interests, Bloch has been something of a maverick in anthropology, pursuing an agenda as wide-ranging as ritual speech and authority in Madagascar to the origins of sacrifice in world myths. In *Prey into Hunter*, he refers to biblical and Greek myths alongside those which are gathered from contemporary anthropological fieldwork from nearly every major continent. He holds degrees from both the London School of Economics and Cambridge University, and his volume on *Marxist Analyses and Social Anthropology* reflects his synthesis of approaches.

In the excerpt, Bloch explores the pattern of rebounding violence in a variety of cultural representations.

FROM *PREY INTO HUNTER*

Chapter 2 began with a discussion of initiation among the Orokaiva. It described how the elders organise a ritual in which the children to be initiated are first associated with pigs, creatures which are seen as very similar to them, and how as pigs the initiates are hunted and symbolically killed by masked men representing ancestral spirits or birds. Then, the initiates are isolated in a dark hut in the forest, where it is said that they, like all those who have gone beyond death, have themselves become a kind of spirit. Finally, the children re-emerge and return from the world of the spirits. They re-emerge associated with the spirits which initially killed them, as hunters and consumers of pigs. However, at this stage the pigs which the initiate will hunt are real pigs. From being conquered and consumed as though they were pigs, the initiates have become conquerors and consumers of pigs and of everything which the pigs evoke: vitality, strength, production, wealth and reproduction.

The initiates' return is accompanied by the whole community, who share in the new-found aggressiveness of the initiates, and all are now predominantly represented as killers of pigs and as eaters of pig meat. As the ritual develops, however, so does the evocation of conquest and soon the killing of pigs is associated with the conquest and killing of people. The pig hunt has come to be a foretaste of warfare and the consumption of enemies.

This matrix of Orokaiva initiation, which is found in many other rituals of initiation, is analogous to the underlying matrix of many of the rituals which have been called sacrifices in anthropological literature. This fundamental connection between sacrifice and initiation has been noted by many commentators. For example Stanner (1960), in a discussion of Australian Aboriginal initiation, shows how the same themes are present there as in biblical sacrifice. Similarly Schwimmer so extends the notion of sacrifice that it includes many aspects of the initiation ritual which was discussed in the previous chapter (1973: 154–59). This continuity will again be argued in this chapter as we compare Orokaiva initiation with a number of rituals which have been called "sacrifice" by the anthropologists who studied them. In the end, however, this comparison will lead to an even wider comparison of ritual forms, taking in such manifestations as funerary rituals, spirit possession and spirit mediumship.

Although this chapter mainly concentrates on two examples of sacrifice, this is not because sacrifice, any more than initiation, is an easily definable term delimiting a distinct type of ritual. To assume this would almost amount to thinking that every case is a variant of a fundamental and original sacrifice. Like a number of recent writers, such as de Heusch (1986), I believe it is right to stress the great variety that exists among the various examples of "sacrifice" as they have been described in the literature. A possible reaction to such a complex state of affairs might be to give a restrictive definition of the term, but this would be to take the very opposite strategy to the one I wish to adopt here. Instead, we need not be too concerned about whether a specific ritual is or is not a sacrifice, since the aim of this book is to include all these phenomena within a wider analytical category, which includes considerably more than even the wide range of rituals which have been labelled as sacrifice. Somewhat similarly, de Heusch concludes his book by saying that trance and sacrifice are part of a more general ritual system than is implied by either term. This is convincingly argued, but the ritual system he suggests goes well beyond phenomena which have been called trance and sacrifice and, indeed, goes beyond even what is commonly referred to as religion.

The anthropological concept of sacrifice should, therefore, be treated like the notion of totemism so effectively discussed by Lévi-Strauss (1962). The phenomena which have been called by names such as totemism or sacrifice are not so varied as to make the words useless as general indicators of linked manifestations. On the other hand these manifestations are so loosely connected that it would be as totally pointless to look for an explanation of sacrifice as such as Lévi-Strauss showed it was useless to look for an explanation of totemism as such. Rather, and again like Lévi-Strauss, we must see what are called sacrifices as a few cases of the very many manifestations of a much wider range of phenomena, some of which may have been labelled sacrifices, some initiations, and so on. It is at this more inclusive level that we must seek explanation.

Two examples of sacrifice have been most prominent in the immense non-anthropological literature on the topic, which proliferated especially at the end of the last century. These are ancient Greek sacrifice and biblical sacrifice. A discussion of these familiar cases can therefore serve as an introduction to the approach to be taken in this chapter.

For the ancient Greeks, as for many of the people who have been studied by anthropologists, all meat eating was a sacrifice. The Greeks never killed domestic animals for food for other purposes than sacrifice (Vernant 1979: 44). As in the case of Orokaiva initiation we therefore find an indissoluble link between religion and consumption. Furthermore, the political and military implications of this link are equally present in all these cases. For the Greeks, sacrifices had necessarily to be performed before any legal process could be initiated or before any major act of government could be envisaged. This was because sacrifice gave the sacrificers power and wisdom. Above all, sacrifices were essential before any military enterprise because the performance of the ritual was believed to be strength-giving.

The story of a particularly famous sacrifice has always dominated the traditional nineteenth-century discussions of ancient Greek sacrifice and it can serve to reveal the essential elements of the practice. This is the story of Iphigenia as found in the Greek dramatists, especially the two plays by Euripides, *Iphigenia in Aulis* and *Iphigenia in Tauris*. The Greeks were about to set sail to attack the Trojans when their warlike intentions were weakened by the lack of wind. This problem is normally explained in the Greek sources as a punishment administered by the goddess Artemis for an unspecified offence. A way out of this predicament was, we are told, found in the suggestion made through divination that Agamemnon, the leader of the expedition, should sacrifice his daughter Iphigenia, and thereby launch quite a number of plays and operas. But, in the Euripides version at least, at the very last moment, just as the knife was about to come down, Iphigenia was replaced by a hind, which was killed instead. No doubt this animal would then have been treated like other Greek sacrificial animals. That is, it would be divided into different parts, some of which would be burnt so that the smell could feed the insubstantial gods, while other parts would be roasted and boiled to be consumed by different groups of humans. For humans, unlike the gods who had escaped the transformative cycles of life and death, need the sustaining and strengthening element which comes from consumed flesh (Vernant 1979). Thus fortified, the Greeks got their favourable wind and were ultimately able to kill the Trojans, rape the women, and burn the town.

The overall pattern of the story is strong and clear. Agamemnon, the leader and representative of the Greeks, submits to an attack on himself, or something close to himself: his daughter. For the ancient Greeks, children were thought of as the extension of their fathers. In agreeing, however unwillingly, to carry out the sacrifice, Agamemnon was co-operating with an attack from a god directed against him. The first element of the sequence of sacrificial violence evoked by this story is therefore the partly self-inflicted violence intended by the chief protagonist. But then the violence rebounds and, from having been the victim, Agamemnon becomes a violent actor towards others. He eats the strengthening flesh of the sacrificial animal and not only is he restored bodily, but so is the whole situation and so are all the Greeks; the wind returns, the outward movement of the fleet towards their prey begins and ultimately the process reaches its climax as the Trojans and their town are consumed with fire. From having been conquered Agamemnon has thus become a conqueror.

The other story which is always referred to in the discussions of sacrifice, which appeared in such profusion during the last century, is the biblical story of Abraham and Isaac. According to Genesis, God ordered Abraham to offer his son Isaac in sacrifice instead of the usual sheep. In the end Abraham unwillingly agreed to carry out the divine instructions and began to make the necessary preparations. It is difficult to escape the implication that if the sacrifice had been carried out Isaac would have been killed and perhaps eaten. However, again at the last minute, God substituted a ram and Isaac was spared. Furthermore, as a mark of his favour and in return for obedience and self-denial, God promised Abraham to "make descendants as many as the stars of heaven and the grains of the sea shore. Your descendants shall gain possession of the gates of their enemies" (Genesis 22:18).

The similarities between the story of Iphigenia and that of Isaac are very striking and have often been pointed out. Furthermore, the connection between these two stories of sacrifice and the Orokaiva practice of initiation is clear. In all three cases we find the same elements. Firstly, a terrifying closeness to death on the part of the living is evoked. It is as if there was an element of dare in these stories. In the case of Orokaiva initiation the participants stress how very probable it is that the children will not survive the seclusion period of the ritual. In our two sacrifice stories death is avoided by a hair's breadth. Secondly, those who come close to death in all three cases are children, that is members of society who have life before them and who promise social continuation. In other words, the threatened killing is a killing of human vitality at its most intense and forward-looking. The abandonment of this form of vitality would be the abandonment of life itself for the whole community. Thirdly, in all three cases an animal is, at the last moment, substituted for the child. This means that the actual victim's vitality can be completely abandoned in fulfillment of the original promise to God, the gods or the ancestors, who, because of their non-bodily nature, are simply satisfied with receiving the insubstantial aspect of the animal. Fourthly, in all cases the substantial part of the victim, that is its potential vitality, is obtained in the form of meat by the human participants, who thereby replace and regain the vitality which they had lost in the initial self-denial. Fifthly, this consumption enables the whole community to regain vitality and life to such an extent that they can turn their strength outwards in the form of military aggression against other peoples and their children. The spatial aspect of this final, aggressive outward movement is particularly strongly evoked in both of our cases of sacrifice: by the image of the sea journey towards Troy in the one and the biblical reference to the "gates" of the enemies in the other. Both are images which recall the final military expeditions of Orokaiva initiation.

Several elements of this pattern shared by initiation and sacrifice, especially the movement out of vitality and back again, provided the framework of Hubert and Mauss's "communication" theory of sacrifice (1968 (1899)). This theory of sacrifice was, until recently, the most widely accepted in anthropology and it was the model for the highly influential study of Nuer sacrifice put forward by Evans-Pritchard (Evans-Pitchard 1956, chapters 8, 9, 10). It was in this form in particular that Hubert and Mauss's theory came largely to supersede an older theory of sacrifice, which goes back to Plato, where the practice is seen as a matter of obligating the gods by means of a gift.

According to Hubert and Mauss, sacrifice is a matter of going towards the divine via the death of the victim and then coming back to the profane. This may be done for two reasons. Communication may be established through sacrifice in order momentarily to enter into contact with the divine so that sins may be forgiven or other benefits obtained. Hubert and Mauss called these cases "rites of sacralisation." Or communication is established with the sacred so that unwanted contact with the supernatural may be brought to an end. These sacrifices were called by the two authors "rites of desacralisation." In both cases sacrifice is above all envisaged as the crossing of the barrier between the sacred and the profane (Hubert and Mauss 1968 (1899)).

In spite of the clear advance which Hubert and Mauss's theory represents over previous work, it has recently been fundamentally criticised by a number of writers. The main thrust of that criticism is that Hubert and Mauss were unjustifiably influenced by the prominence they gave to Vedic sacrifice and sacrifice as it is understood in the Judaeo-Christian tradition. This led them to assume that what are in reality quite specific models, derived from particular places and periods, could be used to build a universal theory. Clearly this is an ever-present danger in any attempt to generalise on such a vast subject and the criticism seems particularly well founded in their case, since any theory which uses terms such as "sacred" and "profane", terms which cannot be given extracultural referents, cannot form the basis of a general theory of sacrifice or of anything else.

What Hubert and Mauss brought from their reading of ancient Sanskrit texts on sacrifice is the notion that the sacrificer enters the area of the sacred by means of purification of both himself and the victim and can thus communicate with the deity by means of the killing of the victim, which has become a sacred object. For these two authors, sacrifice is a kind of sacrilege which both joins and separates the sacred and the profane. But even if this theory is broadly acceptable for Sankritic sacrifice—and this will be discussed more fully in the next chapter—it appears that even for ancient India it needs qualification (Biardeau and Malamoud 1976: 19ff.). Even more significantly it is made perfectly clear by writers such as de Heusch, among others, that the idea of a separation between the sacred and the profane in the terms envisaged by Hubert and Mauss is far from universal, and that, in particular, it does not in any way apply to Africa (de Heusch 1986: 20–21).

The unfortunate effect of the Judaeo-Christian heritage on the work is partly inherited from previous writers and partly indulged in anew by Hubert and Mauss. This problem is lucidly identified in an article by the French classicist Detienne, which introduces a number of studies on Greek sacrifice (Detienne 1979). Detienne shows how Hubert and Mauss's work belongs to a long tradition in Eurpoean history and theology which was already well formulated in the eighteenth century and which reached its apogee in the work of such writers as Cassirer (1972) and Girard (1972). All the writers in this long line implicitly or explicitly sought to make sacrifice the key to the definition of religion and saw Christian ideas of sacrifice as the apogee of lesser forms. As a result they interpreted the phenomena in an evolutionary perspective which saw non-Chrisitian sacrifice as a primitive precursor of the disinterested self-sacrifice of the deity.

Although most of the writers who developed these linked theories were denounced in their time by various orthodox Christians, they were, Detienne convincingly argues, misled by anachronistic or ethnocentric Christian and Jewish concepts. Their work shows, Detienne tells us, "how an all-encompassing Christianity has continued to exercise a secret and surprising hold on the thought of historians and sociologists who were sure that they were inventing a new science" (1979: 35). This comment has been recently further vindicated by de Heusch's severe examination of how much the famous study of Nuer sacrifice by Evans-Pritchard (1956), which largely follows Hubert and Mauss, has been vitiated by the attempt to translate Nuer concepts into Christian theology and vocabulary (de Heusch 1986: 21–33).

According to Detienne, crypto-Christianity leads to three problems and misrepresentations in the way sacrifice has been viewed both in anthropological literature and beyond.

To illustrate this point further I shall, by way of illustration, give two ethnographic examples which are in many ways complementary. These are, first, the classic study of the Dinka of the southern Sudan by Lienhardt (1961) and secondly Gibson's recent study of the Buid of the Philippines (1986), which appears to support the position of Detienne and Vernant. [Editors' note: Only the example of the Dinka is included in this excerpt.]

Dinka ethnography is deservedly famous in anthropology and so I shall refer to it only very quickly in order to stress those aspects which are particularly relevant to the general argument. Under normal circumstances Dinka sacrifice centrally involves the killing of cattle. It is these people's most important religious rite and the same would be true of many other African peoples. Most commonly, sacrifices are carried out in time of trouble or when people need strengthening. Very often the immediate cause is disease. This leads us to ask the simple but centrally relevant question: why does killing cattle cure people? But before answering this question we need to begin at the beginning of the sequence of events which culminates in sacrifice as a form of curing.

The initial reason for carrying out the sacrifice is when someone, or a group of people, feels penetrated by an outside force, which is believed either to cause or actually to *be* the disease. Disease is used here in a very wide sense of the word to mean almost any kind of trouble. Lienhardt shows how permeable the Dinka feel to such outside forces and how all trouble is explained in terms of such a bodily invasion.

The next stage in the progression towards sacrifice occurs when the person (or persons) who has been attacked tries to find the cause of the trouble. To do this the patient turns to divination or some other diagnostic procedure and in the process of divination the sequence which leads to sacrifice quickens. What follows the diagnostic is the diviner's recommendation for bringing about a cure and this is particularly revealing. Two apparently totally different and opposed ways of curing are common, especially in Africa. These two ways may be tried concurrently, but more usually they appear as two successive stages of the process of finding a cure, since, if the first is not successful, the other will then be tried. The first way of dealing with intrusion is found universally. Once the source of the trouble has been identified, a way is sought to expel the intrusive force. This way of going about things is familiar to us from western medicine. Indeed the Dinka themselves recognise this identity of form and therefore readily welcome western medicine for this sort of practice.

If this first approach fails, however, then the second tack is tried and that is completely different. In this the diviner will suggest that the disease is a powerful supernatural being, a clan divinity or a spirit for example, which cannot, or should not, be resisted and so, instead of expelling the intrusion, the patient should rather submit to the disease and its attack on her body. She should even draw in and identify the disease against her body, in other words make her body foreign and accept the intrusion against it. This is not expected to occur without a struggle, but the final victory of the intruding force should not be in doubt.

The lives of Christian saints or the story of Job are well-known examples of this pattern and there are many ethnographic cases of this type of turning round of the person against themselves or rather against the bodily aspect of themselves. For example a particularly fine description of this process is given in the book *Human Spirits* by M. Lambek (1981), where this way of dealing with illness by "welcome" is shown to lead naturally to spirit possession. After a struggle when the diseased person is still trying out the first tack of expelling the intrusive spirit she finally agrees to the second tack and instead welcomes the spirit. What this means in this case is that she allows her body to be made a receptacle without will, which can be used by an immortal and external spirit for its temporary incarnation (Lambek 1981).

In the case discussed by Lambek this second welcoming approach to disease leads to the instituting of a spirit possession cult, but it could just as easily have been a preliminary to sacrifice. The fact that similar preliminaries can lead to either what we call sacrifice or spirit mediumship shows well how closely these two manifestations are related, a point already made, as we saw, by de Heusch. It also shows once again how misleading the divisions can be within the typology of ritual categories which our academic traditions have imposed. Indeed the close connection between sacrifice and possession can help us understand the Dinka case to which we return.

Here, however, yet another preliminary is necessary before we come to the ritual itself. As was the case for the understanding of Orokaiva initiation, it is necessary to sketch how the Dinka view relations with supernatural beings and with animals, especially cattle. In fact, the main points I want to make on these matters are implicit in the very organization of Lienhardt's book. The book begins with a discussion of the Dinka's association and near-identification with their cattle. It is made clear that this identification is particularly strong in the case of boys and young men. To illustrate this we are shown a picture of Dinka youth dancing in a way that imitates cattle. The book ends, however, with a discussion of the ritual of the death-defying burial alive of a Dinka priest, the master of the fishing spear. The priest should be a very old man who is buried alive in such a way that, after he has disappeared from sight, nothing but his disembodied voice can be heard singing or speaking an invocation. This complementary opposition between cattle and speech, between the bovine strength of youth and the verbal power of the old, which Lienhardt constructs by the very organisation of the book, is central to Dinka symbolism.

For the Dinka, cattle and humans are very close and this parallelism, which is evocatively discussed by Lienhardt, is familiar from other parts of Africa. This link between cattle and humans is not unlike that which exists between pigs and humans among the Orokaiva. For the Dinka, cattle represent the beauty of strength, vitality and sexuality to which humans aspire, but which they possess in varying amounts. In particular, cattle are associated with young men.

But the similarity between the Orokaiva and Dinka cases goes further. This is because, even though Dinka cattle are seen as similar to humans in some respects, in other, equally significant respects, cattle and humans are very different. These aspects are not so stressed by Lienhardt but they emerge from a careful reading of his ethnography.

For the Dinka, a clear difference between humans and cattle lies in humans' ability to speak. Although Lienhardt does not discuss speech in general, he discusses at great length the speech of the Dinka prophets and of the members of the priestly clan, the masters of the fishing spear. This is a kind of ideal speech, cool speech, not often achieved by less sacred mortals. The Dinka believe that prophets and masters of the fishing spear are the permanent mediums of Divinity and of lesser divinities which, in any case, are simply avatars of the supreme God. The speech of the chosen vessels of Divinity is, therefore, particularly powerful, but it is not exclusive to them. It seems that all men, and perhaps some women, can occasionally make their speech reach similar heights, for example when possessed or when acting as diviners. Perhaps the most important aspect of this quintessential speech is that it is always true. This means that when it is used to talk of the future it is prophetic. Ideally it should be declaimed clearly and require few words (Lienhardt 1961: 139). Everything about this truth-speech contrasts with the associations of cattle. While cattle are youthfully strong but turbulent, mobile, always being exchanged or killed in sacrifice, the true speech of the Dinka is manifested in the old and frail, but is permanent, unchanging, of no particular time and of all times, sober and immortal, beyond process.

This duality of speech and cattle takes many forms. For example the Dinka think of their society as fundamentally divided between warrior clans who are more closely associated with cattle, and priestly clans who bring order, stability and prophetic speech. This kind of distribution suggests an image of complementarity since it implies that both elements are necessary for life. The Dinka see existence as a combination of bovine animal vitality and a death-defying order crystallised in the invocations of the masters of the fishing spear.

In stressing this duality in Dinka thought I am not doing what Lienhardt rightly warned us against in a recent article on the concept of the self (Lienhardt 1985). There, he very properly stressed how it would misrepresent Dinka thought to argue that they have an explicit theory of what makes up the self. Very sensibly the Dinka say that no one can know what a person is like inside. I believe such justified skepticism is found in most cultures, and I have already tried to stress the dangers of such overexplicit exegesis of ideas of the person in the last chapter. What I am talking about when I say that the Dinka envisage the person as part cattle and part speech is, rather, the dramatic simplifications which are acted out in rituals. In rituals, unlike ordinary, everyday life, an image of the components of interior states is evoked in a way that is partly iconographic and partly allegorical. These dramatic representations are created in order to bring about a symbolic transformation, but they soon fade after the ritual is done, though they never disappear completely.

After the diviner has told the patient that, rather than resist, she must submit to the external invasion, in most cases he will suggest that this is done by sacrificing cattle. Why this is a suitable way of co-operating with the external invader becomes evident in the main actions of the rite. First, the victim is associated with the person for whom the sacrifice is being done. Then, in the first part of the sacrifice proper the animal is threatened for long periods with the spear of the sacrificer and it is weakened in a variety of ways but principally by exposure to the sun. Ultimately it is killed. But simultaneously, as this is happening, the other aspect of human society, the cold speech of truth, is strengthened and conquers. Speech is manifest in sacrifice in the invocations and prayers spoken by the master of the fishing spear which dominate the first part of the ritual. The Dinka say that it is the continual speaking of these invocations which weakens and kills the animal and makes its horns, prime symbols of vitality and virile strength, wilt and droop. The very word which the Dinka use as a verb for "to invoke" suggests the violence that is being done to the sacrificial animal as it can also mean "to attack an enemy" (1961: 263). The drama is a tilting of the balance between vitality and unchanging truth, in which vitality is vanquished.

It is, therefore, right to see Dinka sacrifice as involving an identification between sacrificer and victim, as Lienhardt does in the case of the Dinka and as Evans-Pritchard for the Nuer. In spite of de Heusch's objections much of the ethnography confirms their point of view. However, the proposition has to be qualified since it is only *one* aspect of the sacrificer and the community, the vital cattle aspect, which is symbolically weakened and killed in the ritual, but the other aspect, the speech aspect, is strengthened at the very same time as vitality ebbs away. This is why theories of the identification of sacrificer and victim have often been criticised but never overcome. It is not the whole person, which is identified with the victim, but only one aspect.

Dinka sacrifice is in its first part a drama of conflict between cattle and speech; as the animal is defeated speech and invocation become triumphant. What the ritual creates by evocation is first a reduction of the complexity of the person and society so that it can appear to consist merely of two opposed elements, the cattle and the invocation, which are represented as visually and auditorily in conflict. Once the image has been established the ritual can reach the next stage as, finally, the speech element conquers.

For the sacrificer and the community the conquest and the killing of the cattle is an external drama which can be experienced as corresponding to the weakening and killing of the cattle element by now evoked in the body. It is in this ritual context, and this context only, that [it] is right to speak of elements of the person because, in the ritual, different external entities are brought into action to represent and create an internal conflict. What is happening is similar to a morality play where the struggle of good and evil within a protagonist can be represented as objectified by different actors.

But ritual is more complex and more powerful than this simple comparison suggests. Firstly, as will be discussed below, the second half of the ritual breaks away from the theatrical model. Secondly, even in the first part of the ritual discussed above, we are not just dealing with an externalised representation of an internal state, but also with actions which have an experienced internal effect on the body of the participants.

The drama of the victory of speech over cattle occurs out in the open on the ceremonial ground. But the same division and the same tipping of the balance also occurs experientially for both the sacrificer and for those less centrally concerned. In order to understand how the killing of the cattle is bringing about a cure it is better to concentrate on this aspect first.

The effect of the ritual on the peripheral participants is revealing in many ways. First, it shows how, in a ritual such as this and in society such as that of the Dinka, the boundary between the body of an individual and the wider group is weak (Bloch 1988). Thus, in the Dinka ritual of sacrifice, as in Orokaiva initiation, even though the event might be focused on the central actor (the initiate or the patient), all the others present are not onlookers but co-participants. This continuity manifests itself at the point in the ritual when, as the animal on the ritual ground is weakened and as the speech side is magnified, the onlookers also experience speech overwhelming their internal vitality and they become possessed and speak the words of Divinity. Lienhardt gives a graphic description of the twitching of the flesh of the possessed young men, their cattle side, as it submits to the verbal invasion of Divinity. This twitching of the flesh of the possessed serves well to show how a parallel has been established between the external visible actions of the participants in the ritual and the invisible experiential process which goes on inside their bodies, since the Dinka themselves stress the identity of this twitching of the flesh of the possessed participants with the twitching of the flesh of the animal as it is being slaughtered (1961: 137).

The falling into trance of some of the onlookers is illuminating in a number of ways. First, we have once again demonstrated the close affinity of sacrifice and spirit possession. Secondly, because spirit possession is a matter of the triumphant penetration of a transcendental being into the conquered body of a medium, we can see that this is also what sacrifice is all about, that, like spirit possession, it is an appropriate response to the diviner's advice not to resist disease, but rather join the invader entering into your body. In the ritual the sacrificial animal is made to stand for the vitality of the body of the sacrificer while the transcendental speech of the invocations of the master of the fishing spear appropriately represents and is a manifestation of Divinity. By organising the sacrifice the patient is thus completing the attack on his own vitality in order to let the permanent triumph. The weakening and death of the animal is the culmination of this process and publicly represents the victory of transcendental speech. The first part of sacrifice and possession is the completion of the process of joining the invader against one's vital self.

And, of course, all this is exactly what happens in a ritual such as Orokaiva initiation, or rather in the first part of the ritual when the pig element in the children is weakened and killed so that the spiritual element can dominate. But then, with sacrifice as with initiation, there is a reversal. The abandonment of strength and vitality cannot be final. As with initiation, it must be regained. The internal lack of balance in the body, brought about by the victory of the transcendental, must be redressed if life is to go on. And again this poses the problem of how to avoid contradiction so that the second part of sacrifice is not merely a reincorporation of what has so painfully been got rid of.

The Dinka sacrifice solution is very similar to the Orokaiva initiation solution and it revolves around the change in the relation of the sacrificer and victim which occurs at the moment of the actual killing. Lienhardt, like other ethnographers, notes how a dramatic transformation in mood occurs at this point. This is due to the fact that the close association of sacrificer and victim ends at this moment. Up to then there has been a painfully close experiential analogic relation between the two, but once the killing has been done the sacrificer is freed and the dead animal is merely a dead animal on the ground, ready to be cut up and eaten in the second part of the ritual. When that occurs the relation of the victim, on the one hand, and the sacrificer and community, on the other, changes from the analogic to the physical, just as, among the Orokaiva, the pigs of the first part of the initiation were metaphoric pigs while the pigs of the second half are real pigs.

What happens in the second part of the ritual is that the animal is cut up, distributed and partly eaten there and then amidst a good deal of celebration. By this stage this meat has taken on a quite different meaning from what it had in the first part. No longer does it represent the animal, vital side of the sacrificer; it has become, by the simple fact of killing, the meat of an animal which, because it is an animal, is by nature alien to humans. Its vitality can be consumed without problem by those present in order that, like all meat, it will restrengthen them through its nutritive value.

Unlike Lienhardt, and even more Evans-Pritchard writing of the nearby Nuer, the Dinka attach very great importance to the feast side of sacrifice and to the eating of cattle, in which they revel. Indeed, the Dinka word which Lienhardt translates as "sacrifice" would, according to him, be more straightforwardly translates as "feast," thereby making a nonsense of the refusal to consider the meal as part of the sacrifice (1961: 281). The eating of the meat of the cattle restores vitality which had been analogically lost in the first part of the ritual. Those who had allowed their native vitality to be symbolically vanquished by following the advice of the diviner and performing the sacrifice are now rewarded with the actual vitality of an external being. The meal is that highly pleasurable recovery of this vitality, which has been surrendered in the first part of the proceedings. And here, as with the other consumptions which follow rebounding conquests, this may not be just a restoration of lost vitality. The recovery is triumphalist and outwardly directed. It may indeed lead to a legitimate increase in vitality since the vitality that is now being recovered is conquered and ordered by the transcendental order of the speech of the masters of the fishing spear.

By having allowed one side of themselves to die so that they may become pure speech the Dinka sacrificers can regain the cattle side through the mouth, almost exactly as happened for the Orokaiva initiate. There is a difference in the two cases but it is slight. In the case of Orokaiva initiation it was the children who were representing pigs in the first part of the proceedings, while in the first part of Dinka sacrifice it is the cattle which represents the humans, but this difference is of no significance to the general logic of the proceedings.

And the parallel between the two rituals does not end there. For the Orokaiva the consumption of the external pig was also the promise of further more adventurous conquests of a political and military form and, again, the same is true of the Dinka. As in the case of the Orokaiva, Dinka sacrifice takes on a more military idiom as it proceeds. Lienhardt tells us that to "make a feast or sacrifice often implies war" (1961: 281), indeed that the rituals often ended either in threatened or real military raids. The expansionist reconquest of vitality is shown once again to lead either to restoration, as in the return of the initiates to the village, or to aggrandisement.

It is because the sacrifice ends in such a feast, which involved not just the legitimate recovery of vitality but, by extension, the recovery of more vitality, as much as one can get, that sacrifice can cure disease in all its forms whether physical or, as is often the case, social and moral. What has happened in the sacrifice is that the specific problem, which was the original cause of the ritual, has been dealt with in a way which is not specifically addressed to it but is, rather, an action which generally reactivates the strength and activity of the social group and which, it is hoped, will overcome the particular difficulty with its general force. This is why the same rituals can be used both to cure specific ills and on a non-specific basis to reactivate the right order of man in society and nature.

GEORGES BATAILLE

A COLORFUL FIGURE IN FRENCH and Spanish literary circles in the first half of the twentieth century, Georges Bataille (1897–1962) joined and then was ostracized from the surrealist movement in France. He had trained for the priesthood as a young man but then abandoned his faith. He served twenty-two years as a librarian at the Bibliothèque Nationale in Paris. Bataille wrote novels that center on sensuousness and pain, but he also dabbled in economics and religion. His writing style was highly cryptic, as may be seen in the following excerpt from *Theory of Religion*.

Bataille based his theory of religion on his theory of economics, which he formulated in *The Accursed Share*. According to Bataille, societies are like plants: stimulated by the sun, many plants produce more beauty than they need for utility, just as a society too produces a surplus of energy beyond its utilitarian needs. A society may be evaluated by the ways it expends this surplus energy. Those ways include religious spectacles and sacrifices, among other things. However, Bataille's understanding of religion ultimately went beyond economics. For Bataille, religion stems from a suspicion of "immanence"—a pre-articulate awareness of a realm of being outside of the world of tools, things, and usefulness. The ritual practice of animal sacrifice, for Bataille, reflects an uncomfortable synthesis of the utilitarian viewpoint and the suspicion of immanence.

In the excerpt, Bataille explores the intimacy fostered between the sacrificer and his victim when they leave the world of utility for the world of religious spectacle. There they experience a return to immanence. In actually killing the victim, the sacrificer experiences a moment of raw vitality, wherein he senses the victim's vivid anguish in a profound way. Yet simultaneously, in regarding the victim as a thing to be killed, he also returns it to the realm of things to be squandered in a capricious religious exercise.

FROM *THEORY OF RELIGION*

The Eaten Animal, the Corpse, and the Thing

The definition of the animal as a thing has become a basic human given. The animal has lost its status as man's fellow creature, and man, perceiving the animality in himself, regards it as a defect. There is undoubtedly a measure of falsity in the fact of regarding the animal as a thing. An animal exists for itself and in order to be a thing it must be dead or domesticated. Thus the eaten animal can be posited as an object only provided it is eaten dead. Indeed, it is fully a thing only in a roasted, grilled, or boiled form. Moreover, the preparation of meat is not primarily connected with a gastronomical pursuit: before that it has to do with the fact that a man does not eat anything before he has made an object of it. At least in ordinary circumstances, man is an animal that does not *have a part* in that which he eats. But to kill the animal and alter it as one pleases is not merely to change into a thing that which doubtless was not a thing from the start; it is to define the animal as a thing beforehand. Concerning that which I kill, which I cut up, which I cook, I implicitly affirm that *that* has never been anything but a thing. To cut up, cook, and eat a man is on the contrary abominable. It does no harm to anyone; in fact it is often unreasonable not to do something with man['s corpse]. Yet the study of anatomy ceased to be scandalous only a short time ago. And despite appearances, even hardened materialists are still so religious that in their eyes it is always a crime to make a man into a thing—a roast, a stew. . . . In any case, the human attitude toward the body is formidably complex. Insofar as he is spirit, it is man's misfortune to have the body of an animal and thus to be like a thing, but it is the glory of the human body to be the substratum of a spirit. And the spirit is so closely linked to the body as a thing that the body never ceases to be haunted, is never a thing except virtually, so much so that if death reduces it to the condition of a thing, the spirit is more present than ever: the body that has betrayed it reveals it more clearly than when it served it. In a sense the corpse is the most complete affirmation of the spirit. What death's definitive impotence and absence reveals is the very essence of the spirit, just as the scream of the one that is killed is the supreme affirmation of life. Conversely, man's corpse reveals the complete reduction of the animal body, and therefore the living animal, to thinghood. In theory the body is a strictly subordinate element, which is of no consequence for itself—a utility of the same nature as canvas, iron, or lumber.

The Need That Is Met by Sacrifice and Its Principle

The first fruits of the harvest or a head of livestock are sacrificed in order to remove the plant and the animal, together with the farmer and the stock raiser, from the world of things.

The principle of sacrifice is destruction, but though it sometimes goes so far as to destroy completely (as in a holocaust), the destruction that sacrifice is intended to bring about is not annihilation. The thing—only the thing—is what sacrifice means to destroy in the victim. Sacrifice destroys an object's real ties of subordination; it draws the victim out of the world of utility and restores it to that of unintelligible caprice. When the offered animal enters the circle in which the priest will immolate it, it passes from the world of things which are closed to man and are *nothing* to him, which he knows from the outside—to the world that is immanent to it, *intimate*, known as the wife is known in sexual consumption (*consummation carnelle*). This assumes that it has ceased to be separated from its own intimacy, as it is in the subordination of labor. The sacrificer's prior separation from the world of things is necessary for the return to *intimacy*, of immanence between man and the world, between the subject and the object. The sacrificer needs the sacrifice in order to separate himself from the world of things and the victim could not be separated from it in turn if the sacrificer was not already separated in advance. The sacrificer declares: "*Intimately*, I belong to the sovereign world of the gods and myths, to the world of violent and uncalculated generosity, just as my wife belongs to my desires. I withdraw you, victim, from the world in which you were and could only be reduced to the condition of a thing, having a meaning that was foreign to your intimate nature. I call you back to the *intimacy* of the divine world, of the profound immanence of all that is."

The Unreality of the Divine World

Of course this is a monologue and the victim can neither understand nor reply. Sacrifice essentially turns its back on real relations. If it took them into account, it would go against its own nature, which is precisely the opposite of that world of things on which distinct *reality* is founded. It could not destroy the animal as thing without denying the animal's objective *reality*. This is what gives the world of sacrifice an appearance of puerile gratuitousness. But one cannot at the same time destroy the values that found reality and accept their limits. The return to immanent intimacy implies a beclouded consciousness: consciousness is tied to the positing of objects as such, grasped directly, apart from a vague perception, beyond the always unreal images of a thinking based on participation.

The Ordinary Association of Death and Sacrifice

The puerile unconsciousness of sacrifice even goes so far that killing appears as a way of redressing the wrong done to the animal, miserably reduced to the condition of a thing. As a matter of fact, killing in the literal sense is not necessary. But the greatest negation of the real order is the one most favorable to the appearance of the mythical order. Moreover, sacrificial killing resolves the painful antinomy of life and death by means of a reversal. In fact death is nothing in immanence, but because it is nothing, a being is never truly separated from it. Because death has no meaning, because there is no difference between it and life, and there is no fear of it or defense against it, it invades everything without giving rise to any resistance. Duration ceases to have any value, or it is there only in order to produce the morbid delectation of anguish. On the contrary, the objective and in a sense transcendent (relative to the subject) positing of the world of things has duration as its foundation: no *thing* in fact has a separate existence, has a meaning, unless a subsequent time is posited, in view of which it is constituted as an object. The object is defined as an operative power only if its duration is implicitly understood. If it is destroyed as food or fuel is, the eater of the manufactured object preserves its value in duration; it has a lasting purpose like coal or bread. Future time constitutes this real world to such a degree that death no longer has a place in it. But it is for this very reason that death means everything to it. The weakness (the contradiction) of the world of things is that it imparts an unreal character to death even though man's membership in this world is tied to the positing of the body as a thing insofar as it is mortal.

As a matter of fact, that is a superficial view. What has no place in the world of things, what is unreal in the real world is not exactly death. Death actually discloses the imposture of reality, not only in that the absence of duration gives the lie to it, but above all because death is the great affirmer, the wonder-struck cry of life. The real order does not so much reject the negation of life that is death as it rejects the affirmation of intimate life, whose measureless violence is a danger to the stability of things, an affirmation that is fully revealed only in death. The real order must annul—neutralize—that intimate life and replace it with the thing that the individual is in the society of labor. But it cannot prevent life's disappearance in death from revealing the *invisible* brilliance of life that is not a *thing*. The power of death signifies that this real world can only have a neutral image of life, that life's intimacy does not reveal its dazzling consumption until the moment it gives out. No one knew *it* was there when it was; it was overlooked in favor of real things: death was one real thing among others. But death suddenly shows that the real society was lying. Then it is not the loss of the thing, of the useful member, that is taken into consideration. What the real society has lost is not a member but rather its truth. That intimate life, which had lost the ability to fully reach me, which I regarded primarily as a thing, is fully restored to my sensibility through its absence. Death reveals life in its plenitude and dissolves the real order. Henceforth it matters very little that this real order is the need for the duration of that which no longer exists. When an element escapes its demands, what remains is not an entity that suffers bereavement; all at once that entity, the real order, has completely dissi-pated. There is no more question of it and what death brings in tears is the useless consumption of the intimate order.

It is a naive opinion that links death closely to sorrow. The tears of the living, which respond to its coming, are themselves far from having a meaning opposite to joy. Far from being sorrowful, the tears are the ex-pression of a keen awareness of shared life grasped in its intimacy. It is true that this awareness is never keener than at the moment when ab-sence suddenly replaces presence, as in death or mere separation. And in this case, the consolation (in the strong sense the word has in the "conso-lations" of the mystics) is in a sense bitterly tied to the fact that it cannot last, but it is precisely the disappearance of duration, and of the neutral behaviors associated with it, that uncovers a ground of things that is daz-zlingly bright (in other words, it is clear that the need for duration con-ceals life from us, and that, only in theory, the impossibility of duration frees us). In other cases the tears respond instead to unexpected triumph, to good fortune that makes us exult, but always madly, far beyond the concern for a future time.

The Consummation of Sacrifice

The power that death generally has illuminates the meaning of sacrifice, which functions like death in that it restores a lost value through a relin-quishment of that value. But death is not necessarily linked to it, and the most solemn sacrifice may not be bloody. To sacrifice is not to kill but to relinquish and to give. Killings is only the exhibition of a deep meaning. What is important is to pass from a lasting order, in which all consump-tion of resources is subordinated to the need for duration, to the violence of an unconditional consumption; what is important is to leave a world of real things, whose reality derives from a long term operation and never resides in the moment—a world that creates and preserves (that creates for the benefit of a lasting reality). Sacrifice is the antithesis of produc-tion, which is accomplished with a view to the future; it is consumption that is concerned only with the moment. This is the sense in which it is gift and relinquishment, but what is given cannot be an object of preser-vation for the receiver: the gift of an offering makes it pass precisely into the world of abrupt consumption.

This is the meaning of "sacrificing to the deity," whose sacred essence is comparable to a fire. To sacrifice is to give as one gives coal to a fur-nace. But the furnace ordinarily has an undeniable utility, to which the coal is subordinated, whereas in sacrifice the offering is rescued from all utility.

This is so clearly the precise meaning of sacrifice, that one sacrifices *what is useful*; one does not sacrifice luxurious objects. There could be no sacrifice if the offering were destroyed beforehand. Now, depriving the labor of manufacture of its usefulness at the outset, luxury has already *destroyed* that labor; it has dissipated it in vainglory; in the very moment, it has lost it for good. To sacrifice a luxury object would be to sacrifice the same object twice.

But neither could one sacrifice that which was not first withdrawn from immanence, that which, never having belonged to immanence, would not have been secondarily subjugated, domesticated, and reduced to being a thing. Sacrifice is made of objects that could have been spirits, such as animals or plant substances, but that have become things and that need to be restored to the immanence whence they come, to the vague sphere of lost intimacy.

The Individual, Anguish, and Sacrifice

Intimacy cannot be expressed discursively.

The swelling to the bursting point, the malice that breaks out with clenched teeth and weeps; the sinking feeling that doesn't know where it comes from or what it's about; the fear that sings its head off in the dark; the white-eyed pallor, the sweet sadness, the rage and the vomiting . . . are so many evasions.

What is intimate, in the strong sense, is what has the passion of an absence of individuality, the imperceptible sonority of a river, the empty limpidity of the sky: this is still a negative definition, from which the essential is missing.

These statements have the vague quality of inaccessible distances, but on the other hand articulated definitions substitute the tree for the forest, the distinct articulation for that which is articulated.

I will resort to articulation nevertheless.

Paradoxically, intimacy is violence, and it is destruction, because it is not compatible with the positing of the separate individual. If one describes the individual in operation of sacrifice, he is defined by anguish. But if sacrifice is distressing, the reason is that the individual takes part in it. The individual identifies with the victim in the sudden movement that restores it to immanence (to intimacy), but the assimilation that is linked to the return to immanence is nonetheless based on the fact that the victim is the thing, just as the sacrificer is the individual. The separate individual is of the same nature as the thing, or rather the anxiousness to remain personally alive that establishes the person's individuality is linked to the integration of existence into the world of things. To put it differently, work and the fear of dying are interdependent; the former implies the thing and vice versa. In fact is not even necessary to work in order to be the *thing* of fear: man is an individual to the extent that his apprehension ties him to the results of labor. But man is not, as one might think, a thing because he is afraid. He would have no anguish if he were not the individual (the thing), and it is essentially the fact of being an individual that fuels his anguish. It is in order to satisfy the demands of the thing, it is insofar as the world of things has posited his duration as the basic condition of his worth, that he learns anguish. He is afraid of death as soon as he enters the system of projects that is the order of things. Death disturbs the order of things and the order of things holds us. Man is afraid of the intimate order that is not reconcilable with the order of things. Otherwise there would be no sacrifice, and there would be no mankind either. The intimate order would not reveal itself in the destruction and the sacred anguish of the individual. Because man is not squarely within that order, but only partakes of it through a thing that is threatened in its nature (in the projects that constitute it), intimacy, in the trembling of the individual, is holy, sacred, and suffused with anguish.

KARL MARX

RELIGION PLAYS A SIGNIFICANT ROLE in the critique of society developed by the great socialist philosopher, Karl Marx (1819–1883). Religious belief is a delusion, said Marx, but also an expression of real despair. Offering heavenly rewards, religions divert our deepest yearnings for reward in material life. Religious suffering is thus a symptom of real suffering; it is based in economic realities but exacerbated by heavenly promises that can never be achieved. Marx concluded that religion was "the heart of a heartless world."

Yet Marx did not deny the force of religion. In his *Theses on Feuerbach*, Marx complained that Feuerbach had attempted to reduce religion to its secular basis, but had failed to notice that religion was itself a cultural force in history. For instance, Marx saw that the feudal church continued to play an oppressive social and economic role in the modern German state, but he trusted that economic liberation would lead to freedom from religion, and cravings for religion would dissolve as humans attained material well-being. Marx also accepted Hegel's supposition that there was a forward-moving spirit in human history. Yet Marx recast Hegel's spiritual dialectics—an ongoing play of thesis, antithesis, and synthesis—to the material sphere, envisioning the process of history as leading to ever higher forms of human gratification and well-being.

The young Karl Marx is perhaps nowhere more eloquent than in this excerpt that follows, from his *Critique of Hegel's Philosophy of Right*. Here are his famous words on religion as "the opium of the people" and "the sigh of the oppressed creature." Here he points out that "the criticism of religion ends with the doctrine that *man* is *the highest being for man*," and he concludes with "the *categoric imperative to overthrow all relations* in which man is a debased, enslaved, abandoned, despicable essence" (emphasis in original).

FROM *CRITIQUE OF HEGEL'S PHILOSOPHY OF RIGHT*

For Germany, the *criticism of religion* has been essentially completed, and the criticism of religion is the prerequisite of all criticism.

The *profane* existence of error is compromised as soon as its *heavenly oratio pro aris et focis* ["speech for the altars and hearths" (i.e., for God and country)] has been refuted. Man, who has found only the *reflection* of himself in the fantastic reality of heaven, where he sought a superman, will no longer feel disposed to find the *mere appearance* of himself, the non-man [*Unmensch*], where he seeks and must seek his true reality.

The foundation of irreligious criticism is: *Man makes religion*, religion does not make man. Religion is, indeed, the self-consciousness and self-esteem of man who has either not yet won through to himself, or has already lost himself again. But *man* is no abstract being squatting outside the world. Man is *the world of man*–state, society. This state and this society produce religion, which is an *inverted consciousness of the world*, because they are an *inverted world*. Religion is the general theory of this world, its encyclopaedic compendium, its logic in popular form, its spiritual *point d'honneur*, its enthusiasm, its moral sanction, its solemn complement, and its universal basis of consolation and justification. It is the *fantastic realization* of the human essence since the *human essence* has not acquired any true reality. The struggle against religion is, therefore, indirectly the struggle *against that world* whose spiritual *aroma* is religion.

Religious suffering is, at one and the same time, the *expression* of real suffering and a *protest* against real suffering. Religion is the sigh of the oppressed creature, the heart of a heartless world, and the soul of soulless conditions. It is the *opium* of the people.

The abolition of religion as the *illusory* happiness of the people is the demand for their *real* happiness. To call on them to give up their illusions about their condition is to call on them to *give up a condition that requires illusions*. The criticism of religion is, therefore, in embryo, the *criticism of that vale of tears* of which religion is the *halo*.

Criticism has plucked the imaginary flowers on the chain not in order that man shall continue to bear that chain without fantasy or consolation, but so that he shall throw off the chain and pluck the living flower. The criticism of religion disillusions man, so that he will think, act, and fashion his reality like a man who has discarded his illusions and regained his senses, so that he will move around himself as his own true Sun. Religion is only the illusory Sun which revolves around man as long as he does not revolve around himself.

It is, therefore, the *task of history*, once the *other-world of truth* has vanished, to establish the *truth of this world*. It is the immediate *task of philosophy*, which is in the service of history, to unmask self-estrangement in its *unholy forms* once the *holy form* of human self-estrangement has been unmasked. Thus, the criticism of Heaven turns into the criticism of Earth, the *criticism of religion* into the *criticism of law*, and the *criticism of theology* into the *criticism of politics*. . . .

The weapon of criticism cannot, of course, replace criticism of the weapon, material force must be overthrown by material force; but theory also becomes a material force as soon as it has gripped the masses. Theory is capable of gripping the masses as soon as it demonstrates *ad homi-*

nem, and it demonstrates *ad hominem* as soon as it becomes radical. To be radical is to grasp the root of the matter. But, for man, the root is man himself. The evident proof of the radicalism of German theory, and hence of its practical energy, is that is proceeds from a resolute *positive* abolition of religion. The criticism of religion ends with the teaching that *man is the highest essence for man*–hence, with the *categoric imperative to overthrow all relations* in which man is a debased, enslaved, abandoned, despicable essence, relations which cannot be better described than by the cry of a Frenchman when it was planned to introduce a tax on dogs: Poor dogs! They want to treat you as human beings!

Even historically, theoretical emancipation has specific practical significance for Germany. For Germany's *revolutionary* past is theoretical, it is the *Reformation*. As the revolution then began in the brain of the *monk*, so now it begins in the brain of the *philosopher*.

Luther, we grant, overcame bondage out of *devotion* by replacing it by bondage out of *conviction*. He shattered faith in authority because he restored the authority of faith. He turned priests into laymen because he turned laymen into priests. He freed man from outer religiosity because he made religiosity the inner man. He freed the body from chains because he enchained the heart.

But, if Protestantism was not the true solution of the problem, it was at least the true setting of it. It was no longer a case of the layman's struggle against the *priest outside himself* but of his struggle against his *own priest inside himself*, his priestly nature. And if the Protestant transformation of the German layman into priests emancipated the lay popes, the *princes*, with the whole of their priestly clique, the privileged and philistines, the philosophical transformation of priestly Germans into men will emancipate the *people*. But, *secularization* will not stop at the *confiscation of church estates* set in motion mainly by hypocritical Prussia any more than emancipation stops at princes. The Peasant War, the most radical fact of German history, came to grief because of theology. Today, when theology itself has come to grief, the most unfree fact of German history, our *status quo*, will be shattered against philosophy. On the eve of the Reformation, official Germany was the most unconditional slave of Rome. On the eve of its revolution, it is the unconditional slave of less than Rome, of Prussia and Austria, of country junkers and philistines.

Meanwhile, a major difficulty seems to stand in the way of a *radical* German revolution.

For revolutions require a *passive* element, a material basis. Theory is fulfilled in a people only insofar as it is the fulfilment of the needs of that people. But will the monstrous discrepancy between the demands of German thought and the answers of German reality find a corresponding discrepancy between civil society and the state, and between civil society and itself? Will the theoretical needs be immediate practical needs? It is not enough for thought to strive for realization, reality must itself strive towards thought.

——————

As philosophy finds its material weapon in the proletariat, so the proletariat finds its *spiritual* weapon in philosophy. And once the lightning of thought has squarely struck this ingenuous soil of the people, the emancipation of the *Germans* into *men* will be accomplished.

Let us sum up the result:

The only liberation of Germany which is *practically* possible is liberation from the point of view of *that* theory which declares man to be the supreme being for man. Germany can emancipate itself from the Middle Ages only if it emancipates itself at the same time from the *partial* victories over the *Middle Ages*. In Germany, *no* form of bondage can be broken without breaking *all* forms of bondage. Germany, which is renowned for its *thoroughness*, cannot make a revolution unless it is a *thorough* one. The *emancipation of the German* is the *emancipation of man*. The *head* of this emancipation is *philosophy*, its *heart* the *proletariat*. Philosophy cannot realize itself without the transcendence [*Aufhebung*] of the proletariat, and the proletariat cannot transcend itself without the realization [*Verwirklichung*] of philosophy.

When all the inner conditions are met, the *day of the German resurrection* will be heralded by the *crowing of the cock of Gaul*.

NANCY JAY

NANCY JAY (1929—91) developed the "descent theory" of sacrifice, according to which sacrificial rituals provide experiences of male bonding that privilege men in patrilineal societies. She based this conclusion on her analysis of two anthropological movements in ritualized blood sacrifice: expiation, eliminating unwanted elements as unclean; and communion, which integrates elements into a new whole.

In *Throughout Your Generations Forever,* Jay surveyed sacrificial practices in cultures as diverse as native Hawaiian society and ancient biblical cultures. Jay claimed that sacrificial institutions in these settings attempt to expiate certain qualities from their members in order to inaugurate them into new kinship groups with new identities. The new kinship group's identity is male-oriented and patrilineal. What is expiated from the initiate is matrilineal, his natural descent from the mother. This explains why most sacrificial institutions prohibit female participation; participation is viewed as an exclusively male privilege to be established when an initiate kills a victim. The killing forges a special bond between fathers and sons. The new identity is seen as overcoming the chaos and destiny toward death that results from birth from the mother. Communion with the new exclusively male group implicitly confers a kind of immortality. Thus, sacrificial institutions are ways of transcending death. They are also ways of transcending natural birth. Through ritually killing sacrificial victims, sacrificial societies secure symbolic rebirth and figurative immortality for men.

Nancy Jay's single book, published posthumously, offers the first mainstream feminist critique of sacrificial institutions.

"SACRIFICE AND DESCENT," *THROUGHOUT YOUR GENERATIONS FOREVER*

For the Greeks, the essential features of their social world (those that distinguished it equally from the natural and the divine realms) were sacrifice, marriage, and agriculture. In myth these all share the same origin: marriage and agricultural production were consequences of Prometheus's sacrifice ending the Golden Age. Turning from the myth to its social context, from Pandora to the world of young Greek brides, marriage takes on a more precise meaning: it is not a voluntary personal relation between two individuals, but a relation for and between family groups:

Pleasure is not the object of marriage. Its function is quite different: to unite two family groups within the same city, so that a man can have legitimate children who "resemble their father" despite being the issue of their mother's womb, and who will thus be able, on the social and religious level, to continue the line of their father's house to which they belong. (Vernant 1980: 136.)

The unfortunate defect of being "the issue of their mother's womb" is a quality children share with the beasts. Wild animals also have a mother, "to whom they are linked by the natural animal bond of childbirth; but they have no father. Without marriage there can be no paternal filiation, no male line of descent, no family, all of which presuppose a link which is not natural, but religious and social" (ibid.: 138). The sexual promiscuity of the beasts is precisely the absence of the patrilineal family, and the male purity of the Golden Age is the ideal principle of that family carried to level of absolute perfection. Letting "P" stand for patriliny, the three-tiered structure can be written this way:

Wild (natural level)	Social (religious level)	Golden Age (divine level)
$-P$	$+P$	P^n
Unregulated sex	Regulated sex	Male purity
Death	Social continuity	Immortality

This structure encodes mortality just as it does sexuality. The social and religious continuity of the patrilineal family gives males an attenuated form of immortality in the institutionalized succession of fathers and sons. The beasts, recognizing no fathers, have no continuity at all to mitigate individual mortality. On the other hand, if children only resembled their fathers perfectly they would be identical younger versions, cloning younger exact duplicates in their turn, and the Golden Age of male immortality would have returned. It is only mothers, bearing mortal children, who dim this glorious vision of eternal and perfect patriliny. Remember Pandora: because of a woman, men are mortal.

Only in myth is the fatal flaw of having been born of woman overcome. Herakles was sacrificing bulls to his father, Zeus, when the fire ignited a poisoned shirt his wife had given him. In Ovid's account he bears his Latin name, Hercules:

> All that his mother gave him burned away.
> Only the image of his father's likeness
> Rose from the ashes of his funeral pyre.

So Hercules stepped free of mortal being

And with an air of gravity and power
Grew tall, magnificent as any god.
—*Metamorphoses*, 1958: 248

Purified by the fire (almost like bones and fat), Herakles became a heavenly god. As both mortal hero and immortal god, he received both chthonic and Olympic sacrifice.

That women destroy the ideal of perfect patrilineal continuity has a real foundation in Greek social organization. Women (who fail in such glaring ways to resemble the father) do not contribute to the continuity of their own family line. The above quotation from Vernant needs correction: it is not "legitimate children" but only legitimate sons who "continue the line of their father's house to which they belong." Women marry outside their own family and bear children for the continuity of a different family. Children are born not just of women, but of outsiders. For any boy, "all that his mother gave him" pollutes the purity of the paternal line.

The starkness of the Greek womb/tomb equation is probably unrivaled, but all over the world social structures idealizing "eternal" male intergenerational continuity meet a fundamental obstacle in their necessary dependence on women's reproductive powers. There are various ways to organize over or around this obstacle, to transcend it. Many societies value continuity flowing unilineally from father to son to son's son, and these are probably the most common contexts for intensively sacrificial religions. But they are not the only ones. Even in settings where various kinds of descent through women are valued, and also in social organizations with no actual family base (such as the clerical hierarchy of the Roman Church), sacrificing produces and reproduces forms of intergenerational continuity generated by males, transmitted through males, and transcending continuity through women.

It is important to recognize that all the different ways people create enduring continuity between generations cannot really be sorted into categories like "patrilineal," "matrilineal," or "bilateral." Chapter 2 [of the book *Throughout Your Generations Forever*] emphasizes that the terms "communion" and "expiation" do not actually describe any real sacrifice. They are only abstractions, lenses to look through. What is true of sacrificial traditions is true also of kinship traditions: they are so diverse that concrete general categories become impossible. There is not one real statistical typification "patriliny"; there are countless *different* normative ways in which people envision continuity between fathers and sons and value this intergenerational link as especially important for inheritance, political control, and other forms of social organization. There are also all the ways people do not conform to family norms. For example, Greek brides normatively married outside "the line of their father's house." But marriage inside the extended family did sometimes occur in Athens, especially in the case of an heiress, to keep the dowry in the family (Cantarella 1987: 45). When I use a term like "patrilineal" then, it is only an ideal type, not a real one, a lens for looking at a great variety of different ways of valuing father-son continuity, and of even more ways of leading real family lives.

A century ago W. Robertson Smith recognized an affinity between patriliny and sacrifice. In *The Religion of the Semites* they are so closely linked that he could not err about one without simultaneously distorting the other. Following Wellhausen, Robertson Smith believed that all sacrifice was originally clan sacrifice (1972: 284). Rejecting his contemporaries' utilitarian theories of sacrifice as gift (or even bribery: *do ut des*), he claimed that the purpose of sacrifice was to create and maintain relationships of kinship between "men" and their gods. He did not consider that sacrifice might create and maintain kinship between men and men. He took that kinship for granted as "natural." Nor did he distinguish between the "principle of kinship" and the "tie of blood." There was no difference, for him, between consanguineal relatedness and the ordering of society according to the selective, normative systems that actual kinship groups create and maintain. By his "tie of blood" he meant only unilineal descent. But since this was, for him, "natural" kinship, he did not consider that biological descent had already been (socially and religiously) transformed into something else.

In common with most theorists of his time, he believed that originally everyone recognized only descent from mothers. The possibilities for sacrifice in such a society are limited, however, for "the children are of the mother's kin and have no communion of blood religion with the father. In such a society there is hardly any family life, and there can be no sacred household meal" ibid.: 178). At some unspecified time, and in some unknown way, almost everyone but a few very primitive groups switched to patrilineal descent, still considered by Smith only as a natural blood tie, not as an achievement. It is on the father-son relation that the sacrificial relation of deity to worshiper is founded, although it was later expanded to include patron-client, master-servant, and king-subject.

Smith's lengthy treatment of relations between worshiper and deity was limited to consanguineal and derivative relations. He did not consider marriage as a possible model. Nor did he mention relations between affines (persons and groups related to one another by marriage). Smith's kinship systems are so thoroughly unilineal that there are no affines anywhere, and consequently, no problems of affinal relations in unilineal descent. In fact, "the members of one kindred looked on themselves as one living whole, a single animated mass of blood, flesh and bones" (ibid.: 274). Nowhere in *The Religion of the Semites* is there any indication of how these utterly united kin groups are related to, and differentiated from, other such groups.

For Smith, all kinship relations were entirely benign. In spite of Cain and Abel, Jacob and Esau, Joseph and brethren, and many others, this Hebrew Bible scholar was serenely convinced that "those in whose veins the same life-blood circulates cannot be other than friends bound to serve each other in all the offices of brotherhood" (ibid.: 398). Kinship relations with deities are equally benign. "The habitual temper of the worshippers is one of joyous confidence in their god, untroubled by any habitual sense of human guil . . . ancient religion assumes that ordinary acts of worship are all brightness and hilarity" (ibid.: 255, 257).

In identifying "natural" kinship with totally homogeneous, affineless unilineal descent, and in purging kin relations of all guilt, envy, hatred, and terror, Smith had already done all the work of sacrifice. His purifying process was so complete before anyone killed a victim that there was nothing left to expiate, to get rid of, from kinship structure or from religious life. The clean had already been wholly separated from the unclean. His preliminary atoning work was so perfect that there was no room left for atonement itself. As he himself said, "There was no occasion and no place for a special class of atoning sacrifices" (ibid.: 360). Atonement, expiation, sin offerings, and all the dark side of sacrifice was only a later, secondary development, a consequence of the "Assyrian catastrophe" and the despair that followed the Babylonian exile. As well as being historically inaccurate, this at-one-ment without atonement is logically and sacrificially impossible. Smith had created a Golden Age of his own among the Semites.

A peculiar mixture of error, erudition, and profound insight, *The Religion of the Semites* has been regularly denounced for the last seventy years. Smith has been condemned for leading astray biblical scholars, anthropologists, sociologists, psychoanalysts, and theologians. But bad scholarship is usually forgotten. If his work continued to trouble people, it was because his central idea was partly correct. He was right in linking sacrifice with kinship, even with kinds of kinship rather like what he described: clearly defined patrilineal descent systems, commonly excluding mothers and affines. Although his inattention to kin group differentiation, and to affinal relations, led Smith into absurdities, even his "single animated mass of blood, flesh and bones" has some real basis when the unity is conceived as social, religious, or moral, rather than as physical. (A corporate unilineal descent group, seen from the outside, says Meyer Fortes, "might be defined as a single legal personality.") No matter how corporate, a patrilineage is never "a physical unity of life." Nor is unilineal descent natural, but social and religious. And sacrificing orders relations within and between lines of human fathers and sons, between men and men, at least as effectively as it does relations between men and their divinities.

Maintaining normative modes of family continuity through male or female lines ("unilineal descent") glosses only some of the ways people may order social relations in terms of descent. Descent "systems" are all ideal ways of ordering the social relations of reproduction, and, as is true of all forms of social organization, unilineal descent is associated with specific kinds of economic production. The varieties of enduring intergenerational continuity such groups strive for may be glossed as "lineage" organization. Lineage organization is particularly efficient for control and transmission by inheritance of productive property such as farmland and livestock herds, and also of gainful monopolized skills, including priestly skills and political office. Such enduring descent groups (and blood-sacrificial religions too) are not of significance among people relatively unconcerned with inheritance of important productive property, such as hunter-gatherers, who have little durable property. Nor do they usually survive the introduction of a modern economy with occupational differentiation and monetary media of exchange. Like blood-sacrificial religions, such enduring family groups are concentrated among preindustrial societies with some degree of technological development, in which rights in durable property are highly valued. The symbolic structure in which the Geeks linked agriculture, patriliny, and sacrifice may be unique, but control of agricultural property by patrilineal descent groups as a material base of sacrificial religion is found around the world and across a wide range of societies. These range from extremely poor subsistence farmers, with no central government at all, to highly sophisticated societies like pre-revolutionary China.

Because these are all family groups, the control of the means of production is inseparably linked with the control of the means of reproduction, that is, the fertility of women. As Fortes says,

> I have several times remarked on the connection generally found between lineage structure and the ownership of the most valued productive property of the society, whether it be land, or cattle, or even the monopoly of a craft like blacksmithing. . . . A similar connection is found between lineage organization and control over reproductive resources and relations. (1953: 35)

(For "reproductive resources," read "childbearing women.") "Rights over the reproductive powers of women," says Fortes, "are easily regulated by a descent group system" (ibid.: 30).

The social relations of production may be much the same whether intergenerational continuity through men or through women is more highly valued. But the social relations of reproduction will differ between "matrilineages" and "patrilineages," since matrilineages divide men's rights over women's bodies between brothers and husbands, who are ordinarily members of different lineages. In this sense the identity of the group controlling productive and reproductive property is always imperfect in matrilineages.

It should be recognized that although the different kinds of groups glossed as "patrilineages" are patriarchies, "matrilineages" are not matriarchies. Men ordinarily hold the major positions of authority in matrilineages as well as in patrilineages. It is the descent of authority, and of property, which differs: in patrilineages it is from father to son, in matrilineages from uncle to nephew, from mother's brother to sister's son. Both systems are ways of formally connecting men with women as childbearers, that is, ways of organizing intergenerational continuity between men and men in the face of the fact that it is women who give birth and with whom the next generation begins life already in close relation. Both systems are ways in which men regulate rights over women's reproductive powers, but in matrilineal descent systems these rights are divided: the man with rights of sexual access and the man and group with rights in the offspring are not the same.

Although obviously both types of unilineal descent, father to son and mother's brother to sister's son, are equally dependent on women's powers of reproduction for their continuity, this dependence is structurally recognized in matrilineal descent, but transcended in patrilineal descent. Rights of membership in a matrilineage may be determined by birth alone, providing sure knowledge of maternity. Paternity never has the same natural certainty, and birth by itself cannot be the sole criterion for patrilineage membership. No enduring social structure can be built only upon the shifting sands of that uncertain relation, biological paternity. Social paternity and biological paternity may, and often do, coincide, but it is social paternity that determines patrilineage membership. Some sacrificing societies, such as the Romans or the Nuer, distinguish between biological and social paternity in their vocabulary; for example, the Latin distinction between (biological) *genitor* and (social) *pater*. Only the *pater* was significant sacrificially.

Unilineal descent groups are not concerned merely with an existing order, but with its continuity through time, generation succeeding generation. When the crucial intergenerational link is between father and son, for which birth by itself cannot provide sure evidence, sacrificing may be considered essential for the continuity of the social order. What is needed to provide clear evidence of social and religious paternity is an act as definite and available to the senses as is birth. When membership in patrilineal descent groups is identified by rights of participation in blood sacrifice, evidence of "paternity" is created which is as certain as evidence of maternity, but far more flexible.

Consider patrilineal ancestor cults, whose powerful affinity with sacrificial ritual is widely recognized. Ancestral sacrifice ritually indexes patrilineage boundaries (keeps the difference between members and not-members) by distinguishing between those who have rights to participate and those who do not, and at the same time extends the temporal continuity of the lineage beyond its living members to include the dead.

Sacrificial ancestor cults are commonly features of corporate descent groups whose members are tired to a certain locality by inherited farmland, and also often by ancestral graves. Right of participation in sacrifices can also identify patrilineage membership even when the lineage is not a corporate group and is not clearly defined territorially, but in this case there may not be an ancestor cult, and sacrifice, more "spiritual" as the group is less corporate, may be offered to divinities. The Nuer and Dinka are examples. Sacrificing may be the exclusive privilege of only one descent group in a society: a hereditary priesthood, who may keep their own lineage boundaries absolutely clear while other, non-sacrificing descent groups in the same society lose such clearly defined identity. In this case the ideology of eternal genealogical continuity is also centered in the priesthood. The Israelite Aaronid priesthood is an example.

Sacrificing can identify, and maintain through time, not only social structures whose continuity flows through fathers and sons but also other forms of male to male succession that transcend dependence on childbearing women. Because it identifies social and religious descent, rather than biological descent, sacrificing can identify membership in groups with no presumption of actual family descent. This is the case with the sacrifice of the Mass, offered by members of a formally institutionalized "lineage," the apostolic succession of the clergy in the Roman Church. This social organization is a truly perfect "eternal line of descent," in which authority descends from father to father, through the one "Son made perfect forever," in a line no longer directly dependent on women's reproductive powers for continuity.

Sacrificial ritual can serve in various ways as warrant of, and therefore as means of creating, patrilineal descent—as a principle of social organization, not as a fact of nature. When sacrifice works in this performative way it is what Thomas Aquinas called an "effective sign," one that causes what it signifies: in this case, patrilineage membership (*Summa Theologica*, III, Q62: 1). For Thomas, as well as for tribal sacrificers, the effective work of symbolic action is, of course, reflexively dependent on the existence of other structures (social, religious, linguistic, legal, etc.). That is, sacrifice does not "cause" patrilineage membership where there are not patrilineages.

Sacrifice cannot be infallible evidence of begetting and therefore obviously cannot constitute biological paternity. It is the social relations of reproduction, not biological reproduction, that sacrificial ritual can create and maintain. Where the state and the social relations of production are not separable from patrilineally organized social relations of reproduction, the entire social order may be understood as dependent on sacrifice. "Not just the religious cult but the order of society itself takes shape in sacrifice," says Burkert of the Greeks (1983: 84). This is also true of other entirely unrelated societies, such as nineteenth-century West African city states like Benin and Dahomey and twentieth-century subsistence farmers or pastoral cattle herders, without urban development or centralized organization. The particular Greek elaboration of alimentary symbolism is surely unique, but Detienne's observation that "the city as a whole identifies itself by the eating of meat" (1979b: ix) accurately describes sacrificial maintenance of social organization in other traditions and other societies. The Israelite priesthood, for example, identified itself by eating of meat (the "edible" sin offerings), and so did and do different kinds of patrilineal groups in Africa, Europe, Asia, and the New World.

When a form of social organization is dependent on sacrifice for its identification and maintenance, it can also be lost by failure to sacrifice, and improper sacrifice can endanger it. As Detienne says, "To abstain from eating meat in the Greek city-state is a highly subversive act" (1979b: 72). Georges Dumézil tells the sad story of the end of a Roman family. An official named Appius Claudius persuaded the family to sell its private sacrificial cult to the state for public use.

> According to Festus ... Appius Claudius went blind, and within the year all members of the selling family died. . . .
> Thenceforth it was the urban proctor who each year made the offering of an ox (or a heifer) in the name of Rome. (1979: 435)

According to Dumézil, "Some think . . .that we must understand [this account] by reversing the order of events." That is, the state only assumed control of the cult because the proprietary family had already died out.

But the story's order of events (although not their speed) is quite possibly correct. Having lost its ritual means of identification, and with it the ritual entail of its property, the family line itself disappeared— ot as a number of biological individuals but as the particular kind of social organization it was.

Consider a cautionary tale from M. Herskovits about the problems of maintaining patrilineal descent in the West African kingdom of Dahomey. Only certain ritual specialists could touch victims which had been offered to the ancestors and hope to survive the contact. Without these specialists there could be no sacrifice, but training them involved a long course of rituals in a specially constructed cult house for the dead. This course of training was undertaken as seldom as possible because of the great danger involved, both from the intensity of relations with the ancestral dead and also from the possibility of committing a fatal ritual error. The royal ancestor cult was the apex of the hierarchy of all ancestor cults in the kingdom, and consequently it was the duty of the king to officiate in the centralized training of the kingdom's ancestor cult specialists. After French colonizers ended the monarchy, the head of the royal patrilineal descent group, or sib, continued in the ritual position of the king. In the early thirties, when Herskovits was in Dahomey, the head of the royal sib had neglected to perform his ritual duty of building the cult house because, even if he did not die at once as a consequence of committing some ritual error, he would in any case die soon after from such prolonged and intense contact with the dead.

> This last cult house for the ancestors of the entire kingdom was established so many years ago that most of those who received this training are dead, and it is urgent that another soon be instituted, though it is believed that this will hasten the death of the head of the royal family. In the last one, it is said, some three thousand initiates came from . . . each sib all over the kingdom. . . . When the last of these, now old, die, there will be no one able to touch a sacrificial animal, and thus will even greater evil befall all Dahomeans, and the entire royal family will die out. (1938, vol. I: 228)

This final prophecy of doom is not mere superstition. If the cult house were not built, if the prerequisite for continued sacrifice were not met, the royal sib might indeed die out. The biological individuals forming its membership need not die, but the royal sib, as a social organization constituted and maintained by sacrifice, dependent on repeated sacrifice for its "eternal" continuity, would decay with the end of sacrificing. Evils would befall all Dahomeans because all Dahomean kinships organization was sacrificially maintained and was organized in relation to the royal sib.

Only the Aztecs outdid the Dahomeans in volume, compulsiveness, and cruelty of sacrificing. Dahomean religion was not representative of sacrificial religion, it was an exaggeration of it, a concentration and intensification of many features which occur selectively and less starkly in many other sacrificing societies. In Dahomey, says Herskovits, a child "legally stands in no relation whatever to its mother's kin" (ibid. 153). This is certainly unusual, as is also the degree of continuity with the dead and the desperateness of dependence on sacrifice for maintenance of the social order. All these are only exaggerations of what could be called a common sacrificial principle: that it is by participation in the rule-governed (moral, not biological) relatedness of father and son in a ritually defined social order, enduring continuously through time, that birth and death (continually changing for the membership of the "eternal" lineage) and all other threats of social chaos may be overcome.

Man born of woman may be destined to die, but man integrated into an "eternal" social order to that degree transcends mortality. I use the word "man" advisedly, for in sacrificially maintained descent groups, "immortality," which may be no more than the memory of a name in a genealogy, is commonly a masculine privilege. It is through fathers and sons, not through mothers and daughters, that "eternal" social continuity is maintained. Daughters, who will marry out, are not members of the lineage in the same way as their brothers, nor do their mothers have full membership in their husbands' and sons' lineage. Where participation in "eternal" social continuity is a paternal inheritance, mortality itself may be phrased as a maternal inheritance. (As Job said (14: 1,4), "Man that is born of woman is of few days, and full of trouble .... Who can bring a clean thing out of an unclean?")

Exogamous patrilineal groups, whose members find wives from outside the group, are utterly dependent on alien women for their continuity. But if decent from these women were given full social recognition, the patrilineage would have no boundaries, no identity, and no recognizable continuity. The integration of any unilineal descent group, its continuity through time as the same, as one, can only be accomplished by differentiation from other such groups. There is necessarily an "either/or" about lineage membership (members must be distinguished from not-members), and for patriliny, this either/or requires transcending descent from women.

The twofold movement of sacrifice, integration and differentiation, communion and expiation, is beautifully suited for identifying and maintaining patrilineal descent. Sacrifice can expiate, get rid of, the consequences of having been born of woman (along with countless other dangers) and at the same time integrate the pure and eternal patrilineage.

Sacrificially constituted descent, incorporating women's mortal children into an "eternal" (enduring through generations) kin group, in which membership is recognized by participation in sacrificial ritual, not merely by birth, enables a patrilineal group to transcend mortality in the same process in which it transcends birth. In this sense, sacrifice is doubly a remedy for having been born of woman.

23

ELAINE SCARRY

THE SURPRISING KINSHIP between biblical literature and the work of torturers is one of the intriguing themes explored by Elaine Scarry (1946–)
in *The Body in Pain*. Scarry begins with an examination of the pre-
articulate and private nature of pain—verbally inexpressible and yet absolutely certain for the one experiencing it. After the pain, victims may
offer analogies ("it was like a flame," "it was like a knife"), but witnesses
can only imagine the experience behind these analogies, or project their
own imaginations into the victim's inarticulate screams, cries, and gasps.
For Scarry, the immediate incommunicability of pain is the locus for the
destruction of worlds. Torturers who inflict pain are able to destroy the
layers of conceptualization, interpretation, and imagination that a culture builds up for its members. The victim is reduced to a figurative blank
slate, vulnerable to reinscription by torturers who impress their own
worlds—as in their own pictures and understandings of reality—onto the
victim. The torturer also lifts the objectified attributes of the prisoner's
pain—such as its totalizing power and its incontestable reality—away
from the prisoner and confers them on the regime: now it seems the
regime (not the pain) that has power, the regime (not the pain) that
seems real.

In the following excerpt from *The Body in Pain*, Scarry analyzes the
body of creation and the voice of creator in biblical narratives that show
the figurative making and unmaking of worlds through pain and punishment. The intensification of bodily pain is associated with the generation
of community and the inexorable power of a creator so frequently as to
constitute a biblical habit of mind, says Scarry. Such biblical narratives
do more than illustrate the rigors of belief. Rather, they reveal profound
patterns of constructing God and reality in Western imagination. Scarry's
analysis of biblical scenes of wounding—reprinted here—is in *The Body
and Pain* preceded and followed by benign models of validating God's
existence through two forms of creation, bodily reproduction and the
making of material artifacts.

As Walter M. Cabot Professor of Aesthetics at Harvard University,
Elaine Scarry enjoys a reputation as an intrepid explorer into wide realms
of intellectual inquiry. Her subjects range from war and torture to beauty
and creation.

FROM *THE BODY IN PAIN*

Body and Voice in the Judeo-Christian Scriptures
and the Writings of Marx

The Hebrew scriptures, along with the Christian scriptures they gave rise to, are among all the singular artifacts of western civilization perhaps the single most monumental, for they can be credited with sponsoring a civilization to a degree shared by no other isolated verbal text (*Hamlet, War and Peace*, the United States Constitution) or by any isolated material object (the pyramids, the Panama Canal, the Brooklyn Bridge). Although, however, they are themselves a monumental artifact, they are at the same time a monumental description of the nature of artifice. Product of the human imagination, they are also a tireless laying bare of the workings of the imagination, not merely the record of its aspirations toward disembodiment or of its origins in pain but, more concretely, the record of the very sequence of stages and substitutions by which it regulates and promotes its own acts of self-modification.

As will gradually become apparent over the course of the present chapter, the scriptures can be understood as narratives about created objects that enable the major created object, namely God, to describe the interior structure of all making.

Though scenes of wounding by no means constitute the sole content nor even the major content of these writings, they recur so frequently that no reader, Jewish or Christian, will have failed to notice them, and few readers, Jewish or Christian, will have failed to be troubled by them. God's invisible presence is asserted, made visible, in the perceivable alterations He brings about in the human body: in the necessity of human labor and the pains of childbirth, in a flood that drowns, in a plague that descends on a house, in the brimstone and fire falling down on a city, in the transformation of a woman into a pillar of salt, in the leprous sores and rows of boils that alter the surface of the skin, in an invasion of insects and reptiles into the homes of a population, in a massacre of babies, in a ghastly hunger that causes a people to so glut themselves on quail that meat comes out of their nostrils, in a mauling by bears, in an agonizing disease of the bowels, and so on, on and on. There are, of course, many moments in which God explicitly refrains from an act of wounding, retracts even what is presented as a "deserved" punishment; so, too, there are reassurances about Its mercy and the brief duration of Its anger; there are alternative and profoundly benign images of God ("The Lord is my shepherd"); and above all, the largest framing act of the narrative—the creation and growth of a people and their rescue from their human oppressors—establishes the benevolent context in which these other, themselves terrifying, scenes occur. Yet the positioning of God and humanity at the two vertical ends of the weapon itself recurs so regularly that it seems to become a central and fixed locus toward which and away from which the narrative continually moves. At times, this image seems to define the structure of belief itself. The problematic scenes of hurt, as will be shown, tend to occur in the context of disbelief and doubt: the invisible (and hence periodically disbelieved-in) divine power has a visible substantiation in the alterations in body tissue it is able to bring about. Man can only be created once, but once created, he can be endlessly modified; wounding re-enacts the creation because it re-enacts the power of alteration that has its first profound occurrence in creation.

As an understanding of the nature of material and verbal making requires as prelude attention to the problematic scenes of wounding, so in turn an understanding of these scenes of wounding requires as prelude attention to scenes that center on the growth of the Hebrew population – scenes in which there is a benign alteration in human tissue that comes with procreation, pregnancy, self-replication, and multiplication. Although the nature of what is apprehended to have been the original genesis of man and world is reaffirmed in scenes of hurt, it is also reaffirmed in the human generational act itself, which in its insistent repetitions (especially throughout the opening book of Genesis) becomes the large framing event against which the less frequent but much more problematic scenes of hurt occur. It will become apparent that the two very different kinds of scene, reproduction and wounding, each contain an identifiable relation between the human body and an imagined object (God): in each, the experienceable "reality" of the body is read not as an attribute of the body but as an attribute of its metaphysical referent. The constancy of this relation across the two scenes may explain how the Old Testament mind arrived at its otherwise inexplicable dependence on the rhythmic invocation of scenes of hurt: that is, it may be that such scenes are introduced in order to perpetuate a relation between body and belief once the "begat" sequences can no longer be called on to provide the needed confirmation (as after Genesis, where the next four books of the Torah have as their subject a single generation of the Hebrew people).

Scenes of Wounding and the Problem of Doubt

Sometimes as one reads through the Hebraic scriptures, God's existence seems so absolute and human belief in that existence so assumed and widely shared that doubt within the story of any one individual's life or any one epoch seems like only a small tear in the page, a tiny fold in an almost invisible shred of tissue in the heart, the dropping of a single stitch in the endless rounds of a woven cloth. God's realness, His presence, seems so steady, so immediately available for apprehension, that the individual person or group that fails to apprehend Him seems only an idiosyncratic exception, perversely denying of what is obvious. Yet at other readings—perhaps even almost simultaneously—it seems as though what is on every page described in these writings is the incredible difficulty, the feat of the imagination and agony of labor required in generating an idea of God and holding it steadily in place (hour by hour, day by day) without any graphic image to assist the would-be believer.

Just as the overwhelming power of alteration in the original creation brought forth the physical earth and the species man, so the land and man continue to be two canvases on which God's power of alteration continually re-manifests itself. The subsequent alterations of the land recur not only in Genesis (the flood that for a time obliterates the earth's surface, making it when it again appears a "new" thing) but periodically throughout later books: "The uneven ground shall become level, and the rough places a plain. And the glory of the Lord shall be revealed" (Isaiah 40:4, 5); "What are you, O great mountain? Before Zerubbabel you shall become a plain; and he shall bring forward the top stone amid shouts of 'Grace, grace to it'" (Zechariah 4:7). So, too, this power of alteration repeatedly manifests itself across the surface of the human body.

> Their flesh shall rot while they are still on their feet, their eyes shall rot in their sockets, and their tongues shall rot in their mouths. And on that day a great panic from the Lord shall fall on them, so that each will lay hold on the hand of his fellow, and the hand of the one will be raised against the hand of the other; even Judah will fight against Jerusalem (Zechariah 14:12–14).

Perhaps the continual movement of the people across the land is itself a conflation of the two locations of alteration, land and body. Many of the Genesis chapters open with the instruction to "Arise and go" from this place to another (12, 26, 28, 31, 35, 46). This physical movement, which continues in later books, re-enacts the idea of original world creation because there is a sense of erasing, wiping away, the ground of events, beginning again, starting over. When Moses records the history of the people, he does so by writing down their "starting places" (Numbers 33: 1,2); and the repeated language of "starting places" also calls attention to the kinship between this event and bodily reproduction, the connection between the movement of extending-outward (or going forth) and the movement of extending outward from the "lap of birth," a different kind of "starting place."

It is, however, not the surface of the land but the surface of the body that will be attended to in this section. Throughout the writings of the patriarchs and the prophets, we again and again and again return to a scene of wounding. It is a scene that carries emphatic assurance about the "realness" of God, but one that (for the participants inside) contains nothing that makes his "realness" visible except the wounded human body. The powerful God does not have the power of self-substantiation. The body is not simply an element in a scene of confirmation; it is the confirmation. Apart from the human body, God himself has no material reality except for the countless weapons that he exists on the invisible and disembodied side of. Whether the material object is itself physically present in the story (as in the flaming torch and pot of Genesis 15, or the burning bush of Exodus) or instead verbally invoked (as in the song given by God to Moses in Deuteronomy 32—"I will spend my arrows upon them;/ they shall be wasted with hunger,/ and devoured with burning heat/ and poisonous pestilence . . . If I whet my glittering sword . . . I will make my arrows drunk with blood"), the weapon is a material sign of Him separate from the human body and explaining the path of connection. In this respect, as was suggested earlier, the stories of hurt differ from the stories of reproduction, where there is no immediately available, mediating sign. Here there are many—fire, storm, whirlwind, plague, rod, arrow, knife, sword—and on the other side of these objects, our brooding and terrible heaven. Only the last four objects in this list have the actual physical structure alluded to earlier, a vertical line connecting two radically different ends. But this same structure is implicitly present in all the others as well: a fire, too, has two ends, for at one terminus it is ignited and at the other it burns; just as plague, storm, and wind each has a passive terminus from which it is brought into being and pointed in a certain direction, and an active terminus where it mutilates and imperils.

Across the image of the weapon, the material and the immaterial are severed. As God in the scene of hurt is a bodiless voice, so men and women are voiceless bodies. God is their voice; they have none separate from him. Repeatedly, any capacity for self-transformation into a separate verbal or material form is shattered, as God shatters the building of the tower of Babel by shattering the language of the workers into multiple and mutually uncomprehending tongues (Genesis 11:1–9). The book of Numbers is a book of constant murmuring and complaint:

And the people complained in the hearing of the Lord about their misfortunes; and when the Lord heard it, His anger was kindled. (11:1)

Moses heard the people weeping through their families, every man at the door of his tent; and the anger of the Lord blazed hotly. (11:10)

Then all the congregation raised a loud cry; and the people wept that night. And all the people of Israel murmured against Moses and Aaron . . . "Would that we had died." (14:12)

"How long shall this wicked congregation murmur against me? I have heard the murmurings of the people of Israel, which they murmur against me. . . . [You] who have murmured against me, not one shall come to the land." (14:27, 29, 30)

Their voices whine and murmur. Devoid of any content other than complaint, their utterances are self-trivializing and dissolute, a form of inarticulate pre-language that carries no power to legitimize their suffering, their hunger, their fear, their doubt, their exhaustion, or to legitimize our notice of these things. If their voices were able to form and express these things, the story would be a different story. As it is, their voices deprive them of God's sympathy and of ours: they seem debased and dismissible even if now and then for a moment – as in their expressed longing for meat, fish, melons, cucumbers, leeks, onions, garlic and the longing for a fixed ground that is implicit in this simple enumeration of root fruits (11:5)—one catches a glimpse of the edge of that other story. Physical suffering destroys language, and moral rightness (in the Old Testament as in most other human contexts) tends to lie with the most articulate. So we linger with the people only a moment; then continue on in the hope that their cries will end.

Although an occasion of wounding is often described (within the narrative itself as well as in commentaries on the narrative) as a scene of disobedience and punishment, it is in many ways more comprehensible and accurate to recognize it as a scene of doubt, for it is a failure of belief that continually reoccasions the infliction of hurt. Unable to apprehend God with conviction, they will—after the arrival of the plague or the disease-laden quail or the fire or the sword or the storm—apprehend him in the intensity of the pain in their own bodies, or in the visible alteration in the bodies of their fellows or in the bodies (in only slightly different circumstances) of their enemies. The vocabulary of punishment describes the event only from the divine perspective, obscures the use of the body to make experienceable the metaphysical abstraction whose remoteness has occasioned disbelief.

Moments in which the people have performed an immoral act (other than doubting) and where the idiom of punishment may therefore seem appropriate, must be seen within the frame of the many other moments where the infliction of hurt is explicitly presented as a "sign" of God's realness and therefore a solution to the problem of his unreality, his fictiveness. Such passages openly identify the human body as a source of analogical verification. Specified forms of hurt are overtly presented as demonstrations of His existence:

> And Moses said: "Hereby you shall know that the Lord has sent me to do all these works, and that it has not been of my own accord. If these men die the common death of all men, or if they are visited by the fate of all men, then the Lord has not sent me. But if the Lord creates something new, and the ground opens its mouth and swallows them up, with all that belongs to them, and they go down alive into Sheol, then you shall know that these men have despised the Lord." (Numbers 16:28–30).

The spectacular and self-consciously innovative form of devastation immediately follows (16.31–35). Hurt here, as in many other moments, becomes the vehicle of verification; doubt is eliminated; the incontestable reality of the sensory world becomes the incontestable reality of a world invisible and unable to be touched. Centuries of men and women ready, even longing, to deepen their faith may feel that a small and benign sign, the blossoming of Aaron's rod, would suffice; but belief is not within the mental structures of the Hebraic scriptures an exercise in open choice. As barrenness in the scenes of reproduction may be changed by God to a living presence in the womb, so in the infliction of pain the anterior condition of unfeeling emptiness (doubt) is replaced by an amplification of sentience about which no uncertainty is possible and no decisions need to be made.

This is true whether the hurt actually takes place, as in the narratives of Genesis, Exodus, and Numbers, or whether it takes place in a warning and ritualized form, as in the repeated refrain, "Lest you die," "Lest he die," "Lest I turn my face against you" which follows the enumeration of rules in Leviticus. Moments in the Old Testament where punishment is rendered because of doubt are to a large extent paradigmatic of all other moments of punishment: that is, immoral behavior or disobedience or cruelty are extreme forms of doubt, extreme failures of belief, the failure to absorb into oneself and to embody in one's acts and attitudes a concept of God. To offer incense at a time when this act has been prohibited, to question the authority of the human leader appointed by God, to break a specified rule of ritualized cleansing, to devote one's body to a dance around a golden calf, to turn back for one last look at the cities of Sodom and Gomorrah and their godless behavior, to complain of present hunger and anticipated hunger when one should perceive oneself as under the protection of a bountiful Overseer, are all demonstrations of an inability to incorporate into everyday patterns of gesture and speech a depth and totality of certitude, and thus all demonstrations of doubt. So too to be a foreigner—a second explanation for God's many moments of inflicting hurt—is also an extreme form of disbelief, a state of existing wholly outside the circle of faith.

The failure of belief is, in its many forms, a failure to remake one's own interior in the image of God, to allow God to enter and to alter one's self. Or to phrase it in a slightly different form, it is the refusal or inability to turn oneself inside-out, devoting one's physical interior to something outside itself, calling it by another name. Disobedience or disbelief or doubt in the scriptures is habitually described as a withholding of the body, which in its resistance to an external referent is perceived as covered, or hard, or stiff:

> But they refused to hearken, and turned a stubborn shoulder, and stopped their ears that they might not hear. They made their hearts like adamant lest they should hear the law and the words. . . . (Zechariah 7:11, 12)

> They refused to take correction.
> They have made their faces harder than rock;
> They have refused to repent. (Jeremiah 5:3)

> Blessed is the man who fears the Lord always;
> But he who hardens his heart will fall into
> calamity. (Proverbs 28:14)

> He who is often reproved, yet stiffens his neck
> will suddenly be broken beyond healing. (Proverbs 29:1)

> O that today you would hearken to his voice!
> Harden not your hearts, as at Meribah. . . . (Psalms 95:7, 8)

> Yet they acted presumptuously and did not obey thy
> commandments, but sinned against thy ordinances, by
> the observance of which a man shall live, and
> turned a stubborn shoulder and stiffened their neck
> and would not obey. (Nehemiah 9:29)

> Because I know you are obstinate and your neck is
> an iron sinew and your forehead brass. (Isaiah 48:4)

Perhaps most familiar are the descriptions of the "stiff-necked" Israelites who trouble God while Moses is receiving the ten commandments (Exodus 32:9, 33:3, 33:5, 34:9) and earlier, the opening passages of Exodus in which the Egyptian Pharaoh's refusal to listen, to be moved to belief by the turning of the Nile to blood, the plague of frogs, the invading swarms of gnats and flies, are described in these same terms: "Pharaoh's heart remained hardened and he would not listen" (7:22); "He hardened his heart and would not listen to them" (8:15); "Pharaoh hardened his heart this time also, and did not let the people go" (8:32) "But the heart of the Pharaoh was hardened and he did not let the people go" (9:7). The processes of belief are openly revealed in this story, for the physical hurt is here explicitly designated as a "sign" of God's realness, and even more significantly, the Pharaoh's disbelief in God is itself caused by God in order to occasion the wounding of the Egyptians and thus provide to the watching Israelites the "signs" of God's realness: "I have hardened his heart and the hearts of his servants, that I may show these signs of mine among them, and that you may tell in the hearing of your son and of your son's son how I have made sport of the Egyptians and what signs I have done among them; that you may know that I am the Lord" (10:1,2; see also 10:20; 9:12, 9:35).

In all of the passages cited above, the withholding of the body—the stiffening of the neck, the turning of the shoulder, the closing of the ears, the hardening of the heart, the making of the face like stone—necessitates God's forceful shattering of the reluctant human surface and the repossession of the interior. Perhaps the most overt acting out of this occurs in the final plague on the house of the Pharaoh, the final entry into his hard heart, the massacre of the innocents in which the interior of the body as it emerges in the first-born infant is taken by God (Exodus 12). The fragility of the human interior and the absolute surrender of that interior that does not simply accompany belief, that is not simply required by belief, but that *is itself belief*—the endowing of the most concrete and intimate parts of oneself with an objectified referent, the willing rereading of events within the realm of sentience as themselves attributes of the realm of self-extension and artifice – are in this history acted out with terrible force and unequivocal meaning.

The taking of the Egyptian infants is a few lines later followed by the willing consecration of the Israelite infants, the willing consecration by the Israelites of their own interiors: "The Lord said to Moses, 'Consecrate to me all the first-born; whatever is the first to open the womb among the people of Israel, both of man and of beast is mine'" (13:1, 2).

This, in turn, is itself followed by a second way in which God's entry into the human interior is ensured, the prohibition against leavened bread: "And it shall be to you as a sign on your hand and as a memorial between your eyes, that the Law of the Lord may be in your mouth" (13:9; see also Deuteronomy 11:18). The human child, the human womb, the human hand, the face, the stomach, the mouth, the genitals (themselves circumcised, marked)—it is in the body that God's presence is recorded. Either, as in the case of the Egyptian massacre, the body is unwillingly given and violently entered or, as in the case of the Israelite consecration that follows, it is willingly surrendered.

Although any part of the body may become the focus of this conversion, the essential habit of mind is caught and dramatized in its full force in the stories of the sacrifice of offspring, for here the two extreme forms of physical alteration, self-replication and wounding, converge. It may be in part for this reason that the story of Abraham and Isaac is returned to again and again as containing the central mystery of the Judeo-Christian God. Again, the story does not merely describe the rigors of belief, what is required for belief, but the structure of belief itself, the taking of one's insides and giving them over to something wholly outside oneself, as Abraham agrees to sacrifice the interior of his and Sarah's bodies, and to participate actively in that surrender. The building of the altar externalizes and makes visible the shape of belief; the hidden interior of sentience is lifted out through work into the visible world. Itself the body turned inside-out, it in turn becomes the table on which the body will once more be turned inside-out. Here the stages of materialization, heightened forms of self-presentation, are successively increasing powers of one another. Abraham's three times repeated, "Here I am" is a simple statement of amplified self-presentation. The interior of himself and Sarah—Isaac—is the once heightened and externalized form. Then Isaac himself will be cut open, his own interior exposed. As in the stories of reproduction, we encounter the rhythm of substantiation, more and more emphatic presentation and re-presentation of the body to confer the force and power of the material world on the noumenal and unselfsubstantiating. Who can be ignorant of the risk he takes and the cost he incurs in agreeing to *re-create* God, *to make* an already existing God more immediately apprehensible, to remake of an unapprehensible God an apprehensible One. To be alone on a mountain in the wind and afraid—one might feel only an overwhelming aloneness, the fragility of one's own existence, the distance, dimness, and unreality of God; but the anticipated sight of the interior of the body then makes the dimly apprehended incontestably present; for the object of conviction acquires a compelling and vibrant presence from the compelling and vibrant sequence of actions with which the human willingness to believe, to be convinced, is enacted.

Belief is the act of imagining. It is what the act of imagining is called when the object created is credited with more reality (and all that is entailed in greater "realness," more power, more authority) than oneself. It is when the object created is in fact described as though it instead created you. It ceases to be the "offspring" of the human being and becomes the thing from which the human being himself sprung forth. It is in this act that Isaac yields against all phenomenal assessment to Abraham, that Abraham yields to God, and that the reader yields to the narrative: it is not simply the willingness to give one's interior to something outside oneself but the willingness to become the created offspring of the thing in whose presence one now stands, as Isaac at that moment is not the many things Isaac is but only Isaac-son-of-Abraham, as again Abraham the patriarch, Abraham the husband, Abraham the father of Isaac, Abraham the father of the twelve tribes of Israel all now converge into Abraham-the-created-offspring-of-God, and as the reader in his or her many capacities ceases to be the many things that he or she is and becomes in the stunned and exhausted silence of Genesis 22: 1–19 the created offspring of the text, of this text and of the many stories through which the framework of belief is set in place.

JEAN BAUDRILLARD

ALTHOUGH ASSOCIATED WITH a number of different intellectual movements, the French sociologist Jean Baudrillard (1929–2007) is best known for his interest in modern media and its assault on human consciousness. He has focused on simulacra—an epiphenomenal layer of experience resulting from a numbing blitzkrieg of media-induced images that strip us of contact with "the real." He compares our defenselessness before this onslaught of images to the schizophrenic's break with reality (*America*). We thrash about in a state of helplessness and terror.

Like a schizophrenic patient, the Western television audience was defenseless before the events of September 11, 2001, which Baudrillard saw as a riveting media display of simulated violence that only compounded the actual violence that took the lives of the victims. The events of September 11, 2001 induced Baudrillard to see a destructive impulse as emerging from within the hegemonic power of Western civilization—itself a simulation, a technological self-invention of extraordinary scale. The system had become too elaborate to self-correct and so had imploded "by a kind of unpredictable complicity." In Baudrillard's reckoning, modern society helped to create the conditions in which the attack could be perpetrated and hence joined in "the game of terrorism" ("Requiem for the Twin Towers," in *The Spirit of Terrorism and Other* Essays).

In the excerpt, Baudrillard refers to terrorism as an amoral reclamation of terms and "a terroristic situational transfer." The 9/11 event had nothing to do with Islam, Baudrillard claimed; if Islam were a power so dominant, so invasive of all symbolic spheres, it too would have been attacked. This reasoning leads Baudrillard to the conclusion that the revolt launched by the Muslim activists participating in the 9/11 attack was not ideological but rather an instinctive response to Western dominion in all spheres of life.

FROM *THE SPIRIT OF TERRORISM*

When it comes to world events, we had seen quite a few. From the death of Diana to the World Cup. And violent, real events, from wars right through to genocides. Yet, when it comes to symbolic events on a world scale–that is to say not just events that gain worldwide coverage, but events that represent a setback for globalization itself–we had had none. Throughout the stagnation of the 1990s, events were "on strike" (as the

Argentinian writer Macedonio Fernandez put it). Well, the strike is over now. Events are not on strike any more. With the attacks on the World Trade Center in New York, we might even be said to have before us the absolute event, the "mother" of all events, the pure event uniting within itself all the events that have never taken place.

The whole play of history and power is disrupted by this event, but so, too, are the conditions of analysis. You have to take your time. While events were stagnating, you had to anticipate and move more quickly than they did. But when they speed up this much, you have to move more slowly-- though without allowing yourself to be buried beneath a welter of words, or the gathering clouds of war, and preserving intact the unforgettable incandescence of the images.

All that has been said and written is evidence of gigantic abreaction to the event itself, and the fascination it exerts. The moral condemnation and the holy alliance against terrorism are on the same scale as the prodigious jubilation at seeing this global superpower destroyed--better, at seeing it, in a sense, destroying itself, committing suicide in a blaze of glory. For it is that superpower which, by its unbearable power, has fomented all this violence which is endemic throughout the world, and hence that (unwittingly) terroristic imagination which dwells in all of us.

The fact that we have dreamt of this event, that everyone without exception has dreamt of it–because no one can avoid dreaming of the destruction of any power that has become hegemonic to this degree–is unacceptable to the Western moral conscience. Yet it is a fact, and one which can indeed be measured by the emotive violence of all that has been said and written in the effort to dispel it.

At a pinch, we can say that they *did it*, but we *wished for* it. If this is not taken into account, the event loses any symbolic dimension. It becomes a pure accident, a purely arbitrary act, the murderous phantasmagoria of a few fanatics, and all that would then remain would be to eliminate them. Now, we know very well that this is not how it is. Which explains all the counterphobic ravings about exorcizing evil: it is because it is there, everywhere, like an obscure object of desire. Without this deep-seated complicity, the event would not have had the resonance it has, and in their symbolic strategy the terrorists doubtless know that they can count on this unavowable complicity.

This goes far beyond hatred for the dominant world power among the disinherited and the exploited, among those who have ended up on the wrong side of the global order. Even those who share in the advantages of that order have this malicious desire in their hearts. Allergy to any definitive order, to any definitive power, is–happily–universal, and the two towers of the World Trade Center were perfect embodiments, in their very twinness, of that definitive order.

No need, then, for a death drive or a destructive instinct, or even for perverse, unintended effects, Very logically–and inexorably–the increase in the power of power heightens the will to destroy it. And it was party to its own destruction. When the two towers collapsed, you had the impression that they were responding to the suicide of the suicide-planes with their own suicides. It has been said that "Even God cannot declare war on Himself." Well, He can. The West, in the position of God (divine omnipotence and absolute moral legitimacy), has become suicidal, and declared war on itself.

The countless disaster movies bear witness to this fantasy, which they clearly attempt to exorcize with images, drowning out the whole thing with special effects. But the universal attraction they exert, which is on a par with pornography, shows that acting-out is never very far away, the impulse to reject any system growing all the stronger as it approaches perfection or omnipotence.

It is probable that the terrorists had not foreseen the collapse of the Twin Towers (any more than had the experts!), a collapse which–much more than the attack on the Pentagon–had the greatest symbolic impact. The symbolic collapse of a whole system came about by an unpredictable complicity, as though the towers, by collapsing on their own, by committing suicide, had joined in to round off the event. In a sense, the entire system, by its internal fragility, lent the initial action a helping hand.

The more concentrated the system becomes globally, ultimately forming one single network, the more it becomes vulnerable at a single point (already a single little Filipino hacker had managed, from the dark recesses of his portable computer, to launch the "I love you" virus, which circled the globe devastating entire networks). Here it was eighteen suicide attackers who, thanks to the absolute weapon of death, enhanced by technological efficiency, unleashed a global catastrophic process.

When global power monopolizes the situation to this extent, when there is such a formidable condensation of all functions in the technocratic machinery, and when no alternative form of thinking is allowed, what other way is there but a *terroristic situational transfer*? It was the system itself which created the objective conditions for this brutal retaliation. By seizing all the cards for itself, it forced the Other to change the rules. And the new rules are fierce ones, because the stakes are fierce. To a system whose very excess of power poses an insoluble challenge, the terrorists respond with a definitive act which is also not susceptible of exchange. Terrorism is the act that restores an irreducible singularity to the heart of a system of generalized exchange. All the singularities (species, individuals and cultures) that have paid with their deaths for the installation of a global circulation governed by a single power are taking their revenge today through this *terroristic situational transfer*.

This is terror against terror–there is no longer any ideology behind it. We are far beyond ideology and politics now. No ideology, no cause–not even the Islamic cause–can account for the energy which fuels terror. The aim is no longer even to transform the world, but (as the heresies did in their day) to radicalize the world by sacrifice. Whereas the system aims to realize it by force.

Terrorism, like viruses, is everywhere. There is a global perfusion of terrorism, which accompanies any system of domination as though it were its shadow, ready to activate itself anywhere, like a double agent. We can no longer draw a demarcation line around it. It is at the very heart of this culture which combats it, and the visible fracture (and the hatred) that pits the exploited and the underdeveloped globally against the Western world secretly connects with the fracture internal to the dominant system. The system can face down any visible antagonism. But against the other kind, which is viral in structure–as though every machinery of domination secreted its own counterapparatus, the agent of its own disappearance— against that form of almost automatic reversion of its own power, the system can do nothing. And terrorism is the shock wave of this silent reversion.

This is not, then, a clash of civilizations or religions, and it reaches far beyond Islam and America, on which efforts are being made to focus the conflict in order to create the delusion of a visible confrontation and a solution based on force. There is, indeed, a fundamental antagonism here, but one which points past the spectre of America (which is, perhaps, the epicentre, but in no sense the sole embodiment, of globalization) and the spectre of Islam (which is not the embodiment of terrorism either), to *triumphant globalization battling against itself*. In this sense, we can indeed speak of a world war–not the Third World War, but the Fourth and the only really global one, since what is at stake is globalization itself. The first two world wars corresponded to the classical image of war. The first ended the supremacy of Europe and the colonial era. The second put an end to Nazism. The third, which has indeed taken place, in the form of cold war and deterrence, put an end to Communism. With each succeeding war, we have moved further towards a single world order. Today that order, which has virtually reached its culmination, finds itself grappling with the antagonistic forces scattered throughout the very heartlands of the global, in all the current convulsions. A fractal war of all cells, all singularities, revolting in the form of antibodies. A confrontation so impossible to pin down that the idea of war has to be rescued from time to time by spectacular set-pieces, such as the Gulf War or the war in Afghanistan. But the Fourth World War is elsewhere. It is what haunts every world order, all hegemonic domination–if Islam dominated the world, terrorism would rise against Islam, *for it is the world, the globe itself, which resists globalization.*

Terrorism is immoral. The World Trade Center event, that symbolic challenge, is immoral, and it is a response to a globalization which is itself immoral. So, let us be immoral; and if we want to have some understanding of all this, let us go and take a little look beyond Good and Evil. When, for once, we have an event that defies not just morality, but any form of interpretation, let us try to approach it with an understanding of Evil.

This is precisely where the crucial point lies–in the total misunderstanding on the part of Western philosophy, on the part of the Enlightenment, of the relation between Good and Evil. We believe naively that the progress of Good, its advance in all fields (the sciences, technology, democracy, human rights), corresponds to a defeat of Evil. No one seems to have understood that Good and Evil advance together, as part of the same movement. The triumph of the one does not eclipse the other–far from it. In metaphysical terms, Evil is regarded as an accidental mishap, but this axiom, from which all the Manichean forms of the struggle of Good against Evil derive, is illusory. Good does not conquer Evil, nor indeed does the reverse happen: they are at once both irreducible to each other and inextricably interrelated. Ultimately, Good could thwart Evil only by ceasing to be Good since, by seizing for itself a global monopoly of power, it gives rise, by that very act, to a blowback of a proportionate violence.

In the traditional universe, there was still a balance between Good and Evil, in accordance with a dialectical relation which maintained the tension and equilibrium of the moral universe, come what may–not unlike the way the confrontation of the two powers in the Cold War maintained the balance of terror. There was, then, no supremacy of the one over the other. As soon as there was a total extrapolation of Good (hegemony of the positive over any form of negativity, exclusion of death and of any potential adverse force–triumph of the values of Good all along the line), that balance was upset. From this point on, the equilibrium was gone, and it was as though Evil regained an invisible autonomy, henceforward developing exponentially.

Relatively speaking, this is more or less what has happened in the political order with the eclipse of Communism and the global triumph of liberal power: it was at that point that a ghostly enemy emerged, infiltrating itself throughout the whole planet, slipping in everywhere like a virus, welling up from all the interstices of power: Islam. But Islam was merely the moving front along which the antagonism crystallized. The antagonism is everywhere, and in every one of us. So, it is terror against terror.

But asymmetric terror. And it is this asymmetry which leaves global omnipotence entirely disarmed. At odds with itself, it can only plunge further into its own logic of relations of force, but it cannot operate on the terrain of the symbolic challenge and death–a thing of which it no longer has any idea, since it has erased it from its own culture.

Up to the present, this integrative power has largely succeeded in absorbing and resolving any crisis, any negativity, creating, as it did so, a situation of the deepest despair (not only for the disinherited, but for the pampered and privileged too, in their radical comfort). The fundamental change now is that the terrorists have ceased to commit suicide for no return; they are now bringing their own deaths to bear in an effective, offensive manner, in the service of an intuitive strategic insight which is quite simply a sense of the immense fragility of the opponent–a sense that a system which has arrived at its quasi-perfection can, by that very token, be ignited by the slightest spark. They have succeeded in turning their own deaths into an absolute weapon against a system that operates on the basis of the exclusion of death, a system whose ideal is an ideal of zero deaths. Every zero-death system is a zero-sum-game system. And all the means of deterrence and destruction can do nothing against an enemy who has already turned his death into a counterstrike weapon. "What does the American bombing matter? Our men are as eager to die as the Americans are to live!" Hence the nonequivalence of the four thousand deaths inflicted at a stroke on a zero-death system.

Here, then, it is all about death, not only about the violent irruption of death in real time–"live", so to speak–but the irruption of a death which is far more than real: a death which is symbolic and sacrificial–that is to say, the absolute, irrevocable event.

This is the spirit of terrorism.

Never attack the system in terms of relations of force. That is the (revolutionary) imagination the system itself forces upon you–the system which survives only by constantly drawing those attacking it into fighting on the ground of reality, which is always its own. But shift the struggle into the symbolic sphere, where the rule is that of challenge, reversion and outbidding. *So that death can be met only by equal or greater death.* Defy the system by a gift to which it cannot respond except by its own death and its own collapse.

The terrorist hypothesis is that the system itself will commit suicide in response to the multiple challenges posed by deaths and suicides. For there is a symbolic obligation upon both the system and power [*le pouvoir*], and in this trap lies the only chance of their catastrophic collapse. In this vertiginous cycle of the impossible exchange of death, the death of the terrorist is an infinitesimal point, but one that creates a gigantic suction or void, an enormous convection. Around this tiny point the whole system of the real and of power [*la puissance*] gathers, transfixed; rallies briefly; then perishes by its own hyperefficiency.

It is the tactic of the terrorist model to bring about an excess of reality, and have the system collapse beneath that excess of reality. The whole derisory nature of the situation, together with the violence mobilized by the system, turns around against it, for terrorist acts are both the exorbitant mirror of its own violence and the model of a symbolic violence forbidden to it, the only violence it cannot exert–that of its own death.

That is why the whole of visible power can do nothing against the tiny, but symbolic, death of a few individuals.

We have to face facts, and accept that a new terrorism has come into being, a new form of action which plays the game, and lays hold of the rules of the game, solely with the aim of disrupting it. Not only do these people not play fair, since they put their own deaths into play–to which there is no possible response ("they are cowards")–but they have taken over all the weapons of the dominant power. Money and stock-market speculation, computer technology and aeronautics, spectacle and the media networks–they have assimilated everything of modernity and globalism, without changing their goal, which is to destroy that power.

They have even–and this is the height of cunning–used the banality of American everyday life as cover and camouflage. Sleeping in their suburbs, reading and studying with their families, before activating themselves suddenly like time bombs. The faultless mastery of this clandestine style of operation is almost as terroristic as the spectacular act of September 11, since it casts suspicion on any and every individual. Might not any inoffensive person be a potential terrorist? If *they* could pass unnoticed, then each of us is a criminal going unnoticed (every plane also becomes suspect), and in the end, this is no doubt true. This may very well correspond to an unconscious form of potential, veiled, carefully repressed criminality, which is always capable, if not of resurfacing, at least of thrilling secretly to the spectacle of Evil. So the event ramifies down to the smallest detail–the source of an even more subtle mental terrorism.

The radical difference is that the terrorists, while they have at their disposal weapons that are the system's own, possess a further lethal weapon: their own deaths. If they were content just to fight the system with its own weapons, they would immediately be eliminated. If they merely used their own deaths to combat it, they would disappear just as quickly in a useless sacrifice – as terrorism has almost always done up to now (an example being the Palestinian suicide attacks), for which reason it has been doomed to failure.

As soon as they combine all the modern resources available to them with this highly symbolic weapon, everything changes. The destructive potential is multiplied to infinity. It is this multiplication of factors (which seem irreconcilable to us) that gives them such superiority. The "zero-death" strategy, by contrast, the strategy of the "clean" technological war, precisely fails to match up to this transfiguration of "real" power by symbolic power.

The prodigious success of such an attack presents a problem, and if we are to gain some understanding of it, we have to slough off our Western perspective to see what goes on in the terrorists' organization, and in their heads. With us, such efficiency would assume a maximum of calculation and rationality that we find hard to imagine in others. And, even in this case, as in any rational organization or secret service, there would always have been leaks or slip-ups.

So, the secret of such a success lies elsewhere. The difference is that here we are dealing not with an employment contract, but with a pact and a sacrificial obligation. Such an obligation is immune to any defection or corruption. The miracle is to have adapted to the global network and technical protocols, without losing anything of this complicity "unto death". Unlike the contract, the pact does not bind individuals–even their 'suicide' is not individual heroism, it is a collective sacrificial act sealed by an ideal demand. And it is the combination of two mechanisms–an operational structure and a symbolic pact–that made an act of such excessiveness possible.

We no longer have any idea what a symbolic calculation is, as in poker or potlatch: with minimum stakes, but the maximum result. And the maximum result was precisely what the terrorists obtained in the Manhattan attack, which might be presented as quite a good illustration of chaos theory: an initial impact causing incalculable consequences; whereas the Americans' massive deployment ("Desert Storm") achieved only derisory effects–the hurricane ending, so to speak, in the beating of a butterfly's wing.

Suicidal terrorism was a terrorism of the poor. This is a terrorism of the rich. This is what particularly frightens us: the fact that they have become rich (they have all the necessary resources) without ceasing to wish to destroy us. Admittedly, in terms of our system of values, they are cheating. It is not playing fair to throw one's own death into the game. But this does not trouble them, and the new rules are not ours to determine.

So any argument is used to discredit their acts. For example, calling them "suicidal" and "martyrs"–and adding immediately that martyrdom proves nothing, that it has nothing to do with truth, that it is even (to quote Nietzsche) the enemy number one of truth. Admittedly, their deaths prove nothing, but in a system where truth itself is elusive (or do we claim to possess it?), there is nothing to prove. Moreover, this highly moral argument can be turned around. If the voluntary martyrdom of the suicide bombers proves nothing, then the involuntary martyrdom of the victims of the attack proves nothing either, and there is something unseemly and obscene in making a moral argument out of it (this is in no way to deny their suffering and death).

Another argument in bad faith: these terrorists exchanged their deaths for a place in paradise; their act was not a disinterested one, hence it is not authentic; it would be disinterested only if they did not believe in God, if they saw no hope in death, as is the case with us (yet Christian martyrs assumed precisely such a sublime equivalence). There again, then, they are not fighting fair, since they get salvation, which we cannot even continue to hope for. So we mourn our deaths while they can turn theirs into very high-definition stakes.

Fundamentally, all this–causes, proof, truth, rewards, ends and means– is a typically Western form of calculation. We even evaluate death in terms of interest rates, in value-for-money terms. An economic calculation that is a poor man's calculation–poor men who no longer even have the courage to pay the price.

What can happen now–apart from war, which is itself merely a conventional safety shield [*écran de protection*]? There is talk of bio-terrorism, bacteriological warfare or nuclear terrorism. Yet that is not longer of the order of the symbolic challenge, but of annihilation pure and simple, with no element of risk or glory: it is of the order of the final solution. Now, it is a mistake to see terrorist action as obeying a purely destructive logic. It seems to me that the action of the terrorists, from which death is inseparable (this is precisely what makes it a symbolic act), does not seek the impersonal elimination of the other. Everything lies in the challenge and the duel - that is to say, everything still lies in a dual, personal relation with the opposing power. It is a power which humiliated you, so it too must be humiliated. And not merely exterminated. It has to be made to lose face. And you never achieve that by pure force and eliminating the other party; it must, rather, be targeted and wounded in a genuinely adversarial relation. Apart from the pact that binds the terrorists together, there is also something of a dual pact with the adversary. That is, then, precisely the opposite of what the Americans did in the Gulf War (and which they are currently beginning again in Afghanistan), where the target is invisible and it is liquidated operationally.

ASHIS NANDY

ASHIS NANDY (1937–), one of India's leading intellectuals, has written extensively on ambivalent attitudes toward modernity in society in general and in Indian society in particular. He has focused especially on India's turbulent mix of Asian and European values. An outspoken critic of Indian religious nationalism, Nandy is equally critical of the Western imposition of secular democratic institutions on Indian society. He has proposed a "multiverse" of potential democracies to counter the universal forms extolled by Western thinkers since the Enlightenment.

In the following excerpt, Nandy ponders what he calls "the discreet charms" of Sikh terrorism during a period when airplane hijackers, mostly teenage boys, behaved "very well," were "extremely polite" to the sick and weary, actually wept, "sang to their hearts' fill" the melancholy love songs from Hindi films, humored children and, after their long ordeal, hugged hostages goodbye. Some hostages even collected autographs. He muses over these incidents from the 1980s and their radical disparity from the way "terrorism" is viewed today. Even then, there was a remarkable discrepancy between the description of events offered by participants and by the Western-facing media. Nandy disagrees with India's famous nationalist leader, Mohandas Gandhi, who once remarked that terrorism by nature tends to absolutize competing points of view. Nandy points to the lack of absolutism in these incidents of Sikh terrorism, showing how captors and captives collaborated to establish a unique moral order within the confines of a pirated airplane. His conclusions are several, but include the observation that the concept of terrorism has become reified in Western imagination, so that it precludes local idioms and blinds us to the ambivalence evident in these encounters from the 1980s.

"THE DISCREET CHARM OF INDIAN TERRORISM,"
THE SAVAGE FREUD AND OTHER ESSAYS

Why have I chosen to recount these curious details of two minor airpiracies? Am I trying to show that in an underdeveloped society, even a plane cannot be hijacked efficiently? Or to say that in such societies public life is shaped by the idiom and melodrama of the commercial cinema? That the Indian press is inconsistent and security forces incompetent?

The conclusions I draw from these two events are more modest. Before listing them, however, I have first to point out a few common features of the two events which strike me as being psychologically relevant.

First, in both cases, the hijackers, crew and passengers established and maintained a dialogue among themselves. Not once did they try to place themselves outside each other's interpersonal world. Nor did they presume any incommensurability between their worldview and that of the others. As a result, despite some low-level violence, the social world of the pirated IC 405 and IC 421 did not become a free-for-all or an amoral Hobbesian jungle. Later on, attempts were made to explain the piracies in terms of the standard categories of international terrorism. But these attempts could not obscure the genuine humaneness which had informed the behaviour of the crew, the passengers and the hijackers.

Of course, the events narrated here can be interpreted in other ways. Reading between the lines of Subrahmanyam's articles, one can easily construct another, *realpolitik*-based interpretation of the same events. There are other clues, too. One hostess claimed that she had been taught, as part of anti-hijacking training, to be friendly with hijackers and to ask them questions about their families and their personal lives. That was why she had been so friendly with hijackers and to them and it had helped. The Pakistani authorities, too, saw in the softness of the hijackers evidence of "low morale." In such 'realistic' interpretations, hijackings become a zero-sum game. Each gesture to the passengers becomes a concession extracted through adroit bargaining, and clear-headed, dispassionate politics. Nor can there be any doubt about which of the two interpretations will fit better with the paramount models in the world of knowledge. Any graduate student in a respectable university would be well-advised to assume Subrahmanyam's tone rather than mine.

I claim that neither of the two interpretations is more "true" than the other. While to some, my account of the hijackings will make them appear maudlin or mystifying, to others, Subrahmanyam's account will seem unrealistic and based on a romanticization of *realpolitik*. They will find anti-empirical his assumption that the odds did not favour the hijackers and hence their ploy of good behaviour. For the success rates of hijackers in seizing hostages, escaping punishment and gaining major publicity have ranged between 79 to nearly 100 per cent. That is to say, the hijackers did not have to behave the way they did merely to hedge their bets or save their skins on a possibly doomed mission. Ultimately, the interpretation is a matter of choice, and the choice is both political and moral.

Second, captors and captives collaborated, perhaps unwittingly, to re-establish a moral order in an extreme situation. In this order there was a place for the children and the ill, for the disabled and the injured, for the basic needs of passengers, and for music, humour, and pathos.

The child who called a hijacker "uncle," the airhostess who retained her wits in a crisis, the hijacker who called a passenger *"mātāji"* or the hijacker who sang to the tired, nervous passengers were not merely forging temporary kinship ties. They were refusing to move into the standardized world of international terrorism typified by, say, the Munich massacre, the Tel Aviv airport killings or by our own Mukteshwar bus massacre.

Of course, there is no guarantee that terrorist acts such as the ones I have described will not give place to more ruthless, gory violence. India has perhaps already graduated to the second stage of terrorism and the 1984 hijackings perhaps belong to another age; the hijackings took place before the assassination of prime minister Indira Gandhi by two of her Sikh security guards, and the large-scale slaughter of Sikhs at Delhi, virtually organized by the ruling party under the patronage of the Indian state. Yet the fact remains that when the hijackings took place, they did so within the limits imposed by another moral order, and this order kept in check the desperate youths even when they were cornered and faced total defeat.

Third, though the language of international terrorism was sometimes used, it was explicitly even if indirectly conveyed that the usage was merely a matter of form, not substance. Thus, when the outside world was told that one passenger would be shot every thirty minutes, the passenger chosen as the first victim was told the threat was a sham. The hard-boiled journalists and strategic analysts in the plane may not have got the message but the other passengers and crew did. That is why the hijackers responded so easily to the discipline of the young airhostesses when the need arose, and the hostesses could so effortlessly assume authority over them. That is why, till the end, the crew and passengers retained their faith in the humanity of their captors and the captors also tried to live up to the image of courageous, self-sacrificing, moral rebels fighting for a just cause.

This compact between passengers, hijackers and crew was not lost on the Indian mouth-pieces of the universal language of statecraft, who knowingly or not tried to erase detailed memories of the hijackings. Not only did this leave ordinary newspaper readers with only a vague sketch of the events but it reduced all the moral gestures made in circumstances of great physical and psychological stress to spicy or comic incidents involving the "unthinking Sikhs" of popular *sardārjī* jokes. On the basis of these filtered memories, a set of standard slogans about terrorism was devised for the consumption of the Indian middle classes. (There was at least one rumour after the second hijacking that, when a passenger on her return to Delhi said something positive about the hijackers to the press at the airport, the interview was cut short and she was whisked away by the security agencies). The army major caught in the first hijacking, sensing the mood of the authorities, refused to give his full name to the press and called himself only Vijay. He might have suspected that his views would be considered unpatriotic.

Fourth, all three parties—hijackers, crew and passengers—refused to raise the stakes during the hijackings. . . . Their actions were not equally palatable to all, but they were nevertheless located in a shared moral universe. The leader of the hijackers who brought out bandages and cotton after roughing up the army major, and the major who, despite being ill-treated, never lost his realism and refused to take the assault as a personal affront, illustrate this point neatly.

There is a set of cultural questions relevant to this issue which I shall not try to answer. These questions involve the touches of reparation or atonement in some of the hijackers' actions. What was the source of this atonement in an avowedly martial community, in a context which could be interpreted to be a just war? Did the traditional Sikh concept of just warfare, with its built-in protection for children, women and noncombatants, come into play? Did the non-Sikh passengers and crew share that concept of warfare, so that the hijackers had to protect their self-esteem and the purity of their struggle by making reparative gestures to undo their deviations from the traditional Sikh principles of warfare? I leave the subject to those who are more competent to handle it.

It is, however, clear that the hijackers refused to absolutize the difference between their politics and that of the passengers and crew. If one goes by Gandhi's belief that such absolutization is essential to terrorism, the distinctive nature of these terrorist acts would be obvious. The hijacking of IC 405 and IC 421 were the ninth and tenth in a series. All the earlier ones had ended reasonably peacefully and with little bloodshed. The passengers, especially the women and children, were treated well and, despite melodramatic touches—in one instance, the hijackers ostentatiously ate apples stuck on to knives—in no case was there real panic. As a non-Indian passenger said after one of these occasions, he had experienced a hijacking with a difference.

Fifth, the maudlin and comic aspects—which are certain to jar on the sophisticated sensitivity of the Indian *haute bourgeoisie*—were exactly those that helped to establish the bonds among the three parties involved. These sentimental and comic aspects were vestigial elements of a dialect which everyone had half forgotten but which everyone recognized at crucial moments of crisis and/or truth. The passengers, crew and air-pirates played for very high stakes indeed: their own liberty and lives. They had to back their actions with something more than learnt scientific-rational interpretations—they had to fall back on their real convictions about the nature of their interpersonal world and draw on their deepest private theories about what might work in an extreme situation in their society.

That to articulate these convictions they chose to borrow sentiments from Hindi commercial movies, rather than from the editorial pages of the national English dailies, suggests that the sentiments reflected something more than the half-digested global mass culture these movies are supposed to typify. One suspects that in trying to cater to the lowest common denominator of popular taste, the popular movies of the subcontinent have established a complex relationship with some of the deep but increasingly cornered elements of Indian culture.

The inefficiency, nervousness and amateurishness of the hijackers were also part of the same half-forgotten dialect; they were in fact an indication of another moral universe not known to the world of international terrorism and its cut-and-dried, expert analysts. That this dialect borrowed so heavily from the world of low-brow commercial films is unfortunate from the point of view of the Indian intelligentsia; but it appears that this dialect, despite all the efforts of modern secular India, cannot be entirely driven out of the culture of Indian politics. It manages to return, like Freud's unconscious, to haunt our public life.

Paradoxically, while the hijackers and their victims spoke the language of the fantasy world of commercial films, nevertheless they remained throughout in better touch with ground-level realities than the outside world of what Kupperman and Trent term "counter-theatrics." It was in fact the Indian press, they airlines bureaucracy, the foreign office, the security machinery and defense experts who appeared to be living in an unreal, mythical world created by the Western experience with terrorism. When these outsiders talked of the hijackers, foreign involvement and security lapses in reified terms, they seemed to be totally out of touch with the real world of air piracy as it had been experienced by real persons uninitiated in sophisticated academic theories of terrorism.

A crucial element in this academic, objectivist approach was the pathetic faith in the technology of anti-terrorism. I have mentioned the demand for means of identifying liquid bombs which eluded conventional x-rays. But the two hijackings did not depend on the hijackers' weapons. They were the products of the ingenuity and power to bluff of teenagers whose strength- as well as weakness- was their inexperience. No technological device on earth can identify liquid bombs that do not exist, nor could such a device have given confidence to the crew and passengers to call the bluff at the right moment. They would have had to take the hijackers at their word.

Lastly, a methodological point. The narratives here can be read as studies in mass media and popular culture. I have depended entirely on the national English press and have avoided, for the moment, drawing upon direct interviews with the hijacked passengers and crew. I have tried to show that the data I have marshaled can be cast in either of the two languages I have identified- the universal language of the modern nation-state, which shapes so much of the available theories of terrorism, and the vernacular in which the majority of those in the hijacked IC 405 and IC 421 spoke. In the process, I have tried to create some space for the latter in our contemporary understanding of South Asian politics. For my argument is that there is a semi-articulate public awareness in these societies which has a place for the vernacular. I have called it a dialect earlier to indicate that it does not enjoy the status of a language. Modern political analysis has already successfully discredited it as soft, effeminate, immature and irrational.

Finally, a few comments on the subject of terrorism in South Asia. It is possible to argue that modern terrorism and counterterrorism have become, in some cases, consumption items for the middle classes. Terrorism, too, can now be advertised, sold and purchased as a political spectacle and as a commodity through the TV, the newspapers, the radio and commercial films. Some well-known experts on terrorism have, in fact, said that terrorism thrives on media exposure and cannot survive without publicity. Perhaps this link between terror and the media has helped the Indian middle classes to internalize, rather quickly, a simplistic theory of terrorism and encouraged the Indian journalist, a self-conscious dealer in middle-class opinion, to assume the role of an expert on the subject overnight. Both groups confront the experience of terrorism second-hand, without any scope to reflect on its long-term meaning, political or cultural.

The theory and the expertise converge, in that they both overlie deep ambivalences triggered by the problems of living with a modern nation-state in a traditional, post-colonial society. In such a society, the westernized middle classes see themselves as guardians or custodians, trying desperately to protect the rest of the society – seen as inefficient, anarchic and irrational – through a hard-boiled law-and-order approach and the technology of the state, which is viewed as the major instrument of modern rationality. The expertise that the modernizing middle classes and journalists claim to have follows directly from their perception of the rest of the society.

Opposed to this potent combination of an almost blind faith in the rationality of the state and ambivalence towards the ordinary Indian's unpredictable, non-modern Indianness, are the observed realities of hijacking as they unfold within the culture of everyday life in India.

Existing theoretical and empirical work stresses two differentiae of contemporary terrorism. First, terrorism is primarily a psychological weapon: "its purpose is to instill fear in an attempt to reach specific objectives." Second, terrorism is "essentially indiscriminate" and its choice of victims is arbitrary or random. 'The lack of discrimination helps to spread fear, for if no one in particular is the target, no one can be safe.

By both criteria, the hijackings described here fail to qualify as terrorism. After the first clumsy attempts to instill some fear in the victims, the hijackers of IC 405 and IC 421 consistently attempted to bring down the level of that fear. Not only by the restraint of their behaviour, but also by caring for the captives and reassuring those whom they should have terrorized according to all the books. As we have seen, many "victims" specifically told the press that there was no panic in the aircraft. Likewise, while the choice of aircraft was random, the terrorization of victims was not. Elaborate South Asian concepts of fair play and duty towards non-combatants determined and made predictable the hijackers' behaviour.

The clash between middle-class faith in the state, its technology and expertise, on the one hand, and the "imperfect terrorism" shaped by traditional morality and restraints on violence, on the other, has its counterpart in the latent clash between the dominant language of the nation-state system and the residual traditional language of rebellion, now virtually inaccessible to those who speak the first language. I have argued here that the persistence of the second language allows one a different kind of political play in some societies. However, I have not overemphasized the last point and I have not argued away international power politics and the security aspects of hijacking. I have merely tried to hint at the possibility—alas, being a product of the Indian middle-class culture myself, I can only call it a possibility—that there may be ways of dealing with one's counter-players and enemies which recognize the multi-layered nature of human personality and social relationships.

Some will call this absurd, maudlin moralism; to others it is the heart of politics.

Closing Comments
THE CONNECTION BETWEEN WAR AND SACRIFICE

WHY ARE GORY ACTS OF SACRIFICE prolific in religion, and what is the relationship between sacrifice and violence? The attempt to find answers to the first question has been a preoccupation of scholars for more than a century. As the excerpts in the second section of the book have shown, attempts to understand the meaning of sacrifice have occupied some of the most significant minds in modern scholarship. For some it has led to a search for the meaning of religion itself. Marcel Mauss, following Émile Durkheim, regarded sacrifice as a kind of sacred communion. René Girard, in the manner of Sigmund Freud, regarded it as a symbolic act that displaces the momentum toward real acts of violence in the world.

Whether it involves the killing of chickens in a Haitian rite, the slaughter of goats at a Muslim Eid event, or the cattle blessed and burned at the temple in ancient Israel, sacrifice has been part of the history of religion. It is a rite of destruction that is found, remarkably, in virtually every religious tradition in the world. The term suggests that the very process of destroying is spiritual because the word comes from the Latin, *sacer*, "to make holy." What makes sacrifice so riveting is not just that it involves killing but also that it is, in an ironic way, ennobling. As René Girard has argued, these sacrificial symbols of violence enable religion to play an ultimately nonviolent and socially useful role. The destruction is performed within a religious context that transforms the killing into something positive. Thus, sacrifice provides an image of violence conquered—or at least put in its place—by the larger framework of order that religious language provides.

War is also common to the religious imagination—and it is more than imagined. Some of the most dramatic moments in the histories of religious traditions take place on a battlefield. The literature of virtually all religious traditions is filled with warfare—whether it is the great conflicts of the Hindu epics, the Ramayana and Mahabharata; the wars between Buddhist and Tamil kings in the Sri Lankan Pali Chronicles; the great adventures of Japanese and Chinese warriors; the biblical images of warfare in the books of Exodus, Deuteronomy, and elsewhere; or the great battles at the beginnings of the Islamic tradition, wherein military forces were commanded by the Prophet. In the case of Christianity, it is the ultimate war before the last judgment. In fact, no war could be more cataclysmic than the final confrontation between good and evil that is portrayed in the New Testament book of Revelation.

Images and acts of both sacrifice and warfare are common to religious traditions throughout history. And the two have some similar traits. Though sacrifice usually involves the killing of one individual person or animal, and warfare involves the destruction of a whole group, they are both acts of destruction undertaken—perhaps paradoxically—in order to establish a more ordered and peaceful world. Like sacrifice, religious war is seen from within the perspective of religious traditions often in a positive light. Like the practice of sacrifice, the idea of war is a way of providing a framework of order over a chaotic situation. Like sacrifice, warfare can be a way of making sense of the fundamental moral elements of reality. And like sacrifice, war is central to the religious imagination.

Virtually every religious tradition contains images of ultimate battles. These are often more than fights between competing enemies. Though the warrior Arjuna in the Hindu epic Mahabharata was concerned about the fact that he was being forced into a battle where he would kill or be killed by one of his own cousins, he was ultimately concerned about the meaning of fighting itself. The lesson that was given by Lord Krishna in his response to Arjuna, written as the Bhagavad Gita, was that warlike struggle is intrinsic to life. Wars portrayed in religious traditions are often grand encounters between forces much greater than human foes. They may be seen as struggles over the nature of reality itself: they are contests between order and chaos, the sacred and the mundane, and good versus evil.

The wars imagined in religious traditions can often be described as "cosmic war," because such confrontations are larger than life. They evoke great struggles of the legendary past, and they relate to metaphysical conflicts on a moral and philosophical plane. Not all religious wars have this grand dimension—international political encounters can involve a multitude of limited military activities for defensive or expansive purposes, and religion may be enlisted to achieve political gain. Yet, like the wars described in the Hebrew Bible and the Qur'an, some of these worldly battles are thought to carry much larger significance. They are represented as battles undertaken on behalf of divine order for purposes that are ultimately moral and theologically righteous.

Cosmic war is often described in mythic terms and with a metaphorical sense. When an evangelical Protestant preacher exhorts a congregation to take up arms for Christ and battle for salvation, the preacher usually means this as an allegory. The war for good and evil is imagined as a struggle that is occurring within the souls of the faithful, and their "swords" are spiritual thoughts and deeds. In these instances, notions of cosmic war can be intimately personal, but ultimately they transcend human experience because one's own individual struggle is thought to be part of the larger battle between good and evil in human existence.

When the militant Sikh leader Sant Jarnail Singh Bhindranwale exhorted his faithful followers to take up the sword of battle and destroy the evil in contemporary life, his sermons sounded very much like the exhortations of the evangelical Protestant revival preachers. They also, at times, urged their congregations to become part of the army of God in spiritual battles, the struggles within each soul. The main difference, however, was that Bhindranwale saw the idea of warfare as more than a metaphor. Bhindranwale thought that he knew exactly where evil was located, and it was within the policies and leadership of the secular government of India. His secular opponents were seen as temporary enemies in the timeless drama of cosmic war.

In the case of the Sikh militants and in many other contemporary cases of politicized religion, a spiritual image of divine struggle—cosmic war—has been placed in the service of a worldly political battle. Sometimes these images help to motivate soldiers on the field of battle. Sometimes, also, they help to justify extraordinary and extreme acts of violence. As we have seen in the case of the al Qaeda activists involved in the attacks on the World Trade Center and Pentagon on September 11, 2001, the notion of a grand and cosmic war can inspire horrendous acts of religious terror.

The 9/11 hijackers undertook their suicide missions as acts of religious warfare. The Last Instructions found in luggage and debris from the three crash sites depict the hijackers as participants in a cosmic war that required their sacrifice and martyrdom. Specific instructions appear to have urged the ritual sacrifice of airplane personnel, as if they were animals destined for slaughter. The instructions represent the attacks as glorious acts in a war that ultimately would restore the world to its pristine perfection. In this instance, sacrifice and warfare were intertwined.

These two aspects of religious violence—sacrifice and warfare—are often interconnected, in part because these two forms of sacred killing are strikingly similar. They are both about destruction, of course, but they are about destroying life with a positive intention. Participants in religious sacrifice and cosmic war envision the creation of conditions in which more life and better life will flourish. Whether they are victims or destroyers in this cosmic process, they see their participation as linking them to something greater than ordinary life. They are players in dramas that exemplify—and thus explain—the most profound aspects of reality.

The excerpts in the first section of this book show that sacrifice and war are essential to the religious imagination. One might argue that, given the centrality of these notions to most religious traditions, the task of creating a vicarious experience of sacrifice and warfare—albeit one usually imagined as residing on a spiritual plane—is one of the main businesses of religion. But questions remain as to the relationship and primacy of sacrifice and war. Are they at two ends of a spectrum, two aspects of the same impulse, or does one conceptually encompass the other? Should war be viewed within the context of sacrifice, or the other way around?

At least since the inception of Christianity, sacrifice has riveted popular imagination. As a metaphor, sacrifice extends into many spheres—economics, spirituality, love. Rather than contemplate the bloody altar at which sacrificial victims once were put to death, we often prefer to think that sacrifice implies surrendering some pleasure for the sake of greater gain. On the basis of this assumption, some argue that religious warfare implies the sacrifice of one's own as martyrs and the reciprocal sacrifice of one's enemy.

The editors of this volume think that an argument can be made that war is as much a context for thinking about sacrifice as sacrifice is a way of thinking about war. Images of sacrificial victims intertwine with those of holy warriors and martyrs because there is a profound dimension of human imagination where they coincide. At that dimension, both religious sacrifice and holy war reflect a quest for sacred order.

The quest for ultimate order is woven into the fabric of both sacrifice and cosmic war. As Émile Durkheim has pointed out, religious language contains ideas of an intimate and ultimate tension, one that he described as the distinction between the sacred and the profane. This fundamental dichotomy gives rise to images of a great encounter between cosmic forces—order versus chaos, good versus evil, truth versus falsehood—that worldly struggles mimic. This struggle is a part of many religious images and activities, and the idea of war captures this antinomy as clearly as the idea of sacrifice.

The social activity of organized conflict, whether against an animal in a hunt or against other people in battle, is a primal form of human activity. Warfare organizes people into a "we" and a "they," and it organizes social history into a storyline of persecution, conflict, and the hope of redemption, liberation, and conquest. The enduring and seemingly ubiquitous image of cosmic war from ancient times to the present continues to excite the religious imagination, and it is often given meaning by rites of sacrifice. Occasionally, rites of sacrifice actually initiate wars, from a deer offered to Artemis to the stewardess slaughtered at 9/11. The concept of holy war is sometimes inconceivable without a sacrifice.

The sacrificial victim can represent the destruction that is endemic to battle. Like the enemy—and like violence itself—the victim is often categorically out of place and is therefore a symbol of disorder. Animals used for sacrifice, for instance, are usually domesticated beasts: they lie in the ambiguous middle ground between the animal kingdom and the human. When sacrificial victims were human, they also frequently came from an uncertain category. In India, for example, widows who died in sati were anomalies: married women bereft of living husbands. Among the Huron and Seneca Indians, a sacrifice might be made of a warrior out of place: an enemy soldier captured during tribal conflict, brought into the community, made a member of a household where a son had been lost in battle, who became for a time that missing son. The brave was feted and adored and then, knowing what the outcome would be and yet displaying his courage, he was ritually tortured to death.

Sometimes it was God himself--or herself--who was offered up, or a divinely inspired person such as Jesus or Husayn, whose very existence was extraordinary. It was not just their sacrifices that made them appear divine; rather, their almost inhuman holiness made them candidates for slaughter. The literary theme of the Christ-like figure of perfection becoming the victim of the intolerance in a less-than-perfect human world—found, for instance, in Herman Melville's portrayal of the shipboard execution of the morally pure Billy Budd—plays on a familiar element of martyrdom found in many religious traditions. The very goodness of a holy person is an indication that he or she does not fit into society and may be cast out, even destroyed. A cross-cultural study of sainthood came to a similar conclusion about saints: they must be perceived as morally and spiritually unusual in some way in order for their martyrdom and self-sacrifice to be seen as pure (Hawley, *Saints and Virtues*).

The sacrifices made during warfare—including those associated with religious terrorism in recent years—have been consistent with this theme. The ritualized killing by the hijackers in the 9/11 attacks is one example. Another is the choice of suicide bombers among the Hezbollah and Amal sects in Lebanon. According to Martin Kramer's study, the young men chosen as suicide martyrs against American and Israeli targets had to meet the traditional criteria of purity and anomaly required of sacrificial beings. They were no longer children but were not yet married, they were members of the community but were free from family responsibilities, and they were pious but not members of the clergy. In the case of the youths who volunteered for participation in Hamas suicide missions, interviews with their families and tapes of their last testimonies indicated that they were often regarded as somewhat shy but good kids. They were serious in their manners, perhaps slightly aloof from their crowd, and ultimately accepted in society in a grand way when their suicidal acts were remembered joyously as events of martyrdom.

When the Hamas leader, Dr. Abdul Aziz Rantisi, objected to the use of the term "suicide bombers" to describe his young colleagues in Hamas who chose to blow themselves up in acts of violence against Israel, he was objecting to the idea that their acts were done idiosyncratically or thoughtlessly. He preferred to think of them as "self-chosen martyrs," soldiers in a great war who diligently and reverently gave up their lives for the sake of their community and their religion. The videotapes taken of the young men the night before their deaths indicated that they thought of themselves in just that way. They were trying not to avoid life but to fulfill it in what they considered to be an act of both personal and social redemption. War provided a context for their acts of sacrifice to have meaning.

Thus, both holy war and sacred sacrifice are part of a larger pattern in which religious ideas provide ways of making sense of the world and maintaining some control over it. Even acts of terrorism can be seen as ways to symbolically express power over oppressive forces and regain some nobility in the perpetrators' personal lives. Those who have been involved in these cultural expressions of violence and participated in acts of ritual and martial empowerment—even vicariously—have experienced the exuberance and hope that religion brings to life. Such performances of power can be restorative, even though the experience may be fleeting. Sadly, these sacred moments are sometimes purchased at an awful cost.

Selected Bibliography

Aho, James. 1995. *The Politics of Righteousness: Idaho Christian Patriotism*. Seattle: University of Washington Press.

Aijmer, Göran, and Jon Abbink, eds. 2000. *Meanings of Violence: A Cross-Cultural Perspective*. Oxford: Berg.

Appleby, R. Scott, ed. 1997. *Spokesmen for the Despised*. Chicago: University of Chicago Press.

Argenti-Pillen, Alexandria. 2002. *Masking Terror: How Women Contain Violence in Southern Sri Lanka*. Philadelphia: University of Pennsylvania Press.

Armstrong, Karen. 2000. *The Battle for God*. New York: Knopf.

Aslan, Reza. 2010. *Confronting Religious Extremism in the Age of Globalization*. New York: Random House.

Avalos, Hector. 2005. *Fighting Words: The Origins of Religious Violence*. Amherst, NY: Prometheus.

Bainton, Roland. 1960. *Christian Attitudes toward War and Peace*. New York: Abington Press.

Banerjee, Sikata. 1999. *Warriors in Politics: Hindu Nationalism, Violence, and the Shiv Sena in India*. Boulder, CO: Westview Press.

Barkun, Michael. 2003. *A Culture of Conspiracy: Apocalyptic Visions in Contemporary America*. Berkeley: University of California Press.

Barmash, Pamela. 2005. *Homicide in the Biblical World*. Cambridge: Cambridge University Press.

Bataille, George. 1991. *Theory of Religion*. Trans. Robert Hurley. London: Zone Books.

———. 1991. *The Accursed Share*. Trans. Robert Hurley. Cambridge, MA: MIT Press.

Baudrillard, Jean. 1988. *America*. Trans. Chris Turner. London: Verso Press. Originally published 1986.

———. 1995. *Simulacra and Simulation*. Trans. Sheila Faria Glaser. Ann Arbor: University of Michigan Press.

———. 2002. *The Spirit of Terrorism and Other Essays*. Trans. Chris Turner. London: Verso Press.

Bernat, David, and Jonathan Klawans, eds. 2009. *Religion and Violence: The Biblical Heritage*. Norton, Sheffield: Sheffield Press.

Bloch, Maurice. 1991. *Prey into Hunter*. Cambridge: Cambridge University Press.

———. 1994. *Marxist Analyses and Social Anthropology*. London: Routledge.

Brekke, Torkel, ed. 2006. *The Ethics of War in Asian Civilizations: A Comparative Perspective*. London: Routledge.

Burkert, Walter. 1983. *Homo Necans*. Trans. Peter Bing. Berkeley: University of California Press.

———. 1996. *The Creation of the Sacred*. Cambridge, MA: Harvard University Press.

————. 2001. *Savage Energies*. Trans. Peter Bing. Chicago: University of Chicago Press.

Carrasco, David. 2002. *City of Sacrifice: The Aztec Empire and the Role of Violence in Civilization*. New York: Beacon Press.

Cook, David. n.d. *Suicide Attacks or "Martyrdom Operations" in Contemporary Jihad Literature*. http://www.ozlanka.com/commentary/jihad.htm.

————. 2005. *Understanding Jihad*. Berkeley: University of California Press.

Das, Veena, ed. 1990. *Mirrors of Violence: Communities, Riots and Survivors in South Asia*. New York: Oxford University Press. Reissued 1992, 1994.

————. 2000. *Violence and Subjectivity*. Berkeley: University of California Press.

deHeusch, Luc. 1985. *Sacrifice in Africa*. Bloomington: Indiana University Press.

Detienne, Marcel, and Jean-Pierre Vernant. 1989. *The Cuisine of Sacrifice among the Greeks*. Chicago: University of Chicago Press. Translated by Paula Wissing from the 1979 French edition.

deVries, Hent. 2002. *Religion and Violence: Philosophical Perspectives from Kant to Derrida*. Baltimore: Johns Hopkins University Press.

Dillon, Martin. 1997. *God and the Gun: The Church and Irish Terrorism*. New York: Routledge, 1997.

Dumezil, George. 1970. *The Destiny of the Warrior*. Trans. Alf Hiltebeitel. Chicago: University of Chicago Press, 1970. Originally published 1952.

Durkheim, Émile. 1915. *The Elementary Forms of Religious Life*. Trans. Joseph Ward Swain. New York: Free Press.

————. 1951. *On Suicide: A Study in Sociology*. Trans. John A. Spaulding and George Simpson. New York: Free Press.

Edinger, Edward, and George R. Elder. 2002. *Archetype of the Apocalypse: Divine Vengeance, Terrorism, and the End of the World*. Chicago: Open Court.

Ehrenreich, Barbara. 1997. *Blood Rites*. New York: Metropolitan Books.

Esposito, John. 2003. *Unholy War, Terror in the Name of Islam*. New York: Oxford University Press.

Firestone, Reuven. 1999. *Jihad*. New York: Oxford University Press.

Fouda, Yosri, and Nick Fielding. 2003. *Masterminds of Terror: The Truth behind the Most Devastating Terrorist Attack the World Has Ever Seen*. Edinburgh: Main Stream Press.

Freud, Sigmund. 1918. *Totem and Taboo*. Trans. A. A. Brill. London: G. Routledge & Sons.

————. 1961. *Civilization and Its Discontents*. Trans. James Strachey. New York: W. W. Norton.

Gambetta, Diego, ed. 2005. *Making Sense of Suicide Missions*. New York: Oxford University Press.

Girard, René. 1969. *Violence and the Sacred*. Trans. Patrick Gregory. Baltimore: Johns Hopkins Press.

————. 1987. *Things Hidden since the Foundation of the World*. Trans. Stephen Bann and Michael Metteer. Stanford: Stanford University Press.

————. 1989. *The Scapegoat*. Trans. Yvonne Freccero. Baltimore: Johns Hopkins University Press.

————. 2000. *The Girard Reader*. Ed. James G. Williams. New York: Crossroads.

Habermas, Jürgen, with Joseph Ratzinger. 2007. *The Dialectics of Secularization: On Reason and Religion*. San Francisco: Ignatius Press.

Hall, John R. 2009. *Apocalypse: From Antiquity to the Empire of Modernity*. Cambridge: Polity.

Hammerton-Kelly, Robert G., ed. 1987. *Violent Origins*. Palo Alto, CA: Stanford University Press.

———. 2008. *Politics and Apocalypse*. East Lansing: Michigan State University Press.

Hassner, Ron. 2009. *War on Sacred Ground*. Princeton: Princeton University Press.

Hawley, John Stratton. 1987. *Saints and Virtues*. Berkeley: University of California Press.

Hedges, Chris. 2002. *War Is a Force That Gives Us Meaning*. Garden City, NY: Anchor Books.

Hubert, Henri, and Marcel Mauss. 1981. *Sacrifice: Its Nature and Function*. Chicago: University of Chicago Press.

Ingebretsen, Edward J. 1994. *Maps of Heaven, Maps of Hell: Religious Terror as Memory from the Puritans to Stephen King*. New York: Continuum.

Jay, Nancy. 1992. *Throughout Your Generations Forever*. Chicago: University of Chicago Press.

Jensen, Adolf E. 1973. *Myth and Cult among Primitive Peoples*. Trans. Marianna Tax Choldin and Wolfgang Weissleder. Chicago: University of Chicago Press.

Jerryson, Michael, and Mark Juergensmeyer, eds. 2010. *Buddhist Warfare*. New York: Oxford University Press.

Johnson, James Turner. 2005. *The Holy War Idea in Western and Islamic Traditions*. University Park: Pennsylvania State University Press.

Jones, James W. 2008. *Blood that Cries Out from the Earth*. New York: Oxford University Press.

Juergensmeyer, Mark, ed. 1992. *Violence and the Sacred in the Modern World*. London: Frank Cass.

———. 2000. *Terror in the Mind of God*. Berkeley: University of California Press.

Juergensmeyer, Mark, Margo Kitts, and Michael Jerryson, eds. 2012. *Oxford Handbook of Religion and Violence*. New York: Oxford University Press.

Kaplan, Jeffrey. 1997. *Radical Religion in America: Millenarian Movements from the Far Right to the Children of Noah*. Syracuse, NY: Syracuse University Press.

Kelsay, John. 2007. *Arguing the Just War in Islam*. Cambridge, MA: Harvard University Press.

Kimball, Charles. 2002. *When Religion Becomes Evil*. New York: Harper Collins.

Kippenberg, Hans G., and Tilman Seidensticker. 2006. *The 9/11 Handbook*. London: Equinox.

Kitts, Margo. 2005. *Sanctified Violence in Homeric Society*. Cambridge: Cambridge University Press.

Kitts, Margo, Bernd Schneidmüller, and Gerald Schwedler, eds. 2010. *Ritual Dynamics and the Science of Ritual*, Vol. 3. *State, Power and Violence*. Wiesbaden: Harrassowitz.

Kramer, Martin. 1987. *Shi'ism, Resistance, and Revolution*. Boulder, CO: West-view Press; London: Mansell.

Levenson, Jon D. 1993. *Death and Resurrection of the Beloved Son*. New Haven: Yale University Press.

Lincoln, Bruce. 1991. *Death, War, and Sacrifice: Studies in Ideology and Practice*. Chicago: University of Chicago Press.

———. 2003. *Holy Terrors*. Chicago: University of Chicago Press.

Mahmood, Cynthia Keppley. 1996. *Fighting for Faith and Nation*. Philadelphia: University of Pennsylvania Press.

Marvin, Carolyn. 1999. *Blood Sacrifice and the Nation*. New York: Cambridge University Press.

Marx, Karl. 1843. *Critique of Hegel's "Philosophy of Right."* Trans. Annette Jolin and Joseph O'Malley. Cambridge: Cambridge University Press, 1970.

———. 1845. *Theses on Feuerbach*. In *Marx/Engels Selected Works*, vol. 1, 13–15. Trans. W. Lough. Moscow: Progress Publishers, 1969.

Marx, Karl, and Frederick Engels. 2002. *Marx and Engels on Religion*. New York: Fredonia Books.

Mauss, Marcel. 1990. *The Gift: The Form and Reason for Exchange in Archaic Societies*. London: Routledge.

Mauss, Marcel, and Henri Hubert. 1902. *Outline of a General Theory of Magic*. New York: Routledge Classics, 2005.

McDermott, Terry. 2005. *Perfect Soldiers*. New York: HarperCollins.

McTernan, Oliver. 2003. *Violence in God's Name: Religion in an Age of Conflict*. New York: Orbis Books.

Nandy, Ashis. 1995. *The Savage Freud*. Princeton: Princeton University Press.

———. 2010. *The Intimate Enemy: Loss and Recovery of Self under Colonialism*. Oxford: Oxford University Press.

Nardin, Terry, ed. 1996. *The Ethics of War and Peace: Religious and Secular Perspectives*. Ethikon Series in Comparative Ethics, vol. 1. Princeton: Princeton University Press.

Niditch, Susan. 1993. *War in the Hebrew Bible*. Oxford: Oxford University Press.

Oliver, Anne Marie, and Paul Steinberg. 2005. *The Road to Martyrs' Square*. New York: Oxford University Press.

Partner, Peter. 1997. *God of Battles*. Princeton: Princeton University Press.

Qutb, Sayyid. 1990. *Milestones*. Indianapolis: American Trust Publications.

Raaflaub, Kurt A. 2006. *War and Peace in the Ancient World*. Malden, MA: Blackwell.

Rapoport, David C. 1989. *The Morality of Terrorism: Religious and Secular Justifications*. New York: Columbia University Press.

Reader, Ian. 2000. *Religious Violence in Contemporary Japan: The Case of Aum Shinrikyo*. Honolulu: University of Hawaii Press.

Reeder, John P., Jr. 1996. *Killing and Saving: Abortion, Hunger, and War*. University Park: Pennsylvania State University Press.

Regan, Richard. 1996. *Just War: Principles and Cases*. Washington, DC: Catholic University of America Press.

Reuter, Christoph. 2004. *My Life Is a Weapon: A Modern History of Suicide Bombing*. Princeton: Princeton University Press.

Riley-Smith, Jonathan, ed. 2002. *The Oxford Illustrated History of the Crusades*. New York: Oxford University Press.

Robertson Smith, William. 1995. *Lectures on the Religion of the Semites, Second and Third Series*. Yorkshire: Sheffield Academic Press.

Scarry, Elaine. 1987. *The Body in Pain: The Making and Unmaking of the World*. Oxford: Oxford University Press.

Schmidt, Bettina E., and Ingo Schröeder, eds. 2001. *Anthropology of Violence and Conflict*. London: Routledge.

Selengut, Charles. 2003. *Sacred Fury: Understanding Religious Violence*. Walnut Creek, CA: Altamira Press.

Sells, Michael. 2012. *God of War: America in a World of Religion*. New York: Knopf.

Shay, Jonathan. 1995. *Achilles in Vietnam: Combat Trauma and the Undoing of Character*. New York: Simon and Schuster.

———. 2003. *Odysseus in America: Combat Trauma and the Trials of Homecoming*. New York: Scribner.

Steffen, Lloyd. 2007. *Holy War, Just War: Exploring the Moral Meaning of Religious Violence*. Lanham, MD: Rowman and Littlefield.

Stern, Jessica. 2003. *Terror in the Name of God: Why Religious Militants Kill*. New York: Ecco.

Stewart, P. J., and Andrew Strathern. 2002. *Violence: Theory and Ethnography*. New York: Continuum Publishing for Athlone Press.

Strathern, A., P. J. Stewart, and N. Whitehead, eds. 2006. *Terror and Violence: Imagination and the Unimaginable*. London: Pluto Press.

Tambiah, Stanley. 1992. *Buddhism Betrayed? Religion, Politics, and Violence in Sri Lanka*. Chicago: University of Chicago Press.

Taussig, Michael. 2001. *Shamanism, Colonialism, and the Wild Man*. Chicago: University of Chicago Press.

Taylor, Christopher. 1999. *Sacrifice as Terror: The Rwandan Genocide of 1994*. Oxford: Berg Press.

Toft, Monica Duffy, Daniel Phillpot, and Timothy Samuel Shah. 2011. *God's Century: Resurgent Religion and Global Politics*. New York: W. W. Norton.

van der Veer, Peter. 1994. *Religious Nationalism: Hindus and Muslims in India*. Berkeley: University of California Press.

von Rad, Gerhard. 1991. *Holy War in Ancient Israel*. Trans. Marva J. Dawn. Grand Rapids, MI: Eerdmans.

Walzer, Michael. 1977. *Just and Unjust Wars*. New York: Basic Books.

Wellman, James K., ed. 2007. *Belief and Bloodshed*. Lanham, MD: Rowman and Littlefield.

Wessinger, Catherine. 2000. *How the Millennium Comes Violently: From Jonestown to Heaven's Gate*. New York: Seven Bridges Press.

Whitehead, Neil L. 2002. *Dark Shamans: Kanaima and the Poetics of Violent Death*. Durham, NC: Duke University Press.

Whitehouse, Harvey. 2004. *Modes of Religiosity*. Walnut Creek, CA: Altamira Press.

Wilson, Elizabeth, ed. 2003. *The Living and the Dead: Social Dimensions of Death in South Asian Religion*. Albany, NY: SUNY Press.

Wilson, Elizabeth. 1996. *Charming Cadavers: Horrific Figurations of the Feminine in Indian Buddhist Hagiographic Literature*. Chicago: University of Chicago Press.

Wlodarczyk, Nathalie. 2009. *Magic and Warfare: Appearance and Reality in Contemporary African Conflict and Beyond*. Hampshire: Palgrave Macmillan.

Zizek, Slavoj. 2008. *Violence, Six Sideways Reflections*. New York: Picador.

Zulaika, Joseba, and William A. Douglass. 1996. *Terror and Taboo: The Foibles, Fables, and Faces of Terrorism*. New York: Routledge.

Permissions

Kautilya, *The Arthashastra*, book 10, "Relating to War," chapter 3, "Forms of Treacherous Fights," 2d ed., translated by R. Shamasastry from Sanskrit, edited by Jerome S. Arkenberg (Mysore: Wesleyan Mission Press, 1923). In the public domain.

Sun Tzu, *The Art of War*, chapter 1, "Laying Plans," translated by Lionel Giles; recent edition published by CreateSpace, 2009. In the public domain.

The Bhagavad Gita in the Mahabharata, chapter 23, verse 45 through chapter 25, verse 54, translated by J.A.B. van Buitenen from Sanskrit (Chicago: University of Chicago Press, 1981), pp. 73–79. Used by permission of the publisher.

Soho Takuan, *The Unfettered Mind: Writings of the Zen Master to the Sword Master*, "Annals of the Sword Taia," translated by William Scott Wilson from Japanese (Tokyo: Kodansha International Publishers, 2003), pp. 40–44. Used by permission of the publisher.

The Hebrew Bible (The Old Testament), Deuteronomy 20, Exodus 23, translated in the Revised Standard Version. In the public domain.

The Qur'an, Surah 2, "The Cow," verses 117–218, translated by Yusuf Ali from Arabic. In the public domain.

Thomas Aquinas, *Summa Theologica*, Part II, Question 40, Section 1, "Whether It Is Always Sinful to Wage War?" translated by Fathers of the English Dominican Province from Latin (New York: Benziger Brothers, 1947). In the public domain.

Reinhold Niebuhr, "Why the Christian Church Is Not Pacifist." Used by permission of Elizabeth Sifton, trustee for the Reinhold Niebuhr estate.

Michael Bray, *A Time to Kill*, chapter 9, "A Time for Revolution?" Used by permission of the author.

Abd al-Salam Faraj, *The Neglected Duty*, selected excerpts from Johannes Jensen, *The Neglected Duty*, 1 E. © 1986 Gale, a part of Centage Learning, Inc. Reproduced by permission.

Meir Kahane, *The Jewish Idea*, chapter 13, "War and Peace." Used by permission of the author's estate.

Shoka Asahara, selections from *Declaring Myself the Christ*, pp. 82–84; and *Disaster Comes to the Land of the Rising Sun*. In the public domain.

9/11 Conspirator, *Last Instructions*, translated by David Cook from the Arabic version published in the *New York Times*. Used by permission of the translator.

Émile Durkheim, *Elementary Forms of the Religious Life*, translated by Joseph Ward Swain (Andover, Hampshire, UK: Cengage Learning 1965), pp. 245–55. Used by permission of Taylor and Francis Group.

Henri Hubert and Marcel Mauss, *Sacrifice: Its Nature and Function* (Chicago: University of Chicago Press, 1968), pp. 95–103. Used by permission of the publisher.

Sigmund Freud, *Totem and Taboo*, "Infantile Recurrence," translated by A. A. Brills (New York: Vintage Books, 1946), pp. 185–200. Originally published 1918. Used by permission of the publisher.

René Girard, *Violence and the Sacred*, chapter 1, "Sacrifice," translated by Patrick Gregory from French (Baltimore: Johns Hopkins Press, 1977, pp. 3–23). Originally published as *La violence et le Sacré* (Paris: Grasset, 1972). Used by permission of the publisher.

Walter Burkert, *Homo Necans*, translated from German by Peter Bing (Berkeley: University of California Press, 1983), pp. 1–22. Originally published 1972. Used by permission of the publisher.

Maurice Bloch, *Prey Into Hunter*, chapter 3, "Sacrifice" (Cambridge: Cambridge University Press, 1992), pp. 24–37. Used by permission of the publisher.

Georges Bataille, *Theory of Religion*, chapter 2, translated by Robert Hurley from French (New York: Zone Books, 1989), pp. 39–40, 43–52. Used by permission of the publisher.

Karl Marx, "Marx's Critique of Hegel's Philosophy of Right," translated by Annette Jolin and Joseph O'Malley, edited by Joseph O'Malley (Cambridge: Cambridge University Press, 1970). Used by permission of the publisher.

Nancy Jay, *Throughout Your Generations Forever*, chapter 3, "Sacrifice and Descent" (Chicago: University of Chicago Press, 1992), pp. 30–40. Used by permission of the publisher.

Elaine Scarry, *The Body in Pain*, chapter 4, "The Structure of Belief and Its Modulation into Material Making" (New York: Oxford University Press, 1985), pp. 181–84, 198–205. Used by permission of the author.

Jean Baudrillard, *The Spirit of Terrorism*, chapter 1, "The Spirit of Terrorism," translated from French by Chris Turner (London and New York: Verso Press, 2002), pp. 3–34. Used by permission of the publisher.

Ashis Nandy, *The Savage Freud and Other Essays*, chapter 1, "The Discreet Charms of Indian Terrorism" (New Delhi: Oxford University Press, 1995), pp. 17–25. Used by permission of the author.

About the Editors

Mark Juergensmeyer is professor of sociology and global studies, affiliate professor of religious studies, and director of the Orfalea Center for Global and International Studies at the University of California, Santa Barbara. He is author and editor of twenty books, including *Terror in the Mind of God: The Global Rise of Religious Violence*. He is currently working on subjects related to global religion and war.

Margo Kitts is associate professor of humanities at Hawaii Pacific University. She is author of *Sanctified Violence in Homeric Society*, coeditor of *State, Power and Violence*, vol. 3 of *Ritual Dynamics and the Science of Ritual*, and has written numerous articles on violence in ancient literature. She is currently working on a book on ritual and revenge in the *Iliad*.

Index